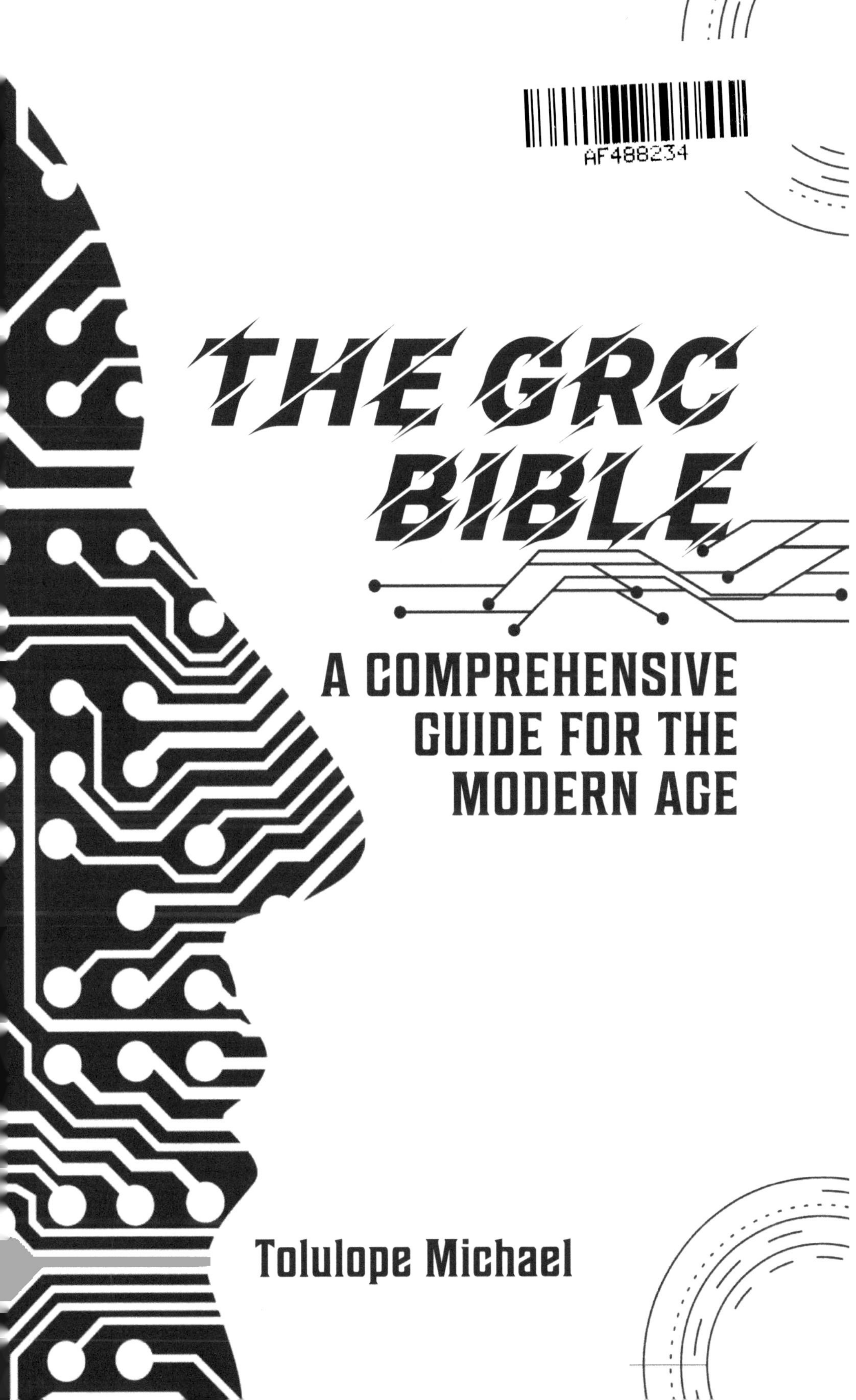

THE GRC BIBLE

A COMPREHENSIVE GUIDE FOR THE MODERN AGE

Tolulope Michael

TABLE OF CONTENTS

The GRC Bible
A Comprehensive Guide for the Modern Age

CHAPTER ONE
THE IMPERATIVE OF GOVERNANCE, RISK AND COMPLIANCE

CHAPTER TWO
RISK MANAGEMENT IN THE DIGITAL ERA: CHALLENGES AND OPPORTUNITIES

CHAPTER THREE
INTRODUCTION TO REGULATORY COMPLIANCE AND ITS IMPORTANCE

CHAPTER FOUR
BUILDING A RESILIENT GOVERNANCE STRUCTURE: FOUNDATIONS AND PRINCIPLES

CHAPTER FIVE

THE ROLE OF TECHNOLOGY IN GRC: INNOVATIONS AND TRANSFORMATIONS

CHAPTER SIX

ETHICAL GOVERNANCE: FOSTERING
A CULTURE OF INTEGRITY

CHAPTER SEVEN

CASE STUDIES: ORGANIZATIONS THAT
HAVE SUCCESSFULLY FOSTERED
ETHICAL GOVERNANCE

CHAPTER EIGHT

DATA GOVERNANCE: SAFEGUARDING INFORMATION IN A
DATA-DRIVEN WORLD

CHAPTER NINE

DATA LIFECYCLE MANAGEMENT

CHAPTER TEN
ANTICIPATING FUTURE TRENDS IN
DATA GOVERNANCE

CHAPTER ELEVEN
STAKEHOLDER ENGAGEMENT:
COLLABORATIVE APPROACHES TO GRC

CHAPTER TWELVE

TRAINING AND DEVELOPMENT IN GRC: EMPOWERING THE MODERN PROFESSIONAL

CHAPTER THIRTEEN

THE PROFILES OF GRC EXCELLENCE: INSPIRING CAREER JOURNEYS

CHAPTER FOURTEEN

CRAFTING YOUR GRC LEGACY IN THE MODERN AGE

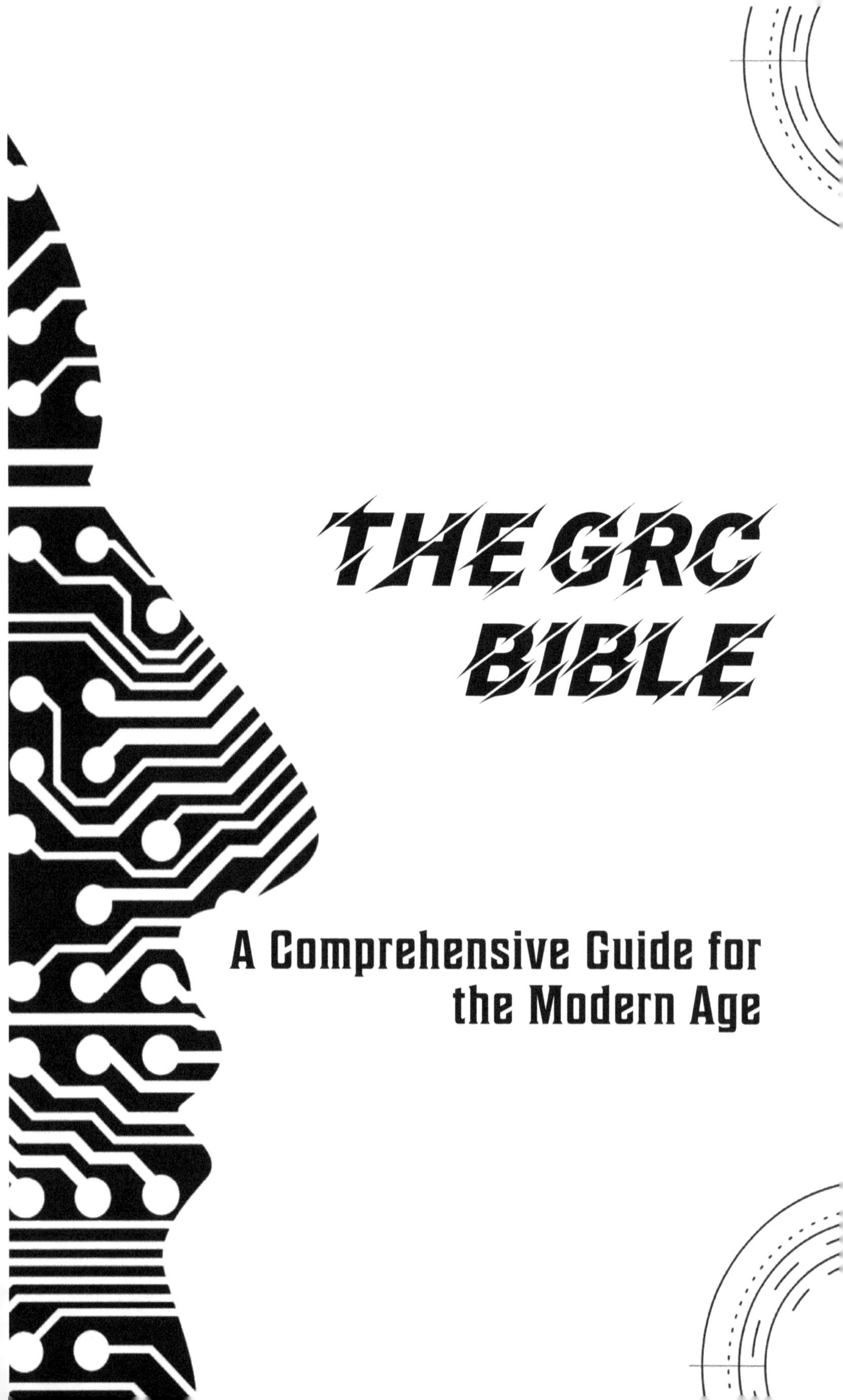

THE GRC
BIBLE
A Comprehensive Guide for
the Modern Age

Welcome to "The GRC Bible: A Comprehensive Guide for the Modern Age," your indispensable companion in navigating the intricate landscapes of Governance, Risk Management, and Compliance (GRC) in today's dynamic world. As we stand at the crossroads of unprecedented technological advancements, global interconnectivity, and ever-evolving regulatory frameworks, the need for a comprehensive and accessible guide to GRC has never been more crucial.

In this era of rapid change, organizations face a myriad of challenges, from the complexities of cybersecurity threats to the demands of ethical and sustainable business practices. "The GRC Bible" is not just a book; it is a roadmap that empowers individuals, businesses, and institutions to not only survive but thrive in the midst of these challenges.

Within these pages, you will embark on a journey that demystifies the intricate world of GRC, unraveling its principles, strategies, and best practices. Whether you are a seasoned executive seeking to enhance your organization's resilience or a newcomer looking to grasp the fundamentals, this guide is tailored to meet you where you are and elevate your understanding to new heights.

Buckle up as we explore the strategic importance of governance in shaping organizational destinies, navigate the ever-shifting landscape of risk management, and unravel the intricate tapestry of compliance requirements that define the boundaries of responsible conduct in the modern age. Along the way, we'll weave in real-world examples, case studies, and actionable insights, ensuring that the theoretical transforms into the practical.

"The GRC Bible" is more than just a reference—it is a call to action. It challenges you to embrace the complexities of the modern age and equips you with the knowledge and tools needed to navigate, adapt, and lead with confidence. Are you ready to embark on a transformative journey towards mastering the art and science of Governance, Risk Management, and Compliance? If so, turn the page, and let the adventure begin.

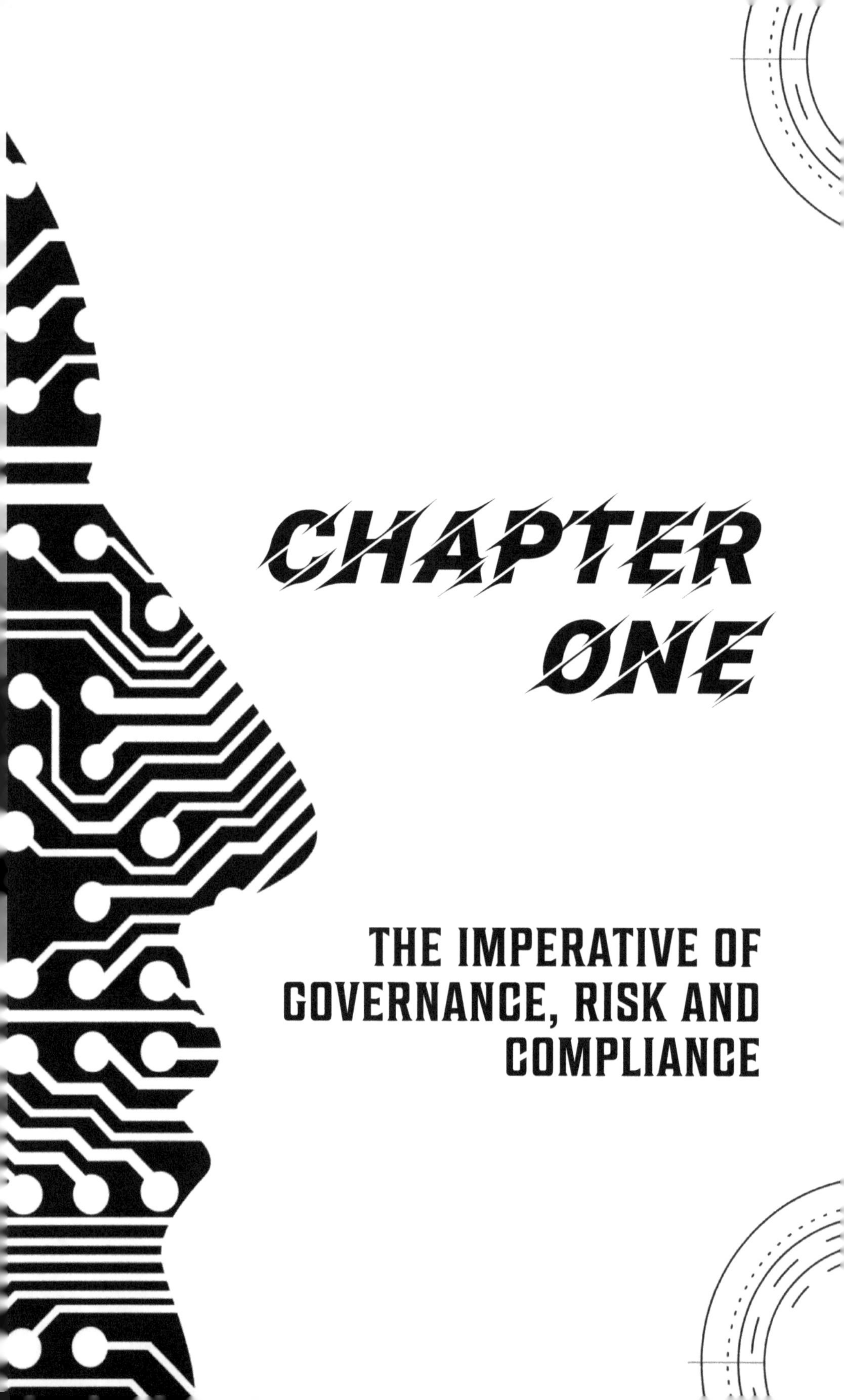

CHAPTER ONE

THE IMPERATIVE OF GOVERNANCE, RISK AND COMPLIANCE

The trajectory of Governance, Risk, and Compliance (GRC) is a narrative that unfolds through distinct epochs, mirroring the dynamic shifts in business paradigms, technological landscapes, and regulatory frameworks. Let us embark on a detailed exploration, beginning with the nuanced definitions that underpin the essence of GRC.

A strategic and proactive approach to GRC contributes not only to an efficient and effective fulfillment of compliance requirements, but also enables companies to realize additional benefits. For example, they are enabled to respond earlier, more flexibly and more comprehensively to new or changed stakeholder requirements. This not only enhances their public image for corporate governance, but also helps them to obtain significant competitive advantage from GRC by demonstrating a firm foundation for the long-term profitability of their business. (PWC, 2007)

1.1 DEFINITION OF GRC

Governance: Governance, the cornerstone of organizational order, encapsulates the processes, structures, and practices instituted by leadership to navigate the intricate web of objectives, risk landscapes, and judicious resource allocation. It establishes the strategic compass, delineating the ethical contours and shaping the cultural ethos that permeates the organizational fabric. Governance is the silent architect behind the scene whose invisible hand that ensures choices align with core values, mission, and long-term objectives. Within its framework lies the ability to adapt, responding to dynamic markets and emerging technologies. But governance is more than a strategic compass; it's the guardian of stakeholder trust, fostering transparency and accountability. In a world where reputation is as valuable as any asset, effective governance becomes the cornerstone of sustainable success.

Risk Management: Risk management, a sentinel against the uncertainties that beset every enterprise, is the systematic endeavor to identify, assess, and mitigate potential pitfalls that could impede the realization of organizational goals. Effective risk management isn't merely about avoiding pitfalls; it's about preserving and creating value. It empowers decision-makers with insights into potential challenges, allowing for informed choices. Beyond this, risk management fortifies organizations, building resilience to weather disruptions and unforeseen events. It is the vigilant watchman, ensuring that organizations not only survive but thrive in the face of uncertainty.

Compliance: Compliance, the ethical lodestar, encompasses the adherence to laws, regulations, standards, and ethical norms that govern an organization's operations. Beyond the legal mandate, it is the pillar of ethical conduct, safeguarding against legal entanglements, preserving reputation, and nurturing a culture of integrity within the organizational ecosystem. It is the embodiment of responsible corporate citizenship, fostering a culture of integrity that resonates both within and beyond organizational walls.

The cost of leaving compliance for later always is always worth much more than what it would cost to put compliance in place. Several surveys have proven this to be true time and time again. One survey of several years ago shows that for every $1 billion in revenue, the cost of compliance programs comes close to $6 million. 2 Another shows the cost of Sarbanes-Oxley compliance alone averaging $4 million for companies with $5 billion in revenue, and $10 million for companies with $10 billion and more in revenue. More telling is that for companies with more than $1 billion in revenue, compliance costs strikingly equaled the salaries of 190 full-time-equivalent employees.

In harmony, Governance, Risk, and Compliance create an imperative triad, each element complementing and reinforcing the others. Together, they form the ethical and strategic backbone of a resilient and successful organization. Recognizing this imperative isn't just a box to tick on a corporate checklist; it's an acknowledgment that in the modern age, where change is constant and challenges are diverse, GRC is not just a necessity—it's a pathway to enduring prosperity and societal contribution.

1.2   SYMBIOTIC RELATIONSHIP AMONG GRC COMPONENTS

1.   **Governance Influencing Risk Management:**

   ✴ *Strategic Alignment:* Effective governance sets the strategic direction for an organization. It involves decision-making structures, leadership practices, and a commitment to ethical conduct. This strategic alignment directly influences how risks are identified, assessed, and managed.

   ✴ *Risk Tolerance and Appetite:* Governance frameworks often define an organization's risk tolerance and appetite. Leadership decisions on risk-taking are rooted in governance structures, shaping risk management strategies. Clear governance guidelines help establish a balance between innovation and risk mitigation.

   ✴ *Cultural Impact:* Governance shapes the organizational culture. A culture that values transparency, accountability, and ethical behavior fosters a proactive risk management environment. Employees, guided by governance principles, are more likely to identify and address risks in alignment with organizational goals.

2. Risk Management Informing Compliance Strategies:

* *Identification of Regulatory Requirements:* The risk management process involves identifying risks, including those related to compliance. Through risk assessments, organizations can pinpoint areas where compliance risks are most prevalent, informing the development of targeted compliance strategies.

* *Proactive Compliance Measures:* Risk management highlights potential vulnerabilities, some of which may be related to regulatory compliance. In response, compliance strategies are designed not only to meet existing requirements but also to proactively address potential risks before they escalate.

* *Adaptive Compliance:* As risks evolve, so do compliance requirements. A dynamic risk management process ensures that compliance strategies are adaptive and responsive to changing circumstances, enabling organizations to stay ahead of regulatory shifts.

3. Compliance Ensuring Ethical Governance:

* *Legal and Ethical Alignment:* Compliance, by nature, requires adherence to legal standards. Ethical governance goes beyond legal requirements, encompassing moral principles and societal expectations. Compliance strategies, when crafted within an ethical framework, ensure alignment with both legal and moral imperatives.

* *Reputation Management:* Ethical governance is foundational for sustaining a positive reputation. Compliance efforts that prioritize ethical conduct contribute to building and maintaining trust with stakeholders. This, in turn, safeguards the organization's reputation, a vital asset in today's interconnected world.

✱ *Cultural Embedding:* Compliance initiatives, rooted in ethical considerations, contribute to the embedding of ethical values within the organizational culture. When compliance is viewed not as a checkbox but as an ethical responsibility, it becomes a driver for ethical governance throughout all levels of the organization.

1.3   EVOLUTION OF GRC

The journey of GRC is a saga marked by transformative epochs, each reflective of the zeitgeist of its time.

SILOS AND FRAGMENTATION

In the annals predating the 21st century, GRC found itself shackled within organizational silos. Governance, risk management, and compliance operated as discrete entities, leading to inefficiencies, redundancy, and a myopic view of the holistic risk landscape.

The early 2000s witnessed a paradigm shift as organizations recognized the imperative of integration. Enterprise-wide GRC solutions emerged as the panacea, breaking down silos and fostering collaboration. These solutions sought to streamline processes, enhance efficiency, and provide a consolidated, panoramic view of GRC activities.

As the second decade of the 21st century dawned, GRC metamorphosed in the crucible of technological innovation. Automation, powered by big data analytics and artificial intelligence, took center stage. Routine tasks were automated, and predictive analytics became the vanguard of risk management. Real-time monitoring emerged as the fulcrum, imbuing GRC with unprecedented accuracy, speed, and agility.

In environments where data silos are the norm, a culture of transparency and trust is very difficult to maintain. Instead, you might be creating rivalry and competition between teams focusing on their own micro-goals (Amresan 2022).

INTEGRATION WITH STRATEGIC PLANNING

The latter part of the second decade witnessed a profound transformation as GRC transcended its conventional role and melded seamlessly with strategic planning. GRC ceased to be a compliance-centric endeavor; instead, it became an integral component of strategic decision-making. Organizations embraced GRC as a strategic enabler, recognizing its pivotal role in driving innovation, mitigating risks, and creating enduring value.

In the contemporary landscape, GRC has evolved beyond the confines of procedural adherence. A cultural renaissance is underway, accentuating the role of ethics and integrity. The focus has shifted from mere compliance to instilling a culture where ethical behavior is ingrained in the organizational DNA. This cultural emphasis is viewed not only as a shield against risks but as a proactive catalyst for organizational resilience and sustainability.

1.4 THE DYNAMIC NATURE OF THE MODERN BUSINESS ENVIRONMENT

The modern business environment is characterized by a dynamic and ever-changing landscape, shaped by a myriad of interconnected factors that influence how organizations operate and thrive. This dynamism reflects a complex interplay of economic, technological, social, and environmental forces, creating a challenging yet opportunity-rich backdrop for businesses. Here are key aspects that illustrate the dynamic nature of the modern business environment:

GLOBAL INTERCONNECTEDNESS:

International Trade and Supply Chains: Globalization has intensified economic interdependence, making international trade and supply chains integral to business operations. Organizations must navigate diverse markets, cultural nuances, and geopolitical influences, amplifying both opportunities and risks.

TECHNOLOGICAL ADVANCEMENTS:

Digital Transformation: Rapid technological progress is reshaping industries. Digitalization, automation, artificial intelligence, and data analytics are not only optimizing processes but fundamentally altering business models. Organizations need to continually adapt to stay competitive and exploit the benefits of technological advancements.

CONSUMER BEHAVIOR AND EXPECTATIONS:

Changing Consumer Dynamics: Evolving consumer preferences and expectations, influenced by social trends and technological advancements, compel businesses to be agile and responsive. Customer-centricity is no longer a choice but a prerequisite for sustained success.

REGULATORY COMPLEXITY:

Evolving Regulatory Landscape: Increasing scrutiny and changes in regulations across industries demand heightened compliance efforts. Organizations must stay abreast of evolving legal frameworks, ethical standards, and industry-specific regulations to avoid legal consequences and protect their reputations.

ENVIRONMENTAL AND SOCIAL RESPONSIBILITY:

Sustainability and Corporate Social Responsibility: Environmental consciousness and social responsibility have become integral to organizational strategies. Businesses are expected to operate ethically, reduce their environmental footprint, and contribute positively to the communities in which they operate.

TALENT AND WORKFORCE DYNAMICS:

Changing Workforce Expectations: The workforce is experiencing a shift in expectations, valuing flexibility, purpose-driven work, and ongoing learning opportunities. Organizations need to adapt their talent strategies to attract and retain skilled professionals.

COMPETITIVE LANDSCAPE:

Rapid Innovation and Disruption: Industries face continuous innovation and disruption, challenging established business models. The competitive landscape is fluid, with nimble startups often posing threats to traditional incumbents.

ECONOMIC UNCERTAINTIES:

Global Economic Variables: Businesses operate in an environment influenced by global economic factors, including market fluctuations, currency exchange rates, and geopolitical events. Economic uncertainties can impact investment decisions, consumer spending, and overall market stability.

CYBERSECURITY RISKS:

Digital Security Challenges: The increased reliance on digital infrastructure exposes organizations to cybersecurity risks. Threats such as data breaches, ransomware attacks, and information theft require robust risk management strategies to safeguard sensitive information.

Understanding and navigating this dynamic environment requires organizations to be agile, innovative, and strategically adaptive. Continuous monitoring, flexibility in operations, and a proactive approach to risk management are essential for success in the contemporary business landscape.

1.5 IMPORTANCE OF GRC IN THE MODERN BUSINESS LANDSCAPE

The modern business environment is constantly evolving and organizations need to ensure they are keeping up. Governance, Risk, and Compliance (GRC) play a paramount role in ensuring the sustainability, resilience, and ethical conduct of organizations. The importance of GRC lies in its ability to provide a structured framework that fosters effective decision-making, mitigates risks, and ensures adherence to regulatory standards.

HERE ARE KEY REASONS GRC IS CRUCIAL:

i. Enhanced Decision-Making: A well-defined governance structure facilitates transparent decision-making processes. In the absence of such structure, decisions may be inconsistent, leading to confusion and potentially detrimental outcomes.

ii. Risk Mitigation: Robust risk management, a component of GRC, helps organizations identify and mitigate potential threats. Failure to manage risks adequately can result in financial losses, reputational damage, and operational disruptions.

iii. Regulatory Adherence: Compliance with industry regulations and legal standards is critical. Non-compliance can lead to hefty fines, legal actions, and reputational harm. For instance, data breaches due to lax data governance may result in severe financial penalties under data protection regulations.

iv. Ethical Business Conduct: Governance principles within GRC frameworks promote ethical behavior. Organizations that neglect ethical considerations may face public backlash, eroded trust, and damage to their brand reputation.

v. Operational Resilience: GRC practices enhance operational resilience by preparing organizations for unforeseen disruptions. In contrast, a lack of preparedness may lead to prolonged downtime, customer dissatisfaction, and financial losses in the wake of crises such as natural disasters or cyberattacks.

vi. Stakeholder Confidence: Effective GRC builds trust among stakeholders, including investors, customers, and employees. Poor GRC practices can erode this trust, leading to investor withdrawal, customer loss, and talent attrition.

vii. Strategic Alignment: GRC ensures that organizational strategies align with risk tolerance and regulatory requirements. Organizations without this alignment may find themselves pursuing strategies that expose them to unacceptable risks or legal consequences.

1.6 REAL-WORLD CONSEQUENCES OF POOR GRC PRACTICES

ENRON SCANDAL (2001):

Issue: Lack of governance oversight and ethical misconduct.

Consequences: Enron's bankruptcy, loss of shareholder value, legal actions against executives, and a significant blow to investor confidence in financial markets.

VOLKSWAGEN EMISSIONS SCANDAL (2015):

Issue: Deceptive compliance practices and lack of transparent governance.

Consequences: Substantial financial penalties, damaged brand reputation, lawsuits, and a decline in market value.

WELLS FARGO ACCOUNT SCANDAL (2016):

Issue: Systemic failures in risk management and compliance.

Consequences: Regulatory fines, CEO resignations, erosion of customer trust, and long-term damage to the bank's reputation.

EQUIFAX DATA BREACH (2017):

Issue: Inadequate data governance and cybersecurity practices.

Consequences: Legal settlements, financial losses, reputational damage, and increased regulatory scrutiny.

BOEING 737 MAX CRISIS (2019):

Issue: Governance and risk management failures in the development of the 737 Max aircraft.

Consequences: Grounding of the aircraft, financial losses, legal actions, and damage to Boeing's reputation.

These real-world examples underscore the critical importance of GRC in safeguarding organizations from ethical lapses, operational disruptions, financial losses, and reputational damage. In today's complex business landscape, effective GRC is not just a regulatory requirement but a strategic imperative for sustainable success.

1.7 INTRODUCTION TO POPULAR GRC FRAMEWORKS AND MODELS

Organizations seeking effective Governance, Risk, and Compliance (GRC) management often turn to established frameworks and models to guide their processes. These frameworks provide structured methodologies, best practices, and guidelines for integrating GRC seamlessly into organizational operations. Here are some widely adopted GRC frameworks and models:

ISO 31000 - RISK MANAGEMENT:

Overview: Developed by the International Organization for Standardization (ISO), ISO 31000 provides principles, framework, and a process for risk management. It emphasizes a systematic and proactive approach to identifying, assessing, and managing risks.

Role in GRC: ISO 31000 guides organizations in integrating risk management into their governance structures, ensuring a consistent and standardized approach to risk across the enterprise.

COSO - ENTERPRISE RISK MANAGEMENT (ERM):

Overview: The Committee of Sponsoring Organizations of the Treadway Commission (COSO) developed the Enterprise Risk Management (ERM) framework, which provides a comprehensive approach to managing risks across the entire organization.

Role in GRC: COSO ERM helps organizations align risk management with their strategic goals, integrate risk into decision-making processes, and enhance overall governance effectiveness.

COBIT - CONTROL OBJECTIVES FOR INFORMATION AND RELATED TECHNOLOGIES:

Overview: COBIT, developed by ISACA, is a framework designed to help organizations achieve their objectives through effective governance and management of information and technology.

Role in GRC: COBIT aids in aligning IT processes with business goals, ensuring compliance with regulations, and providing a holistic view of IT-related risks to enhance overall GRC capabilities.

NIST CYBERSECURITY FRAMEWORK:

Overview: Developed by the National Institute of Standards and Technology (NIST), the Cybersecurity Framework provides a risk-based approach to managing cybersecurity risks. It offers guidelines for identifying, protecting, detecting, responding to, and recovering from cybersecurity incidents.

Role in GRC: The NIST Cybersecurity Framework helps organizations integrate cybersecurity into their overall GRC strategy, ensuring a proactive approach to managing cybersecurity risks.

ITIL - INFORMATION TECHNOLOGY INFRASTRUCTURE LIBRARY:

Overview: ITIL is a set of practices for IT service management. It provides guidance on aligning IT services with the needs of the business, emphasizing continuous improvement and efficiency.

Role in GRC: ITIL helps organizations align IT processes with business objectives, ensuring that IT services support overall governance and compliance requirements.

1.7.1 How These Frameworks Help Structure and Streamline GRC Processes

a. Providing a Common Language: These frameworks offer a standardized vocabulary and set of terms that facilitate communication across different departments and functions within an organization. This common language helps ensure clarity and consistency in GRC activities.

b.   Structured Approach to Risk Management: GRC frameworks provide a structured and systematic approach to identifying, assessing, and managing risks. This ensures that risks are consistently evaluated, and mitigation strategies are effectively implemented throughout the organization.

c.   Aligning GRC with Business Objectives: The frameworks help align GRC activities with the broader strategic objectives of the organization. This ensures that GRC processes contribute directly to the achievement of business goals and priorities.

d.   Enhancing Accountability and Responsibility: By clearly defining roles and responsibilities, these frameworks help establish accountability for GRC activities. This clarity ensures that individuals and teams understand their roles in maintaining effective governance, managing risks, and ensuring compliance.

e.   Promoting Continuous Improvement: GRC frameworks emphasize the importance of continuous improvement. Regular assessments, feedback loops, and monitoring mechanisms ensure that GRC processes evolve in response to changes in the business environment, regulations, and risk landscapes.

f.   Integrating GRC with IT Processes: For organizations where information technology plays a significant role, frameworks like COBIT and ITIL facilitate the integration of GRC with IT processes. This integration ensures that IT activities align with overall business objectives and comply with relevant regulations.

g.   Enhancing Transparency and Reporting: GRC frameworks often include guidelines for transparent reporting of governance, risk, and compliance activities. This transparency is crucial for stakeholders, regulators, and internal decision-makers to understand the organization's GRC posture.

1.8 OVERVIEW OF THE REGULATORY ENVIRONMENT FOR ORGANIZATIONS

The regulatory environment in which organizations operate is a complex and multifaceted system of rules, laws, and standards established by governmental bodies and regulatory agencies. This environment is designed to ensure fair competition, protect consumers, uphold ethical standards, and address industry-specific challenges. Here is a detailed overview of key elements within the regulatory landscape:

1. **Regulatory Framework**

   Legal Foundations: Regulations are grounded in legal frameworks created by legislative bodies. These laws define the rules and boundaries within which businesses must operate.

   Regulatory Agencies: Governmental bodies and agencies are tasked with creating, implementing, and enforcing regulations. Examples include the Securities and Exchange Commission (SEC), Environmental Protection Agency (EPA), and the Food and Drug Administration (FDA).

2. **Industry-Specific Regulations:**

   Financial Industry: Regulations govern financial institutions to ensure market integrity, protect investors, and maintain financial stability. Examples include the Dodd-Frank Act and Basel III.

   Healthcare Industry: Regulations focus on patient safety, data privacy, and the approval of pharmaceuticals and medical devices. Notable regulations include the Health Insurance Portability and Accountability Act (HIPAA) and FDA guidelines.

Environmental Regulations: These regulations address environmental protection, emissions standards, and sustainable practices. Examples include the Clean Air Act and regulations related to waste disposal.

Telecommunications Industry: Regulations in this sector cover competition, consumer protection, and spectrum allocation. Regulatory bodies, such as the Federal Communications Commission (FCC), oversee compliance.

3. **Compliance and Corporate Governance**

Corporate Governance: Regulations often include guidelines for corporate governance, ethics, and responsible business conduct. The Sarbanes-Oxley Act, for instance, focuses on corporate governance and financial reporting.

Ethical Standards: Organizations are expected to adhere to ethical standards in their operations, and non-compliance may lead to legal consequences and reputational damage.

4. **Data Protection and Privacy Laws**

Global Data Protection Laws: With the rise of digital technologies, data protection and privacy laws have become crucial. The General Data Protection Regulation (GDPR) in the EU and the California Consumer Privacy Act (CCPA) in the U.S. are examples of comprehensive data protection laws.

5. **International Regulations**

Trade Regulations: Organizations involved in international trade must navigate regulations shaped by global trade agreements and organizations such as the World Trade Organization (WTO).

International Standards: Certain industries adhere to global standards set by organizations like the International Organization for Standardization (ISO).

6. Compliance Challenges

Complexity: The regulatory environment is characterized by its complexity, with a multitude of rules and requirements that organizations must interpret and comply with.

Rapid Changes: Regulations are subject to frequent updates and changes, requiring organizations to stay informed and adapt their practices accordingly.

7. Enforcement and Consequences

Regulatory Enforcement: Regulatory agencies have enforcement powers to ensure compliance. This may involve inspections, audits, and penalties for non-compliance.

Consequences of Non-Compliance: Failure to comply with regulations can lead to legal action, fines, reputational damage, and operational disruptions.

8. Global Regulatory Considerations:

Diversity Across Geographies: Regulatory requirements vary significantly across different countries and regions, adding complexity for organizations with global operations.

Harmonization Efforts: Some industries aim for global harmonization of regulations to streamline compliance. However, achieving this remains a complex challenge.

9. Evolving Regulatory Landscape

Emerging Technologies: New technologies, such as artificial intelligence, blockchain, and biotechnology, pose regulatory challenges, requiring authorities to adapt and establish guidelines.

10. **Compliance Management Systems**

GRC Frameworks: Governance, Risk, and Compliance (GRC) frameworks help organizations establish systematic approaches to compliance, risk management, and ethical governance.

Compliance Management Software: Technology solutions aid in tracking and managing compliance activities, ensuring timely updates and adherence to regulatory changes.

Effectively navigating this regulatory environment necessitates a proactive and strategic approach to GRC. Organizations must establish robust compliance programs, stay informed about regulatory developments, and cultivate a culture of ethical governance to thrive in this intricate landscape.

1.9 COMMON CHALLENGES FACED BY ORGANIZATIONS IN IMPLEMENTING GRC

Implementing effective Governance, Risk, and Compliance (GRC) processes poses several common challenges for organizations. These challenges, often inherent to the complex nature of GRC, can impact the efficiency and success of GRC initiatives:

FRAGMENTED PROCESSES

Challenge: GRC processes can become fragmented, residing in silos across different departments. Lack of integration may lead to inefficiencies, duplication of efforts, and difficulties in maintaining a cohesive GRC framework.

RESOURCE CONSTRAINTS

Challenge: Limited resources, both in terms of personnel and budget, can hinder the establishment and maintenance of robust GRC systems. Organizations may struggle to allocate sufficient resources to adequately address governance, risk management, and compliance requirements.

RAPID REGULATORY CHANGES

Challenge: The dynamic nature of regulatory environments means that organizations must continually adapt to evolving compliance requirements. Keeping pace with regulatory changes and ensuring timely updates to GRC processes is a persistent challenge.

COMPLEXITY OF RISK ASSESSMENT

Challenge: Accurately assessing and prioritizing risks across diverse business activities is a complex task. The sheer variety and interconnectedness of risks make it challenging for organizations to develop a comprehensive and effective risk assessment strategy.

CULTURAL RESISTANCE

Challenge: Establishing a culture of compliance and risk awareness can face resistance within organizational culture. Employees may be resistant to change, and there might be a lack of awareness about the importance of GRC.

LACK OF STANDARDIZATION

Challenge: Standardizing GRC processes across different business units or geographical locations is often challenging. Variations in processes and procedures can lead to inconsistencies and hinder the development of a unified GRC framework.

DATA MANAGEMENT AND INTEGRATION

Challenge: Efficient GRC relies on accurate and timely data. Integrating data from various sources, ensuring data quality, and maintaining data integrity can be complex, particularly when dealing with diverse systems and formats.

TECHNOLOGY COMPLEXITY

Challenge: Implementation and integration of GRC technologies can be intricate. The complexity of technology solutions, coupled with the need for interoperability, can pose challenges in selecting, implementing, and maintaining suitable GRC tools.

COMMUNICATION AND TRAINING

Challenge: Inadequate communication and training on GRC processes can impede their effectiveness. Employees need to be well-informed about compliance requirements, risk mitigation strategies, and their role in supporting GRC efforts.

CONTINUOUS MONITORING AND REPORTING

Challenge: Establishing effective mechanisms for continuous monitoring and reporting is crucial. GRC processes require ongoing oversight, and organizations may struggle to implement real-time monitoring systems that provide timely insights into potential risks and compliance issues.

VENDOR AND SUPPLY CHAIN RISKS

Challenge: Organizations are increasingly reliant on external vendors and supply chains. Managing the risks associated with third-party relationships, ensuring compliance throughout the supply chain, and mitigating vendor-related risks present ongoing challenges.

Addressing these challenges requires a strategic and holistic approach to GRC implementation. Organizations must foster a culture of awareness, invest in the right technologies, ensure effective communication, and adapt their GRC processes to the evolving regulatory landscape and internal dynamics.

1.10 OPPORTUNITIES FOR INNOVATION AND IMPROVEMENT WITHIN THE GRC FRAMEWORK

Technology Integration: Embrace innovative technologies such as artificial intelligence, machine learning, and data analytics to enhance risk identification, automate compliance monitoring, and streamline reporting processes within the GRC framework.

Predictive Analytics for Risk Management: Implement predictive analytics to anticipate potential risks and vulnerabilities. By analyzing historical data and patterns, organizations can proactively address emerging risks, enhancing the effectiveness of risk management strategies.

Blockchain for Data Integrity: Leverage blockchain technology to enhance data integrity and security within the GRC framework. Blockchain's decentralized and tamper-resistant nature can ensure the trustworthiness of critical data, reducing the risk of manipulation.

Integrated GRC Platforms: Invest in integrated GRC platforms that provide a centralized view of governance, risk, and compliance activities. Such platforms facilitate collaboration, streamline processes, and provide real-time insights, fostering efficiency and transparency.

Automated Compliance Management: Automate compliance processes using technology solutions to monitor regulatory changes, assess impacts, and ensure timely updates. Automation can reduce manual efforts, minimize errors, and enhance the agility of compliance management.

Behavioral Analytics for Fraud Prevention: Implement behavioral analytics to detect anomalies and potential fraudulent activities. Analyzing user behavior within an organization's systems can enhance fraud prevention measures and strengthen the security aspect of GRC.

Continuous Monitoring: Move towards continuous monitoring of risks and compliance rather than relying solely on periodic assessments. Real-time monitoring allows organizations to promptly identify and address issues, enhancing agility and responsiveness.

Gamification for Training and Awareness: Use gamification techniques to make GRC training engaging and effective. Creating interactive and scenario-based training programs can improve employee awareness and understanding of governance, risk, and compliance principles.

Robotic Process Automation (RPA): Implement RPA to automate routine and rule-based tasks within GRC processes. This allows employees to focus on more strategic activities, reduces the risk of human error, and enhances operational efficiency.

Supply Chain Visibility: Enhance supply chain risk management by leveraging technologies like the Internet of Things (IoT) and blockchain. These technologies provide real-time visibility into the supply chain, enabling better risk assessment and mitigation strategies.

Strengthening Cybersecurity Measures: Innovate cybersecurity measures within the GRC framework, adopting advanced technologies like threat intelligence, behavior analytics, and zero-trust architectures to fortify defenses against cyber threats.

Collaborative Risk Assessment: Foster a culture of collaboration by involving employees across departments in risk assessments. This ensures diverse perspectives, identifies risks more comprehensively, and encourages a proactive approach to risk management.

Environmental, Social, and Governance (ESG) Integration: Integrate ESG considerations into the GRC framework to address sustainability and ethical concerns. This proactive approach aligns with evolving stakeholder expectations and regulatory trends.

Dynamic Compliance Dashboards: Develop dynamic dashboards that provide real-time compliance status, key performance indicators, and actionable insights. This empowers decision-makers with timely information for strategic planning and decision-making.

Adaptive GRC Frameworks: Develop GRC frameworks that are adaptive to change. This includes flexible structures that can easily accommodate new regulations, emerging risks, and evolving business models without significant disruptions.

1.11 APPLICATION OF GRC PRINCIPLES IN VARIOUS SECTORS

1. **Finance Sector:**

GRC Principles Application:

Governance: Ensures effective board oversight, transparency in financial reporting, and ethical conduct.

Risk Management: Identifies and mitigates financial risks, such as market volatility, credit risk, and operational risk.

Compliance: Adheres to financial regulations (e.g., Basel III) and standards to ensure fair and transparent financial practices.

Example:

Banking Institutions: Banks implement GRC frameworks to manage financial risks, ensure compliance with regulatory requirements (e.g., Dodd-Frank Act), and maintain strong governance structures. Regular audits and risk assessments are conducted to identify and mitigate potential threats.

2. **Healthcare Sector:**

GRC Principles Application:

Governance: Establishes ethical standards, patient care policies, and oversight to ensure quality healthcare delivery.

Risk Management: Addresses patient safety risks, data security concerns, and compliance with healthcare regulations like HIPAA.

Compliance: Adheres to strict healthcare regulations (e.g., HIPAA) to protect patient privacy and ensure data security.

Example: Hospital Systems: Healthcare organizations implement GRC practices to ensure compliance with regulations, manage medical errors, and maintain ethical standards. Robust governance structures help in decision-making, and risk management strategies address patient safety and data protection.

3. **Technology Sector:**

GRC Principles Application:

Governance: Establishes ethical guidelines, corporate policies, and strategic oversight for technology companies.

Risk Management: Addresses cybersecurity threats, intellectual property risks, and compliance with data protection regulations.

Compliance: Adheres to technology regulations (e.g., GDPR) and industry standards to protect user data and maintain trust.

Example:

Tech Companies: Technology firms integrate GRC principles to manage cybersecurity risks, ensure compliance with data privacy laws (e.g., GDPR), and uphold ethical standards in product development. Regular audits and assessments are conducted to evaluate and improve cybersecurity measures.

4. **Manufacturing Sector:**

GRC Principles Application:

Governance: Establishes ethical manufacturing practices, quality control policies, and strategic oversight.

Risk Management: Addresses supply chain risks, operational risks, and compliance with environmental regulations.

Compliance: Adheres to manufacturing standards and environmental regulations to ensure product safety and sustainability.

Example:

Automotive Industry: Manufacturing companies in the automotive sector implement GRC practices to manage supply chain risks, ensure compliance with safety standards, and address environmental concerns. Governance structures oversee ethical manufacturing practices and strategic decision-making.

5. **Energy Sector:**

GRC Principles Application:

Governance: Establishes ethical energy production practices, safety protocols, and strategic oversight.

Risk Management: Addresses operational risks, environmental risks, and compliance with energy regulations.

Compliance: Adheres to energy regulations and environmental standards to ensure sustainable and responsible energy production.

Example:

Renewable Energy Companies: Companies in the renewable energy sector integrate GRC practices to manage environmental risks, comply with regulations (e.g., Renewable Portfolio Standards), and ensure ethical energy production. Robust governance structures oversee decision-making processes.

In each sector, GRC principles are tailored to address industry-specific challenges, regulatory requirements, and ethical considerations. The implementation of GRC practices is essential for fostering responsible and sustainable business operations across diverse sectors.

1.12 IMPACT OF TECHNOLOGY ON GRC PROCESSES

Technology plays a transformative role in Governance, Risk, and Compliance (GRC) processes, reshaping traditional approaches and enhancing overall effectiveness. The integration of tools, software, and data analytics has ushered in a new era of efficiency, transparency, and agility in managing GRC. Here's an exploration of the impact of technology on GRC processes:

Efficiency and Automation: Technology enables the automation of routine GRC tasks, reducing manual efforts and minimizing the risk of errors. This efficiency allows organizations to focus resources on strategic aspects of GRC, such as risk analysis and decision-making.

Real-Time Monitoring: Advanced tools facilitate real-time monitoring of risks and compliance. Organizations can receive instant insights into emerging risks, regulatory changes, and deviations from compliance standards, enabling proactive responses and decision-making.

Data Integration and Centralization: Technology allows the integration and centralization of data from various sources, providing a holistic view of GRC activities. This centralized data repository enhances collaboration, streamlines reporting, and ensures consistency across the organization.

Advanced Analytics for Risk Prediction: Data analytics tools enable organizations to analyze vast datasets to predict and identify potential risks. Predictive analytics models can forecast trends, allowing proactive risk management strategies to be implemented before issues escalate.

Regulatory Compliance Management: GRC software provides features for tracking regulatory changes, ensuring that organizations stay updated on evolving compliance requirements. Automated compliance management tools help in assessing the impact of new regulations and adapting processes accordingly.

Cybersecurity Measures: Technology is instrumental in enhancing cybersecurity measures within the GRC framework. Tools such as intrusion detection systems, encryption, and threat intelligence platforms strengthen defenses against cyber threats, protecting sensitive data and ensuring compliance with data protection regulations.

Governance and Policy Management: GRC software facilitates the creation, communication, and management of governance policies. This ensures that employees have access to up-to-date policies, fostering a culture of compliance and ethical conduct within the organization.

Audit and Monitoring Tools: Technology-driven audit tools streamline the audit process by automating data collection, analysis, and reporting. These tools enhance the accuracy and effectiveness of audits, providing a comprehensive view of governance and compliance adherence.

Supply Chain Visibility: Technologies like the Internet of Things (IoT) and blockchain enhance supply chain visibility within the GRC framework. These technologies provide real-time data on supply chain activities, enabling organizations to assess and mitigate risks throughout the supply chain.

Training and Awareness Platforms: Technology supports interactive and engaging training platforms within the GRC framework. Gamification, e-learning, and virtual training tools enhance employee awareness of GRC principles, ensuring a well-informed workforce.

Integrated GRC Platforms: Integrated GRC platforms provide a unified view of governance, risk, and compliance activities. These platforms streamline processes, improve communication, and offer a centralized hub for managing GRC initiatives across the organization.

Continuous Monitoring and Reporting: Continuous monitoring tools enable organizations to track key performance indicators, risk indicators, and compliance metrics in real-time. This capability enhances the organization's ability to respond promptly to changing conditions and emerging risks.

CHALLENGES

Despite the positive impact of technology on GRC processes, organizations may face challenges related to the selection, implementation, and integration of these technologies. These challenges include ensuring data security, addressing the learning curve for new tools, and adapting to the rapid pace of technological advancements.

1.13 EMERGING TRENDS AND FUTURE DEVELOPMENTS IN THE GRC LANDSCAPE

Integrated Risk Management (IRM): Organizations are shifting towards a more holistic approach by integrating risk management across the enterprise. IRM encompasses not only financial risks but also operational, strategic, and cybersecurity risks.

RegTech Advancements: Regulatory Technology (RegTech) is evolving to streamline compliance processes. AI-driven RegTech solutions can automate regulatory reporting, monitor changes in regulations, and enhance overall compliance efficiency.

Focus on Environmental, Social, and Governance (ESG): Increasing emphasis on ESG factors reflects a broader understanding of corporate responsibility. Organizations are integrating ESG considerations into their GRC frameworks to address sustainability, social impact, and ethical governance.

Advanced Analytics and Predictive Risk Intelligence: GRC is leveraging advanced analytics and machine learning for predictive risk intelligence. This trend enables organizations to anticipate and proactively address emerging risks based on historical data and real-time analytics.

Cybersecurity Risk Management: With the growing threat landscape, there is a heightened focus on cybersecurity risk management within GRC. Technologies like threat intelligence, behavior analytics, and zero-trust architectures are becoming integral to GRC strategies.

Supply Chain Resilience: The importance of supply chain resilience is on the rise. GRC frameworks are adapting to address supply chain risks, incorporating technologies like blockchain and IoT to enhance visibility, traceability, and risk mitigation.

Regulatory Sandboxes and Innovation Hubs: Some jurisdictions are establishing regulatory sandboxes and innovation hubs to encourage experimentation with new technologies in a controlled environment. This approach fosters innovation while maintaining compliance.

Crisis Management and Business Continuity: GRC is evolving to include more robust crisis management and business continuity planning. Organizations are placing greater emphasis on preparing for unforeseen events and disruptions.

Dynamic Compliance Dashboards: Dynamic compliance dashboards are becoming more prevalent, providing real-time insights into an organization's compliance status, key performance indicators, and potential areas of improvement.

Cultural Shift towards Ethical Governance: There is a cultural shift towards emphasizing ethical governance within organizations. GRC frameworks are incorporating ethical considerations, and a strong ethical culture is seen as a key component of effective governance.

HOW ORGANIZATIONS CAN PREPARE FOR AND ADAPT TO THESE CHANGES

Invest in Technology Adoption: Organizations should invest in adopting advanced technologies such as AI, machine learning, and analytics to enhance GRC processes. This includes selecting and implementing tools that align with the organization's specific needs and objectives.

Continuous Training and Skill Development: As technology evolves, organizations should prioritize continuous training and skill development for GRC professionals. This ensures that the workforce is equipped to leverage new technologies and adapt to changing GRC landscapes.

Stay Informed About Regulatory Changes: Establish processes for staying informed about regulatory changes. Regularly review and update compliance protocols to address new regulations promptly.

Embrace a Culture of Innovation: Foster a culture of innovation within the organization. Encourage experimentation with new technologies and methodologies to enhance GRC practices. Implementing pilot projects in regulatory sandboxes can be a part of this approach.

Enhance Collaboration Across Departments: Facilitate collaboration between different departments involved in GRC activities. Integrated GRC platforms and communication tools can enhance collaboration and ensure a cohesive approach to risk management and compliance.

Integrate ESG Considerations: Organizations should integrate ESG considerations into their GRC frameworks. This involves evaluating and addressing environmental, social, and governance risks and opportunities in a comprehensive manner.

Enhance Cybersecurity Measures: Given the increasing focus on cybersecurity risk management, organizations should continuously enhance their cybersecurity measures. This includes implementing advanced cybersecurity technologies and conducting regular assessments of cyber risks.

Develop Robust Crisis Management Plans: Strengthen crisis management and business continuity planning. Organizations should regularly review and update these plans to ensure they remain effective in the face of evolving risks and disruptions.

Promote Ethical Governance: Promote a culture of ethical governance within the organization. This involves establishing ethical guidelines, providing ethics training, and ensuring that ethical considerations are embedded in decision-making processes.

Engage with Regulatory Sandboxes: In jurisdictions where regulatory sandboxes or innovation hubs exist, organizations can engage with these environments to test and implement new technologies and methodologies in a controlled setting.

By proactively preparing for emerging trends and adapting to changes in the GRC landscape, organizations can position themselves to navigate complexities, capitalize on opportunities, and maintain effective governance, risk management, and compliance practices in the future. Continuous monitoring of industry trends, regulatory environments, and technological advancements will be essential for staying ahead in the dynamic GRC landscape.

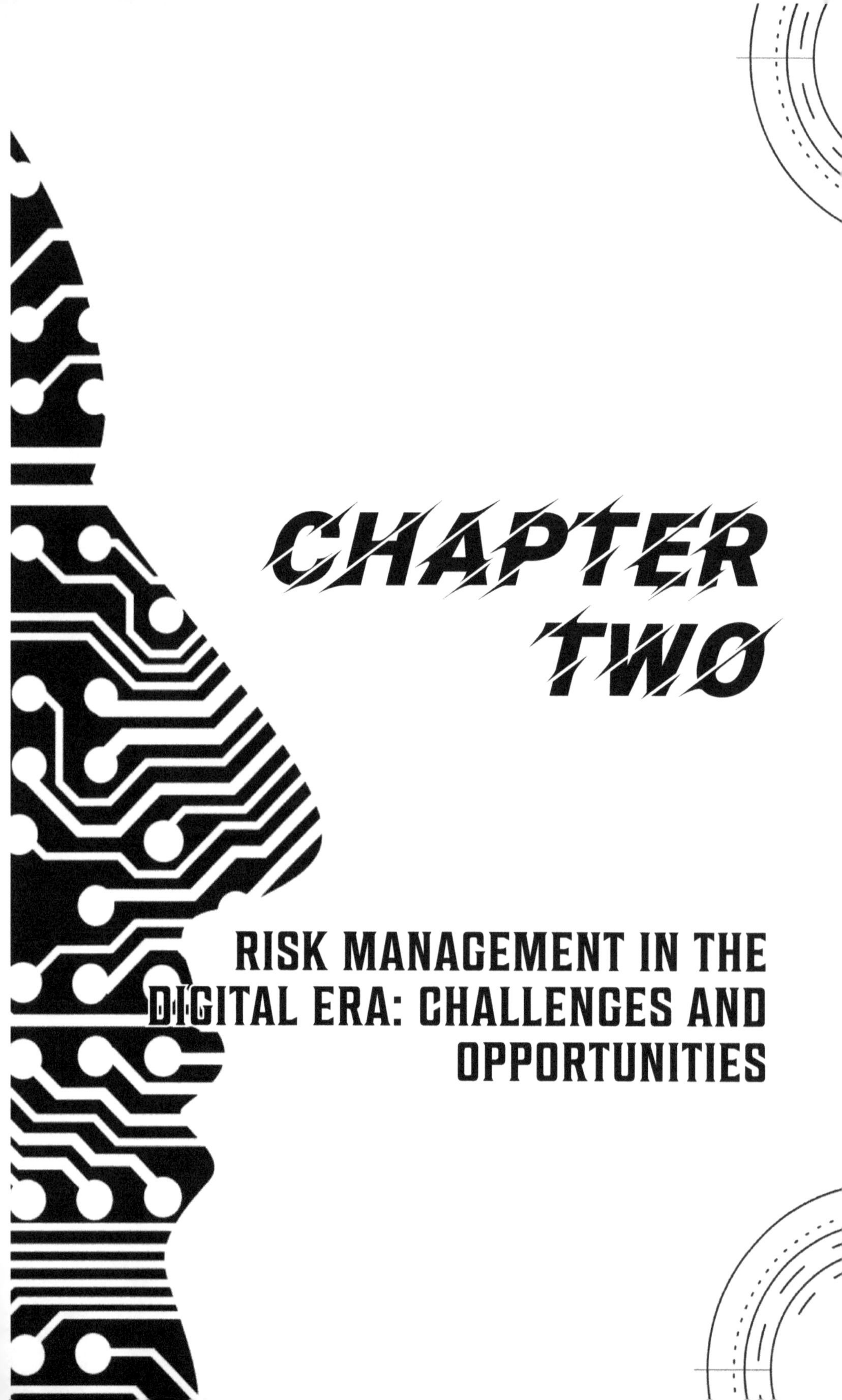
CHAPTER
TWO

RISK MANAGEMENT IN THE
DIGITAL ERA: CHALLENGES AND
OPPORTUNITIES

This chapter is focused on exploring the peculiarities involved in the mama of organizations in an age of digital transformation. Without a doubt, there are advantages to be enjoyed but organizations are also faced with unique risks they need to either overcome or find a way to work around.

2.1   DIGITAL TRANSFORMATION

Digital transformation refers to the integration of digital technologies into various aspects of an organization's operations, processes, products, and services. It involves leveraging advanced technologies to fundamentally alter how businesses operate, interact with customers, and deliver value. Digital transformation is not merely about adopting new technologies; it represents a strategic and cultural shift that enables organizations to stay competitive, agile, and responsive to the evolving demands of the digital age.

2.1.1   SIGNIFICANCE OF DIGITAL TRANSFORMATION IN RESHAPING BUSINESS OPERATIONS

Enhanced Efficiency and Productivity: Digital transformation streamlines processes, automates routine tasks, and facilitates data-driven decision-making, leading to increased operational efficiency and productivity.

Improved Customer Experience: Organizations leverage digital tools to enhance customer interactions, personalize experiences, and provide seamless services across multiple channels, resulting in improved customer satisfaction and loyalty.

Innovation and Agility: Embracing digital technologies fosters a culture of innovation and agility. Organizations can rapidly adapt to market changes, experiment with new ideas, and bring innovative products and services to market faster.

Data-Driven Insights: Digital transformation enables the collection and analysis of vast amounts of data. This data-driven approach provides valuable insights into customer behavior, market trends, and operational performance, guiding strategic decision-making.

Competitive Advantage: Businesses that effectively undergo digital transformation gain a competitive edge. They can respond to market dynamics, outpace competitors, and capitalize on emerging opportunities more effectively than those relying on traditional methods.

Flexibility and Scalability: Digital transformation allows organizations to build flexible and scalable infrastructures. Cloud computing, for example, enables scalable and cost-effective solutions, reducing the dependency on traditional IT infrastructure.

Collaboration and Communication: Digital tools facilitate seamless collaboration and communication within and across organizations. This is especially crucial in a globalized business environment where teams may be geographically dispersed.

Security and Compliance: With the increasing reliance on digital technologies, organizations must prioritize cybersecurity and compliance. Digital transformation initiatives often include measures to enhance data security, privacy, and regulatory compliance.

The Digital Era and Its Impact on Risk Management: The digital era has ushered in a paradigm shift in the risk management landscape, introducing new challenges and opportunities:

Increased Cybersecurity Risks: The digital era has brought about a surge in cyber threats. Organizations face sophisticated cyberattacks, data breaches, and ransomware, necessitating advanced cybersecurity measures and continuous risk monitoring.

Data Privacy Concerns: The proliferation of digital data raises concerns about data privacy. Stringent regulations (e.g., GDPR) require organizations to manage and protect personal and sensitive information, adding a layer of complexity to risk management.

Digital Supply Chain Risks: Digitalization has interconnected global supply chains, introducing new risks related to cyber threats, disruptions, and the dependency on digital platforms. Effective risk management must encompass the entire digital supply chain.

Rapid Technological Changes: The digital era is characterized by rapid technological advancements. Managing the risks associated with adopting new technologies, staying compliant, and ensuring the compatibility of systems becomes crucial.

Social Media and Reputational Risks: Social media amplifies the impact of reputational risks. Negative events, whether real or perceived, can quickly go viral, affecting brand reputation. Organizations need proactive risk management strategies for social media.

Regulatory Complexity: Digital business operations often span multiple jurisdictions, each with its own regulatory requirements. Navigating the complex regulatory landscape and ensuring compliance poses challenges for organizations in the digital era.

Integration of Third-Party Technologies: Organizations increasingly rely on third-party technologies and services. Managing the associated risks, including cybersecurity and compliance with contractual agreements, is integral to effective risk management.

Data Governance and Ethical Considerations: As organizations leverage data for insights, risk management must address issues related to data governance, ethical use of data, and ensuring that data-driven decisions align with regulatory and ethical standards.

2.1.2 DIVERSE RANGE OF RISKS ASSOCIATED WITH DIGITAL TECHNOLOGIES

The adoption of digital technologies has brought about transformative benefits for organizations, but it also introduces a diverse range of risks. Understanding and managing these risks is crucial for ensuring the security, privacy, and resilience of digital operations.

Here's an exploration of key risks, with a focus on cybersecurity threats, data breaches, and challenges posed by interconnected systems:

Cybersecurity Threats: Cybersecurity threats encompass a broad spectrum of malicious activities targeting digital systems, networks, and data. Examples include:

Malware: Software designed to harm or exploit digital systems, including viruses, ransomware, and spyware.

Phishing: Deceptive attempts to trick individuals into revealing sensitive information, often through fraudulent emails or websites.

Denial of Service (DoS) Attacks: Overwhelming a system, network, or website with traffic to disrupt normal functioning.

Advanced Persistent Threats (APTs): Long-term, sophisticated cyberattacks aimed at stealing sensitive information or disrupting operations.

Data Breaches: Unauthorized access, acquisition, or disclosure of sensitive or confidential data. Examples:

Unauthorized Access: Hackers gaining access to systems through vulnerabilities or weak passwords.

Insider Threats: Employees or trusted individuals intentionally or unintentionally compromising data security.

Third-Party Breaches: Security incidents originating from vulnerabilities in external service providers or partners.

Lost or Stolen Devices: Physical loss or theft of devices containing sensitive data.

2.1.3 Challenges Posed by Interconnected Systems

This is the interconnected nature of digital systems introduces challenges related to the seamless flow of data, dependencies, and potential cascading effects of failures.

SUPPLY CHAIN RISKS:

Description: Risks arising from dependencies and interconnections within the supply chain, including vendors, partners, and third-party service providers.

CHALLENGES:

Third-Party Vulnerabilities: Weaknesses in the security practices of external partners can expose an organization to risks.

Dependency Risks: Overreliance on a single supplier can amplify the impact of disruptions or breaches.

Regulatory Compliance: Ensuring that all entities within the supply chain adhere to relevant regulations and standards can be challenging.

IOT VULNERABILITIES:

Description: Security weaknesses in interconnected Internet of Things (IoT) devices.

CHALLENGES:

Diversity of Devices: A wide variety of IoT devices with varying security features pose challenges in maintaining a consistent security posture.

Firmware and Software Issues: Security vulnerabilities in device firmware or software can be exploited by attackers.

Scalability: As the number of IoT devices increases, managing security across a large-scale network becomes more complex.

CLOUD SECURITY CONCERNS:

Description: Security challenges associated with the use of cloud computing services.

CHALLENGES:

Data Privacy: Concerns about the security and privacy of data stored in the cloud.

Shared Responsibility: Clarifying the responsibilities of both the cloud service provider and the user for security measures.

Data Migration Risks: Moving data between on-premises systems and the cloud can introduce vulnerabilities.

CROSS-SYSTEM INTEGRATION ISSUES:

Description: Challenges related to the seamless integration of diverse systems and platforms.

CHALLENGES:

Interoperability Challenges: Ensuring that different systems can communicate and share data effectively.

Data Consistency: Maintaining consistency and accuracy of data across interconnected systems.

Security Standards: Establishing and adhering to security standards for cross-system communication.

MITIGATION STRATEGIES:

IMPLEMENT ROBUST CYBERSECURITY MEASURES:

Utilize firewalls, antivirus software, and intrusion detection systems to detect and prevent cybersecurity threats.

EMPLOYEE TRAINING AND AWARENESS:

Conduct regular training sessions to educate employees about cybersecurity risks, including phishing and social engineering.

REGULAR SYSTEM UPDATES AND PATCHING:

Ensure that software, operating systems, and applications are regularly updated with the latest security patches to address vulnerabilities.

MULTI-FACTOR AUTHENTICATION (MFA):

Implement MFA to add an extra layer of security, reducing the risk of unauthorized access in the event of compromised credentials.

INCIDENT RESPONSE AND RECOVERY PLANNING:

Develop and regularly update incident response plans to effectively respond to and recover from cybersecurity incidents.

SUPPLY CHAIN SECURITY ASSESSMENTS:

Conduct thorough security assessments of third-party vendors and partners to identify and mitigate supply chain risks.

IOT SECURITY BEST PRACTICES:

Follow security best practices for IoT devices, including regular firmware updates, strong authentication, and encryption of data in transit.

CLOUD SECURITY FRAMEWORKS:

Adhere to established cloud security frameworks and standards to ensure the secure use of cloud computing services.

INTERCONNECTED SYSTEM SECURITY STANDARDS:

Implement security standards for cross-system integration, emphasizing interoperability, data consistency, and secure communication.

2.1.4 POTENTIAL CONSEQUENCES OF CYBERATTACKS ON ORGANIZATIONS

DATA BREACH:

Consequence: Unauthorized access or theft of sensitive data, leading to privacy violations and potential legal and regulatory repercussions.

Impact on Organization: Damage to reputation, loss of customer trust, financial penalties, and legal consequences.

OPERATIONAL DISRUPTION:

Consequence: Cyberattacks, especially ransomware, can disrupt critical business operations, leading to downtime and financial losses.

Impact on Organization: Loss of productivity, revenue, and potential long-term damage to the business.

FINANCIAL LOSS:

Consequence: Cyberattacks may result in direct financial losses, including ransom payments, costs of remediation, and expenses associated with legal and regulatory compliance.

Impact on Organization: Erosion of profitability, increased expenses, and potential impact on stock value.

REPUTATION DAMAGE:

Consequence: Public disclosure of a cyberattack can damage an organization's reputation, eroding customer trust and confidence.

Impact on Organization: Long-term damage to brand image, customer attrition, and difficulty in attracting new business.

INTELLECTUAL PROPERTY THEFT:

Consequence: Cyberattacks targeting intellectual property may result in the theft of proprietary information, trade secrets, or research and development data.

Impact on Organization: Loss of competitive advantage, potential legal disputes, and impact on innovation.

REGULATORY AND LEGAL CONSEQUENCES:

Consequence: Non-compliance with data protection regulations or failure to protect sensitive information can lead to legal actions and regulatory fines.

Impact on Organization: Financial penalties, legal liabilities, and ongoing regulatory scrutiny.

OPERATIONAL INEFFICIENCY:

Consequence: Cyberattacks, especially those causing operational disruption, can result in inefficiencies, delays, and difficulties in meeting customer demands.

Impact on Organization: Increased operational costs, customer dissatisfaction, and potential loss of business opportunities.

CUSTOMER TRUST AND LOYALTY:

Consequence: Data breaches and other cyber incidents erode customer trust, leading to a decline in loyalty and potential customer churn.

Impact on Organization: Difficulty in retaining existing customers, challenges in acquiring new customers, and long-term impact on revenue.

LEGAL LIABILITY AND LAWSUITS:

Consequence: Organizations may face legal liability and lawsuits from affected parties, including customers, partners, or shareholders.

Impact on Organization: Legal expenses, potential financial settlements, and damage to the organization's legal standing.

LOSS OF OPERATIONAL CONTROL:

Consequence: Successful cyberattacks may result in the loss of control over critical systems or infrastructure.

Impact on Organization: Potential compromise of business secrets, disruption of operations, and loss of control over sensitive data.

CYBER EXTORTION:

Consequence: Ransomware attacks may lead to extortion demands for the release of encrypted data or systems.

Impact on Organization: Financial losses, potential damage to reputation, and increased vulnerability to future extortion attempts.

Understanding the potential consequences of cyberattacks underscores the critical importance of implementing robust cybersecurity measures, conducting regular risk assessments, and fostering a proactive cybersecurity culture within organizations.

A comprehensive approach that includes technology, policies, employee training, and incident response planning is essential to mitigate the impact of cyber threats on organizational resilience and success.

2.1.5 CHALLENGES RELATED TO DATA PRIVACY IN THE DIGITAL ERA

The digital era has brought about significant advancements in technology and data-driven practices, but it has also introduced a myriad of challenges related to data privacy. As organizations increasingly collect, process, and share vast amounts of personal and sensitive information, addressing these challenges becomes paramount. Here's an examination of the key challenges:

PROLIFERATION OF DATA:

Challenge: The sheer volume of data generated and collected in the digital era poses challenges in managing and securing personal information effectively.

Impact: Increased risk of unauthorized access, data breaches, and difficulty in implementing granular access controls.

GLOBALIZATION AND CROSS-BORDER DATA FLOW:

Challenge: Globalized business operations and cloud-based services often involve the cross-border transfer of personal data, raising concerns about varying data protection regulations.

Impact: Complexity in ensuring compliance with diverse international data protection laws and regulations.

LACK OF AWARENESS AND EDUCATION:

Challenge: Many individuals are not fully aware of the extent to which their data is collected, processed, and shared, leading to a lack of informed consent.

Impact: Increased potential for privacy violations and challenges in establishing a transparent and trustworthy relationship between organizations and individuals.

DATA BROKERAGE AND THIRD-PARTY RELATIONSHIPS:

Challenge: The widespread practice of data brokerage and reliance on third-party services for data processing create challenges in tracking and controlling the flow of personal information.

Impact: Increased risk of data misuse, profiling, and the potential for data breaches through third-party vulnerabilities.

EMERGENCE OF NEW TECHNOLOGIES:

Challenge: Emerging technologies such as artificial intelligence, machine learning, and the Internet of Things (IoT) introduce complexities in managing and protecting personal data.

Impact: Increased risk of algorithmic bias, loss of control over data flow, and challenges in implementing privacy-preserving measures.

DATA SECURITY AND BREACH INCIDENTS:

Challenge: The prevalence of data breaches and cybersecurity incidents poses a significant challenge to safeguarding personal information.

Impact: Compromised confidentiality, reputational damage, and potential legal and financial consequences for organizations.

LEGISLATIVE AND REGULATORY LANDSCAPE:

Challenge: Evolving and diverse data protection regulations, such as the GDPR in Europe and CCPA in the United States, create compliance challenges for organizations operating across regions.

Impact: Increased compliance costs, legal risks, and the need for ongoing adaptation to changing regulatory environments.

DATA SUBJECT RIGHTS AND CONSENT:

Challenge: Ensuring that individuals have control over their personal data, including the right to access, correct, and delete it, presents challenges in implementation and verification.

Impact: Striking a balance between honoring data subject rights and maintaining necessary data for legitimate business purposes.

BIOMETRIC DATA AND ADVANCED IDENTIFICATION:

Challenge: The increasing use of biometric data for identification purposes introduces challenges in protecting highly sensitive personal information.

Impact: Heightened risks of identity theft, unauthorized access, and the potential for irreversible harm if biometric data is compromised.

INTERNET AND SOCIAL MEDIA PRIVACY:

Challenge: The widespread use of social media platforms and online services raises concerns about the privacy of personal interactions, preferences, and behaviors.

Impact: Increased surveillance, targeted advertising, and the potential for data misuse for social engineering or manipulation.

ETHICAL CONSIDERATIONS AND ACCOUNTABILITY:

Challenge: The ethical use of data and establishing accountability for data processing practices pose challenges in aligning organizational conduct with societal expectations.

Impact: Potential loss of trust, reputational damage, and legal consequences for organizations that do not uphold ethical standards in data handling.

DATA RETENTION POLICIES:

Challenge: Determining appropriate data retention periods and implementing effective data disposal practices pose challenges for organizations.

Impact: Accumulation of unnecessary data, increased risk of data breaches, and potential non-compliance with data protection principles.

EDUCATIONAL AND HEALTHCARE DATA PRIVACY:

Challenge: Protecting sensitive personal data in sectors such as education and healthcare, where the information is particularly sensitive, presents unique challenges.

Impact: Enhanced risks of identity theft, discrimination, and potential harm to individuals if sensitive educational or health-related data is mishandled.

Addressing these challenges requires a comprehensive approach that encompasses robust data protection policies, privacy-enhancing technologies, regular risk assessments, and ongoing education for both organizations and individuals. As the digital landscape continues to evolve, the effective protection of data privacy is essential for fostering trust, maintaining compliance, and safeguarding the fundamental rights of individuals in the digital era

IMPACT OF REGULATIONS (E.G., GDPR, CCPA) ON ORGANIZATIONS' RISK MANAGEMENT STRATEGIES

Regulations such as the General Data Protection Regulation (GDPR) in Europe and the California Consumer Privacy Act (CCPA) in the United States have significantly altered the landscape of data protection and privacy. The impact on organizations' risk management strategies is profound, influencing how they collect, process, and protect personal data. Here's an exploration of the key impacts:

HEIGHTENED COMPLIANCE REQUIREMENTS:

Impact: The introduction of stringent data protection regulations imposes heightened compliance requirements on organizations. They are required to adhere to specific principles and guidelines for the lawful and ethical handling of personal data.

DATA GOVERNANCE AND ACCOUNTABILITY:

Impact: Regulations emphasize the importance of data governance and accountability. Organizations are now required to implement robust policies, procedures, and documentation to demonstrate compliance with data protection principles.

ENHANCED DATA SUBJECT RIGHTS:

Impact: GDPR and similar regulations provide individuals with enhanced rights regarding their personal data, including the right to access, correct, and delete their information. Organizations must establish mechanisms to fulfill these rights, impacting how data is managed and processed.

RISK ASSESSMENT AND IMPACT ANALYSIS:

Impact: Regulations mandate organizations to conduct risk assessments and data protection impact assessments (DPIAs). This requires a systematic evaluation of the risks associated with data processing activities, influencing risk management strategies.

SECURITY MEASURES AND BREACH NOTIFICATION:

Impact: GDPR and CCPA require organizations to implement appropriate security measures to protect personal data. In the event of a data breach, timely notification to affected individuals and regulatory authorities is mandatory, influencing incident response and risk mitigation strategies.

DATA MINIMIZATION AND PURPOSE LIMITATION:

Impact: Regulations emphasize the principles of data minimization and purpose limitation, encouraging organizations to collect and process only the necessary data for specific, lawful purposes. This impacts data collection practices and influences risk associated with excessive data handling.

VENDOR AND THIRD-PARTY MANAGEMENT:

Impact: Organizations are held accountable for the actions of their vendors and third-party processors. This influences risk management strategies as organizations must carefully assess and manage the risks associated with third-party data processing activities.

INTERNATIONAL DATA TRANSFERS:

Impact: GDPR introduces strict requirements for the transfer of personal data outside the European Economic Area (EEA). Organizations must ensure that international data transfers comply with GDPR standards, influencing cross-border data flow risk assessments.

PENALTIES AND FINES:

Impact: GDPR and CCPA have introduced significant penalties and fines for non-compliance. This creates a financial risk for organizations that fail to implement adequate data protection measures and highlights the importance of robust risk management strategies.

TRAINING AND AWARENESS PROGRAMS:

Impact: Regulations underscore the importance of training and awareness programs for employees handling personal data. This influences risk management by addressing the human factor and reducing the risk of data breaches due to human error.

LEGAL AND REPUTATIONAL RISKS:

Impact: Non-compliance with data protection regulations introduces legal and reputational risks. Organizations must consider the potential damage to their reputation and the legal consequences of failing to uphold data protection standards in their risk management strategies.

CONSENT MANAGEMENT:

Impact: GDPR emphasizes the need for valid consent for processing personal data. Organizations must implement transparent consent management practices, impacting how they collect and document consent and manage the associated risks.

RECORD-KEEPING AND DOCUMENTATION:

Impact: Regulations require organizations to maintain detailed records and documentation related to data processing activities. This influences risk management by ensuring transparency, accountability, and the ability to demonstrate compliance.

INCORPORATION OF PRIVACY BY DESIGN AND DEFAULT:

Impact: Privacy by Design and Default principles, mandated by GDPR, require organizations to integrate data protection measures into the design of systems and processes. This influences risk management by embedding privacy considerations from the outset.

DATA PROTECTION OFFICERS (DPOS):

Impact: Certain organizations are required to appoint Data Protection Officers (DPOs) under GDPR. DPOs play a crucial role in overseeing data protection practices and influencing risk management strategies.

2.3 TECHNOLOGY ADOPTION RISKS

RISKS ASSOCIATED WITH RAPID TECHNOLOGY ADOPTION:

Rapid technology adoption, while offering numerous benefits and opportunities, also introduces a range of risks that organizations must carefully navigate. The pace at which new technologies are integrated into business operations can sometimes outstrip the ability to address associated challenges. Here are key risks associated with the rapid adoption of technology:

Security Vulnerabilities:

Risk: Rapidly adopting new technologies may result in insufficient time for thorough security assessments. This increases the likelihood of security vulnerabilities that could be exploited by malicious actors.

DATA BREACHES AND CYBERSECURITY THREATS:

Risk: The integration of new technologies may expose organizations to data breaches and cybersecurity threats. Inadequate cybersecurity measures or a lack of awareness about emerging threats can lead to unauthorized access and data compromise.

COMPLIANCE CHALLENGES:

Risk: Rapid adoption may lead to non-compliance with industry regulations or data protection laws. Failure to align technology implementations with regulatory requirements can result in legal consequences and financial penalties.

LACK OF INTEROPERABILITY:

Risk: The rapid adoption of diverse technologies may result in a lack of interoperability between systems. Incompatible technologies may hinder seamless communication and data exchange, leading to operational inefficiencies.

OPERATIONAL DISRUPTIONS:

Risk: The integration of new technologies can disrupt existing workflows and processes. Poorly managed technology transitions may lead to downtime, loss of productivity, and delays in delivering products or services.

EMPLOYEE RESISTANCE AND SKILL GAPS:

Risk: Rapid technology adoption may face resistance from employees who are unfamiliar with or resistant to change. Moreover, there may be skill gaps as employees need time to acquire the necessary expertise, potentially impacting productivity.

OVERLOOKING ETHICAL CONSIDERATIONS:

Risk: In the haste to adopt new technologies, organizations may overlook ethical considerations related to privacy, data use, and societal impact. This can result in reputational damage and legal issues.

FINANCIAL OVERCOMMITMENT:

Risk: Rapid adoption of technology may lead to overcommitment of financial resources without a clear understanding of the long-term returns on investment. This can strain budgets and financial sustainability.

INADEQUATE TESTING AND QUALITY ASSURANCE:

Risk: Insufficient testing and quality assurance processes, often due to time constraints, can result in the deployment of technologies with undetected bugs or flaws, leading to operational disruptions and potential security issues.

VENDOR RELIABILITY AND DEPENDENCY:

Risk: Relying on a limited number of vendors for critical technologies may create dependency and vulnerability. If a vendor experiences issues, goes out of business, or faces security breaches, it can significantly impact the organization.

RAPID CHANGES IN TECHNOLOGY TRENDS:

Risk: Rapid technology adoption may result in organizations investing in technologies that become outdated quickly. Keeping up with evolving trends can be challenging and may necessitate frequent technology upgrades.

INSUFFICIENT CHANGE MANAGEMENT:

Risk: The speed of technology adoption may lead to inadequate change management practices. Poorly managed change can result in resistance, confusion, and a lack of alignment with organizational goals.

ENVIRONMENTAL IMPACT:

Risk: Some technologies may have unforeseen environmental consequences. Rapid adoption without considering sustainability factors can contribute to electronic waste, energy consumption, and other environmental issues.

LACK OF SCALABILITY:

Risk: Technologies adopted hastily may lack scalability, hindering the organization's ability to accommodate future growth or increased demand effectively.

HIDDEN COSTS:

Risk: Rapid adoption may lead to overlooking hidden costs associated with technology implementation, such as ongoing maintenance, training, and integration with existing systems.

2.4 CHALLENGES OF IMPLEMENTING NEW TECHNOLOGIES AND POTENTIAL DISRUPTIONS TO EXISTING PROCESSES

Implementing new technologies in an organization can bring about transformative benefits, but it is not without challenges. The introduction of novel technologies often disrupts existing processes, workflows, and even organizational cultures. Here are key challenges and potential disruptions associated with implementing new technologies:

RESISTANCE TO CHANGE:

Challenge: Employees may resist changes to established workflows and processes. Fear of the unknown, concerns about job security, or lack of familiarity with the new technology can contribute to resistance.

SKILL GAPS AND TRAINING NEEDS:

Challenge: Introducing new technologies may require skills that employees currently lack. Training programs are often necessary to bridge these skill gaps, and the time needed for training can disrupt regular operations.

INTEGRATION WITH LEGACY SYSTEMS:

Challenge: Compatibility issues between new technologies and existing legacy systems can pose significant challenges. Seamless integration is crucial to avoid disruptions and ensure data consistency.

DATA MIGRATION CHALLENGES:

Challenge: Transferring data from old systems to new ones is a complex process. Data migration challenges, such as data loss, integrity issues, or extended downtime during the migration process, can disrupt operations.

INITIAL PRODUCTIVITY DIP:

Challenge: During the initial stages of implementation, there is often a temporary dip in productivity as employees adjust to the new tools and processes. This can impact deadlines and deliverables.

UNCERTAIN RETURN ON INVESTMENT (ROI):

Challenge: Organizations may face uncertainty about the expected return on investment for new technologies. The initial costs of implementation and disruptions may not immediately translate into tangible benefits.

VENDOR RELIABILITY AND SUPPORT:

Challenge: Reliance on external vendors for technology solutions introduces risks. Dependence on a vendor's reliability, support responsiveness, and long-term stability can lead to disruptions if issues arise.

SCOPE CREEP AND OVER-CUSTOMIZATION:

Challenge: Over-customizing new technologies to fit specific organizational needs may lead to scope creep. This can result in delays, increased costs, and unintended disruptions to existing processes.

CHANGE MANAGEMENT ISSUES:

Challenge: Inadequate change management can lead to confusion and resistance. Clear communication, involving stakeholders, and managing expectations are crucial to navigate the human side of technological change.

DATA SECURITY CONCERNS:

Challenge: Introducing new technologies may raise concerns about data security. Organizations must ensure that robust security measures are in place to protect sensitive information from breaches and unauthorized access.

REGULATORY COMPLIANCE RISKS:

Challenge: Implementing new technologies may introduce risks related to regulatory compliance. Failure to comply with industry-specific regulations can result in legal consequences and disruptions to operations.

CULTURAL SHIFTS:

Challenge: The introduction of new technologies may necessitate cultural shifts within the organization. Resistance to cultural changes can lead to disruptions in collaboration and communication.

DEPENDENCY ON EXTERNAL FACTORS:

Challenge: External factors, such as changes in industry standards or regulations, may impact the functionality and relevance of newly implemented technologies, introducing uncertainties.

OVERLOOKING USER EXPERIENCE:

Challenge: Focusing solely on the technical aspects of implementation without considering the user experience can result in dissatisfaction among employees, leading to disruptions in productivity and engagement.

OPERATIONAL DOWNTIME:

Challenge: Transitioning from old to new systems may require temporary operational downtime. Organizations need to plan for this downtime to minimize disruptions to essential business functions.

2.5 UNDERSTANDING THE ROLE OF SOCIAL ENGINEERING IN CYBER THREATS AND ADDRESSING HUMAN FACTORS IN CYBERSECURITY

The subtle tactics of social engineering relies not on exploiting technical vulnerabilities but on manipulating the very human elements that constitute the front line of defense in any organization.

Understanding the role of social engineering and recognizing the intricate dance of human factors in cybersecurity is pivotal for effective risk mitigation.

Here, we delve into these nuances and explore strategies for enlightening and engaging employees to fortify the human firewall.

THE ESSENCE OF SOCIAL ENGINEERING:

Social engineering encompasses a spectrum of deceptive techniques, skillfully crafted to exploit the inherent traits of human behavior. Phishing, spear phishing, vishing, and impersonation are but a few facets of this multifaceted approach. Attackers, leveraging psychological triggers, trick individuals into divulging sensitive information, initiating unauthorized actions, or unwittingly compromising security protocols.

HUMAN FACTORS IN THE CYBERSECURITY EQUATION:

At the heart of cybersecurity challenges lies the intricate interplay of human factors. Lack of awareness serves as a breeding ground for susceptibility, where employees may unwittingly fall prey to the snares of social engineering. The inherent trust in authority, be it in the form of familiar entities or seemingly credible sources, can be manipulated to breach the defense perimeter. Curiosity, urgency, fear, and intimidation become tools wielded by cyber adversaries, exploiting the emotional undercurrents to gain compliance.

2.6 STRATEGIES FOR BUILDING A RESILIENT HUMAN FIREWALL

COMPREHENSIVE TRAINING PROGRAMS:

Establish regular cybersecurity training programs that transcend the perfunctory and delve into the intricacies of social engineering.

Convey the gravity of potential threats through real-world examples, fostering a deeper understanding among employees.

SIMULATED PHISHING EXERCISES:

Initiate simulated phishing exercises to gauge the organization's vulnerability to social engineering attempts.

Utilize the results to tailor targeted training sessions, addressing specific areas of susceptibility.

CLEAR AND ACCESSIBLE POLICIES:

Institute transparent and easily accessible cybersecurity policies, delineating acceptable practices and potential threats.

Foster a culture where employees not only comprehend but actively incorporate these policies into their daily activities.

CONTINUOUS AWARENESS CAMPAIGNS:

Implement ongoing awareness campaigns, utilizing diverse communication channels such as newsletters, posters, and email reminders.

Cultivate a pervasive culture of vigilance, ensuring that cybersecurity remains a constant consideration.

ENCOURAGE REPORTING:

Foster an environment that encourages the reporting of any suspicious activity or perceived social engineering attempts.

Establish a straightforward and confidential reporting mechanism, empowering employees to be proactive in safeguarding the organization.

MULTI-FACTOR AUTHENTICATION (MFA):

Implement MFA as an additional layer of defense, mitigating the impact even if credentials are compromised through social engineering.

Elevate the overall security posture by fortifying access controls.

REGULAR SECURITY UPDATES:

Keep employees informed about the ever-evolving landscape of cybersecurity threats and best practices.

Regularly disseminate updates, spotlighting emerging social engineering tactics and ways to preemptively thwart them.

ENGAGING TRAINING MATERIALS:

Develop engaging and interactive training materials, employing mediums such as videos, quizzes, and gamified modules.

Craft scenarios that resonate with employees, making the training not only informative but relatable to their daily roles.

EXECUTIVE SUPPORT AND INVOLVEMENT:

Ensure active support and participation from executive leadership in cybersecurity initiatives.

Leadership involvement serves as a compelling endorsement, emphasizing the organizational commitment to robust cybersecurity practices.

CONDUCT INCIDENT RESPONSE DRILLS:

Stage regular incident response drills, providing employees with practical experience in dealing with simulated social engineering attacks.

Instill a sense of readiness and preparedness, enhancing the organization's resilience to potential threats.

REWARD AND RECOGNITION PROGRAMS:

Institute reward and recognition programs, acknowledging employees who exemplify exceptional cybersecurity awareness and practices.

Positive reinforcement becomes a catalyst for cultivating a proactive approach to security.

2.7 EVOLVING REGULATORY LANDSCAPE IN DIGITAL TECHNOLOGIES

The regulatory landscape concerning digital technologies is undergoing a constant evolution, driven by the rapid advancements in technology, increased digitalization across industries, and growing concerns about data privacy and cybersecurity. Several key aspects define this dynamic regulatory environment:

DATA PRIVACY REGULATIONS:

Regulations such as the General Data Protection Regulation (GDPR) in Europe and the California Consumer Privacy Act (CCPA) in the United States focus on protecting individuals' privacy rights and regulating the collection, processing, and storage of personal data.

CYBERSECURITY FRAMEWORKS:

Governments and industry bodies are developing and updating cybersecurity frameworks to address the escalating threats in the digital realm. These frameworks provide guidelines for organizations to enhance their cybersecurity measures.

ARTIFICIAL INTELLIGENCE (AI) GOVERNANCE:

As AI technologies advance, there's a growing emphasis on establishing ethical guidelines and governance frameworks to ensure responsible AI development and deployment. This includes considerations for bias, transparency, and accountability.

DIGITAL FINANCIAL SERVICES REGULATIONS:

The rise of digital financial services, including cryptocurrencies and blockchain technology, has prompted regulatory bodies to formulate frameworks to address issues such as fraud prevention, consumer protection, and financial stability.

TELECOMMUNICATIONS AND 5G REGULATIONS:

The deployment of 5G technology is subject to specific regulations to ensure the security and resilience of critical infrastructure. Governments are also addressing issues related to the deployment of telecommunications networks from national security perspectives.

CHALLENGES OF STAYING COMPLIANT WITH RAPIDLY CHANGING REGULATIONS

LACK OF UNIFORMITY:

Different regions and countries often have varying regulations, making it challenging for global organizations to maintain uniform compliance standards across all jurisdictions.

RAPID CHANGES AND UPDATES:

Regulatory bodies frequently update and amend rules to adapt to technological advancements and emerging risks. Staying abreast of these changes demands continuous monitoring and adaptability.

INTERCONNECTED COMPLIANCE REQUIREMENTS:

Digital technologies often involve multiple facets (e.g., data privacy, cybersecurity, AI), each with its own set of regulations. Ensuring compliance across these interconnected requirements adds complexity.

RESOURCE INTENSIVENESS:

Compliance efforts demand significant resources, both in terms of personnel and technology. Smaller organizations may face challenges allocating the necessary resources for comprehensive compliance programs.

LEGAL AND REGULATORY UNCERTAINTY:

The dynamic nature of the regulatory landscape can create uncertainty. Organizations may struggle to interpret and anticipate how regulations will evolve, making long-term compliance planning challenging.

2.8.1   ASSOCIATED RISKS OF NON-COMPLIANCE

FINANCIAL PENALTIES:

Regulatory bodies impose substantial fines for non-compliance, aiming to incentivize organizations to adhere to established standards. These fines can be financially crippling for businesses.

REPUTATIONAL DAMAGE:

Non-compliance can lead to reputational damage, eroding trust among customers, partners, and stakeholders. Negative publicity surrounding regulatory violations can have lasting effects on brand perception.

LEGAL CONSEQUENCES:

Non-compliance may result in legal action, including lawsuits and regulatory investigations. Legal consequences can extend beyond financial penalties to include court-mandated actions and restrictions.

OPERATIONAL DISRUPTIONS:

Regulatory actions may require organizations to make operational changes or cease certain practices, leading to disruptions in business operations and potential financial losses.

LOSS OF COMPETITIVE EDGE:

Organizations that fail to keep up with evolving regulatory standards may lose their competitive edge. Compliance with industry-specific regulations can be a key differentiator in certain markets.

DATA BREACH CONSEQUENCES:

Non-compliance with data protection regulations can increase the risk of data breaches. The consequences of a data breach, including reputational damage and legal liabilities, can be severe.

SUPPLY CHAIN IMPACT:

Many regulations require organizations to ensure compliance not only within their operations but also throughout their supply chains. Non-compliance at any level of the supply chain can have cascading effects.

LIMITED MARKET ACCESS:

Some regions restrict market access for organizations that do not comply with local regulations. Non-compliance can limit expansion opportunities and hinder access to lucrative markets.

2.8.2   NAVIGATING THE REGULATORY LANDSCAPE

To navigate the evolving regulatory landscape, organizations should adopt a proactive approach:

* Establish a robust compliance management system.

* Invest in ongoing training for staff on regulatory changes.

* Engage legal and compliance experts to interpret and apply regulations.

* Leverage technology solutions for compliance monitoring and reporting.

Digital transformation introduces a myriad of positive aspects and opportunities for risk management, revolutionizing traditional approaches and fostering resilience in the face of evolving challenges.

Here are key highlights of the positive impacts and opportunities brought about by digital transformation in risk management:

ENHANCED DATA ANALYTICS:

Positive Aspect: Digital transformation enables organizations to harness the power of advanced data analytics. Analyzing vast datasets in real-time facilitates proactive risk identification and assessment.

Opportunity: Predictive analytics and machine learning algorithms provide insights into emerging risks, allowing organizations to adopt a proactive stance in risk mitigation.

IMPROVED DECISION-MAKING:

Positive Aspect: Access to real-time data and analytics empowers decision-makers with more accurate and timely information.

Opportunity: Decision-makers can make informed choices, optimizing risk responses and maximizing the potential for positive outcomes.

AUTOMATION OF ROUTINE TASKS:

Positive Aspect: Automation of routine risk management tasks reduces the likelihood of human error and streamlines operational efficiency.

Opportunity: Teams can focus on higher-value tasks, such as strategic risk planning and response, while automation handles repetitive processes.

INTEGRATION OF RISK MANAGEMENT SYSTEMS:

Positive Aspect: Digital transformation facilitates the integration of diverse risk management systems, creating a cohesive and comprehensive risk management framework.

Opportunity: Integrated systems enable a holistic view of risks across the organization, promoting a more coherent and efficient risk management strategy.

REAL-TIME MONITORING AND ALERTS:

Positive Aspect: Digital tools enable real-time monitoring of risk indicators, allowing for prompt detection of anomalies.

Opportunity: Automated alerts ensure that risk events are identified promptly, enabling rapid response and mitigation efforts.

CLOUD-BASED SOLUTIONS:

Positive Aspect: Cloud-based risk management solutions offer scalability, flexibility, and accessibility.

Opportunity: Organizations can leverage cloud infrastructure for efficient collaboration, data storage, and real-time updates, enhancing the agility of risk management processes.

ENHANCED CYBERSECURITY MEASURES:

Positive Aspect: Digital transformation prompts organizations to invest in robust cybersecurity measures.

Opportunity: Advanced cybersecurity technologies, such as threat intelligence and behavioral analytics, strengthen the organization's defense against cyber risks and data breaches.

INCREASED STAKEHOLDER ENGAGEMENT:

Positive Aspect: Digital platforms facilitate enhanced communication and engagement with stakeholders.

Opportunity: Organizations can involve stakeholders in risk identification and response, fostering a collaborative risk management culture.

SCENARIO PLANNING AND MODELING:

Positive Aspect: Digital tools enable sophisticated scenario planning and risk modeling.

Opportunity: Organizations can simulate various risk scenarios, allowing for proactive strategizing and the development of effective risk response plans.

BIG DATA UTILIZATION:

Positive Aspect: Digital transformation unlocks the potential of big data, enabling organizations to analyze vast datasets for risk insights.

Opportunity: Big data analytics provides a comprehensive understanding of trends, enabling organizations to anticipate and address emerging risks before they escalate.

REGULATORY COMPLIANCE MANAGEMENT:

Positive Aspect: Digital tools simplify regulatory compliance management through automated tracking and reporting.

Opportunity: Organizations can efficiently adapt to changing regulations, ensuring continuous compliance and mitigating legal and financial risks.

CONTINUOUS MONITORING OF EXTERNAL FACTORS:

Positive Aspect: Digital platforms facilitate continuous monitoring of external factors such as geopolitical events, economic shifts, and industry trends.

Opportunity: Proactive identification of external risks allows organizations to adjust strategies and operations in response to changing external conditions.

IMPROVED REPORTING AND TRANSPARENCY:

Positive Aspect: Digital transformation enhances reporting capabilities, enabling organizations to communicate risk information more effectively.

Opportunity: Transparent reporting builds trust with stakeholders, showcasing the organization's commitment to robust risk management practices.

2.9 INTEGRATED RISK MANAGEMENT (IRM) SYSTEMS: NAVIGATING COMPLEXITY WITH COHESION

Integrated Risk Management (IRM) systems represent a comprehensive approach to managing risk throughout an organization. In the face of increasing complexity, a myriad of risks, and the dynamic nature of the business environment, IRM systems aim to unify disparate risk management processes into a cohesive and interconnected framework. Here's an exploration of the concept of Integrated Risk Management:

1. **Defining Integrated Risk Management (IRM):**

   Holistic Approach: IRM is a holistic methodology that goes beyond traditional risk silos. It seeks to integrate risk management practices across various functions and levels of an organization, fostering a unified understanding of risks.

   End-to-End Risk Management: IRM encompasses the entire risk management lifecycle, from risk identification and assessment to monitoring and response. It recognizes that risks are interconnected and can have cascading effects on different aspects of the organization.

2. **Key Components of IRM Systems:**

   Risk Identification: IRM systems facilitate the identification of a broad spectrum of risks, including operational, financial, strategic, compliance, and reputational risks. This involves engaging stakeholders across the organization in a collaborative process.

   Risk Assessment and Quantification: IRM systems incorporate advanced analytics and risk quantification techniques to assess the impact and likelihood of identified risks. This provides a basis for prioritizing risks and allocating resources effectively.

   Risk Mitigation and Response Planning: IRM involves developing comprehensive risk mitigation and response plans. It goes beyond risk acceptance and aims to proactively address risks through a combination of preventive measures and contingency plans.

   Monitoring and Reporting: Continuous monitoring of key risk indicators is a fundamental aspect of IRM. It ensures that organizations have real-time visibility into changes in the risk landscape. Reporting mechanisms provide insights to stakeholders at various levels.

Governance and Compliance: IRM systems emphasize strong governance structures and compliance with relevant regulations. This involves integrating compliance efforts with overall risk management strategies.

3. **Benefits of Integrated Risk Management:**

Comprehensive Risk Understanding: IRM provides organizations with a comprehensive understanding of their risk landscape by considering the interdependencies between different types of risks.

Efficient Resource Allocation: By prioritizing risks based on their impact and likelihood, IRM allows organizations to allocate resources more efficiently, focusing on the most significant threats.

Improved Decision-Making: The holistic view provided by IRM enhances decision-making processes. Leaders can make more informed choices considering the broader context of risks and opportunities.

Enhanced Communication and Collaboration: IRM fosters collaboration among different departments and stakeholders. Improved communication ensures that risk information is shared effectively across the organization.

Adaptability to Change: The dynamic nature of IRM allows organizations to adapt quickly to changes in the business environment, emerging risks, and evolving regulatory requirements.

4. **Technology's Role in Enabling IRM:**

Integrated Technology Platforms: IRM is facilitated by integrated technology platforms that bring together various risk management processes. These platforms often include modules for risk assessment, incident management, compliance tracking, and reporting.

Data Analytics and Artificial Intelligence: Advanced data analytics and artificial intelligence play a crucial role in IRM systems. They enable organizations to analyze vast datasets, identify patterns, and make predictions about future risks.

Automation of Workflows: IRM systems leverage automation to streamline workflows and reduce manual effort in routine risk management tasks. This ensures consistency and accuracy in risk-related processes.

Real-Time Monitoring Tools: Technology enables real-time monitoring of key risk indicators, providing organizations with timely information to respond to emerging risks promptly.

Cloud-Based Solutions: Cloud technology facilitates the accessibility and scalability of IRM systems. It allows organizations to access risk information from anywhere, ensuring that the system remains responsive to the needs of a dynamic business environment.

5. **Challenges and Considerations:**

Cultural Shift: Implementing IRM often requires a cultural shift within organizations. It involves breaking down silos and promoting a collaborative approach to risk management.

Data Quality and Integration: The success of IRM relies on the quality and integration of data from various sources. Ensuring data accuracy and consistency is a key challenge.

Change Management: Adapting to an integrated risk management approach requires effective change management. Resistance to change and lack of awareness can hinder the successful implementation of IRM systems.

Complexity and Customization: Organizations vary in size, structure, and industry, leading to varying risk profiles. Designing IRM systems that are both comprehensive and tailored to specific organizational needs can be complex.

6. **Implementation Steps:**

Assessment of Current State: Understand existing risk management processes, identify gaps, and assess the maturity of current risk management practices.

Stakeholder Engagement: Involve key stakeholders across departments to ensure a holistic perspective on risks and garner support for IRM initiatives.

Technology Selection: Choose integrated technology platforms that align with the organization's size, complexity, and industry requirements.

Training and Communication: Provide training to employees and stakeholders about the new IRM approach. Effective communication is crucial for successful implementation.

Continuous Improvement: Implement a feedback loop for continuous improvement. Regularly reassess the effectiveness of the IRM system and make adjustments as needed.

2.10 BUILDING ORGANIZATIONAL RESILIENCE IN THE FACE OF DIGITAL RISKS

In the digital age, organizations are navigating a landscape characterized by unprecedented connectivity, rapid technological advancements, and evolving cyber threats. In this complex environment, the importance of building organizational resilience cannot be overstated. Organizational resilience goes beyond mere risk mitigation; it embodies an organization's ability to adapt, recover, and thrive in the face of digital risks. Here's a detailed exploration of the critical importance of fostering resilience in the digital era:

1. **Adaptation to Digital Transformation**

   In the relentless pursuit of innovation, organizations are undergoing digital transformations to stay competitive. However, this very transformation introduces new risks. Building resilience means fostering an adaptive culture that embraces change while proactively addressing the associated risks. Resilient organizations integrate cybersecurity measures seamlessly into their digital strategies.

2. **Dynamic Response to Cyber Threats:**

   The digital landscape is rife with cyber threats, from sophisticated cyberattacks to data breaches. Resilience involves not only preventing these threats but also having a dynamic response mechanism. Organizations with a resilient mindset are prepared to detect and respond swiftly to cyber incidents, minimizing the potential impact on operations and reputation.

3. **Continuous Learning and Improvement:**

   Resilience is a journey, not a destination. It involves a commitment to continuous learning and improvement. Organizations must analyze past incidents, learn from them, and adjust their strategies accordingly. This iterative process ensures that the organization becomes more robust over time, evolving in tandem with the ever-changing digital risk landscape.

4. **Supply Chain Resilience:**

   In an interconnected global economy, supply chains are vulnerable to disruptions. Resilient organizations recognize the importance of building resilience not only within their walls but also across their supply chains. This involves assessing and fortifying the cyber defenses of suppliers and partners, creating a collective shield against digital risks.

5. **Crisis Communication and Reputation Management:**

   Digital risks can extend beyond operational disruptions to affect an organization's reputation. Resilience encompasses effective crisis communication strategies. Being transparent and communicative during a cyber incident can help mitigate reputational damage. Resilient organizations are prepared with communication plans that address stakeholders' concerns and maintain trust.

6. **Investment in Employee Training:**

   Human factors play a crucial role in digital risks, with phishing attacks and social engineering being prevalent threats. Building organizational resilience involves investing in comprehensive employee training programs. An informed workforce is better equipped to recognize and respond to digital threats, contributing to the overall cyber resilience of the organization.

7. **Regulatory Compliance and Risk Governance:**

   The digital landscape is subject to a myriad of regulations, and non-compliance can lead to severe consequences. Resilient organizations prioritize regulatory compliance and establish robust risk governance frameworks. This involves regular assessments, audits, and the integration of compliance measures into daily operations.

8. **Incident Simulation and Testing:**

   Proactive organizations go beyond theoretical preparation and engage in incident simulation and testing. Resilience is demonstrated through the ability to simulate cyber incidents, test response plans, and identify areas for improvement. This hands-on approach ensures that the organization is not only prepared on paper but also in practice.

9. **Integration of Business Continuity:**

   Digital risks have the potential to disrupt not only cybersecurity but also overall business continuity. Resilient organizations integrate cybersecurity considerations into their broader business continuity plans. This holistic approach ensures that the organization can continue critical operations even in the aftermath of a digital incident.

10. **Strategic Leadership and Vision:**

    Building organizational resilience requires strategic leadership and a clear vision. Resilient leaders understand the evolving nature of digital risks and champion a culture of resilience throughout the organization. They prioritize investments in cybersecurity, promote collaboration across departments, and communicate the importance of resilience as a strategic imperative.

STRATEGIES FOR ENSURING BUSINESS CONTINUITY IN THE EVENT OF DIGITAL DISRUPTIONS

Digital disruptions, ranging from cyberattacks to technology failures, can have severe consequences for business operations. Ensuring business continuity in the face of digital disruptions requires a comprehensive strategy that encompasses technology, people, processes, and communication. Here are key strategies to mitigate the impact of digital disruptions and maintain business continuity:

1. **Develop a Comprehensive Business Continuity Plan (BCP):**

   Assessment and Risk Analysis:

   Conduct a thorough assessment of potential digital risks, considering cybersecurity threats, system failures, and other technology-related disruptions.

Perform a risk analysis to identify critical business processes and their dependencies on digital systems.

Establish a BCP Team:

Form a dedicated business continuity team responsible for creating, maintaining, and executing the BCP.

Ensure representation from key departments to address diverse operational needs.

Define Recovery Objectives and Timeframes:

Clearly outline recovery objectives for each critical business process.

Set realistic timeframes for restoring operations and prioritize based on criticality.

2. **Implement Robust Cybersecurity Measures:**

Cyber Hygiene Practices:

Enforce strong cybersecurity practices, including regular software updates, use of firewalls, antivirus software, and secure configurations.

Educate employees on cybersecurity best practices, emphasizing the role they play in preventing cyber threats.

Incident Response Plan:

Develop and regularly update an incident response plan that outlines the steps to be taken in the event of a cybersecurity incident.

Conduct drills and simulations to ensure a swift and effective response.

3. **Establish Redundancy and Data Backups:**

Redundant Systems:

Implement redundant systems and infrastructure to ensure that critical operations can continue in the event of a system failure.

Consider cloud-based solutions for increased flexibility and accessibility.

Regular Data Backups:

Conduct regular data backups of critical information, ensuring that backup systems are geographically separate from primary systems.

Test data restoration processes to verify the integrity and accessibility of backups.

4. **Diversify Technology Providers:**

Vendor Risk Management:

Assess and manage risks associated with technology vendors and service providers.

Diversify technology providers to reduce dependency on a single source and minimize the impact of disruptions.

5. **Employee Training and Awareness:**

Cybersecurity Training:

Provide comprehensive cybersecurity training to employees, emphasizing the importance of vigilance against phishing, social engineering, and other cyber threats.

Promote a culture of security awareness throughout the organization.

6. **Enhance Communication Protocols:**

Internal Communication Plan:

Establish clear communication protocols for internal stakeholders during a digital disruption.

Ensure that employees are aware of the channels and procedures for reporting disruptions and seeking assistance.

External Communication Plan:

Develop a communication plan for external stakeholders, including customers, suppliers, and partners.

Communicate transparently about the situation, recovery efforts, and expected timelines.

7. **Regular Testing and Exercises:**

BCP Testing:

Conduct regular testing of the business continuity plan, including tabletop exercises and simulated disruptions.

Identify weaknesses in the plan and make necessary adjustments.

Collaborative Drills:

Collaborate with external partners, such as cybersecurity experts and emergency services, in conducting drills to enhance preparedness.

8. **Continuous Monitoring and Threat Intelligence:**

Real-Time Monitoring:

Implement real-time monitoring of digital systems to detect anomalies and potential threats.

Utilize security information and event management (SIEM) tools for comprehensive monitoring.

Threat Intelligence Integration:

Integrate threat intelligence feeds to stay informed about emerging cyber threats.

Use threat intelligence to proactively adjust security measures and fortify defenses.

9. Regulatory Compliance and Legal Preparedness:

Regulatory Compliance:

Ensure that the business continuity plan aligns with industry regulations and compliance standards.

Regularly update the plan to address changes in regulatory requirements.

Legal Preparedness:

Collaborate with legal experts to understand legal implications of digital disruptions.

Have legal contingency plans in place, including communication with regulatory authorities if required.

10. Continuous Improvement and Lessons Learned:

Post-Incident Review:

Conduct thorough post-incident reviews after any digital disruption.

Analyze the response and identify areas for improvement in the business continuity plan.

Continuous Adaptation:

Adapt the business continuity plan based on lessons learned from each disruption.

Stay informed about evolving digital threats and update strategies accordingly.

By integrating these strategies into a comprehensive business continuity plan, organizations can enhance their resilience in the face of digital disruptions. The goal is not only to respond effectively to incidents but also to proactively minimize the impact and ensure the continuity of critical business operations.

2.11   USING AI IN RISK MANAGEMENT

Artificial Intelligence (AI) is revolutionizing the field of risk management, providing organizations with advanced tools and capabilities to identify, assess, and mitigate risks more effectively. The integration of AI in risk management processes enhances decision-making, automates tasks, and enables a proactive approach to addressing emerging threats. Here's a comprehensive exploration of the use of AI in risk management:

1.   **Risk Identification and Assessment:**

     Data Analysis and Pattern Recognition:

     AI systems excel at analyzing vast datasets, identifying patterns, and recognizing anomalies that may indicate potential risks.

     Machine learning algorithms can learn from historical data to enhance risk identification and assess the likelihood of future events.

     Predictive Analytics:

     AI facilitates predictive modeling by considering various factors that contribute to risk.

     Predictive analytics enables organizations to anticipate and assess potential risks before they materialize, allowing for proactive risk management.

2. Cybersecurity and Threat Detection:

Behavioral Analytics:

AI-powered behavioral analytics analyze user and system behavior to detect unusual patterns that may indicate a cybersecurity threat.

The continuous monitoring of activities helps identify potential security breaches in real-time.

Threat Intelligence Integration:

AI systems integrate threat intelligence feeds, constantly updating risk profiles based on the latest information.

This integration ensures that organizations stay ahead of evolving cyber threats and adjust their security measures accordingly.

3. Fraud Detection and Prevention:

Anomaly Detection:

AI employs anomaly detection algorithms to identify irregularities in financial transactions, procurement processes, or any other area susceptible to fraudulent activities.

The ability to learn from historical data enhances the accuracy of fraud detection.

Natural Language Processing (NLP):

NLP enables AI systems to analyze unstructured data, such as text and documents, to detect signs of fraudulent behavior or non-compliance.

This is particularly valuable in industries where regulatory compliance is critical.

4. **Automation of Routine Tasks:**

Automated Compliance Monitoring:

AI automates the monitoring of regulatory changes, ensuring that organizations stay compliant with evolving regulations.

Automated compliance checks reduce the risk of regulatory penalties and streamline adherence to complex regulatory frameworks.

Operational Risk Management:

AI automates routine operational risk management tasks, such as data collection, analysis, and reporting.

This allows risk management teams to focus on strategic aspects and complex decision-making.

5. **Decision Support Systems:**

Cognitive Computing:

AI-driven decision support systems leverage cognitive computing to assist human decision-makers.

These systems analyze a wide range of data sources to provide insights, helping organizations make more informed and timely decisions in the face of risks.

Scenario Analysis:

AI enables the simulation of various risk scenarios, allowing organizations to assess the potential impact of different events on their operations.

Scenario analysis assists in developing effective risk mitigation strategies.

6. **Portfolio Risk Management:**

Algorithmic Trading and Investment:

In financial services, AI algorithms analyze market trends, assess portfolio risks, and execute trades autonomously.

AI-powered trading systems adapt to market changes in real-time, optimizing investment portfolios and managing financial risks.

7. **Continuous Monitoring and Early Warning Systems:**

Real-time Monitoring:

AI facilitates real-time monitoring of key risk indicators, providing organizations with immediate insights into changing risk landscapes.

Early warning systems based on AI algorithms alert organizations to potential risks, enabling proactive responses.

Supply Chain Risk Management:

AI enhances supply chain risk management by continuously monitoring factors such as supplier performance, geopolitical events, and market trends.

Predictive analytics in supply chain AI systems help organizations anticipate and mitigate potential disruptions.

8. **Natural Language Processing in Compliance:**

Regulatory Compliance Analysis:

AI-powered natural language processing analyzes regulatory documents, contracts, and legal texts to ensure compliance.

This technology assists in identifying and understanding complex regulatory requirements.

CHALLENGES AND CONSIDERATIONS:

INTERPRETABLE AI MODELS:

Ensuring transparency and interpretability of AI models is crucial for building trust and understanding the decision-making process.

DATA QUALITY AND BIAS:

The effectiveness of AI in risk management depends on the quality and diversity of the data it is trained on. Biases in training data must be addressed to avoid skewed results.

CYBERSECURITY RISKS:

As AI becomes integral to risk management, organizations need to be vigilant against potential AI-specific cybersecurity threats and attacks.

ETHICAL USE OF AI:

Organizations must adopt ethical practices in the use of AI, ensuring that AI technologies are applied responsibly and do not inadvertently contribute to unethical decision-making.

2.12 AI-POWERED ADVANCEMENTS IN PREDICTIVE ANALYTICS AND DECISION-MAKING

Artificial Intelligence (AI) has emerged as a transformative force in predictive analytics and decision-making processes, reshaping the way organizations leverage data for insights and strategic choices. Through sophisticated algorithms and machine learning capabilities, AI enhances the accuracy, speed, and depth of predictive analytics, enabling more informed and proactive decision-making. Here's an exploration of how AI contributes to these critical facets of organizational strategy:

1. **Advanced Data Processing and Pattern Recognition:**

Enhanced Data Analysis:

AI excels in processing vast and complex datasets, extracting meaningful patterns, and identifying correlations that may be challenging for traditional analytics methods.

The ability to handle big data allows organizations to derive more nuanced insights, uncover hidden relationships, and make predictions with greater confidence.

Real-time Pattern Recognition:

AI-powered predictive analytics operate in real-time, continuously learning from incoming data and adapting predictions accordingly.

Real-time pattern recognition is particularly valuable in dynamic environments where swift decision-making is essential.

2. **Predictive Modeling and Forecasting:**

Machine Learning Algorithms:

AI employs machine learning algorithms to build predictive models that can forecast future trends, outcomes, or events.

These models evolve and improve over time as they learn from new data, contributing to more accurate predictions and better decision support.

Dynamic Adaptation to Change:

AI-driven predictive analytics adapt dynamically to changes in the underlying data patterns, allowing organizations to respond promptly to shifts in market conditions, consumer behavior, or other factors influencing predictions.

This adaptability enhances the resilience of predictive models in complex and evolving scenarios.

3. Personalized and Context-Aware Insights:

Individualized Predictions:

AI enables the generation of personalized predictions based on individual user behaviors, preferences, and historical interactions.

Personalization enhances the relevance of predictions, catering to the specific needs and contexts of users, whether in marketing, healthcare, or other domains.

Contextual Understanding:

AI algorithms consider the broader context in which data is generated, providing a more holistic understanding of situations.

Context-aware insights help decision-makers grasp the full picture, enabling them to make well-informed and contextually relevant choices.

4. Decision Support Systems:

Cognitive Computing Capabilities:

AI contributes to decision support systems by incorporating cognitive computing capabilities.

Decision-makers benefit from AI's ability to analyze diverse data sources, identify patterns, and provide comprehensive insights to inform strategic choices.

Reduced Decision Fatigue:

AI automates routine decision-making tasks, reducing decision fatigue and allowing human decision-makers to focus on more complex and strategic aspects.

This enables leaders to allocate their cognitive resources more efficiently.

5. Risk Mitigation and Scenario Analysis:

Proactive Risk Management:

AI aids in identifying potential risks and assessing their likelihood and impact through predictive modeling.

Organizations can proactively manage risks by simulating various scenarios and developing mitigation strategies based on AI-driven insights.

Complex Scenario Analysis:

AI facilitates sophisticated scenario analysis, considering multiple variables simultaneously.

Decision-makers gain a clearer understanding of the potential outcomes of different scenarios, aiding in strategic planning and risk mitigation.

6. Natural Language Processing (NLP) in Decision Support:

Conversational Interfaces:

AI-driven natural language processing enables conversational interfaces in decision support systems.

Users can interact with AI systems using natural language, making it more accessible and intuitive for decision-makers.

Data Extraction and Understanding:

NLP capabilities allow AI to extract insights from unstructured data sources, such as text documents and social media.

Decision-makers benefit from a more comprehensive view of information, even when it's in non-numeric formats.

7. **Continuous Learning and Improvement:**

Adaptive Algorithms:

AI systems continually learn and adapt based on new data inputs.

Continuous learning ensures that predictive models and decision-making processes evolve over time, becoming more accurate and relevant.

Feedback Loop Integration:

Organizations can establish feedback loops where the outcomes of decisions are fed back into the AI system.

This iterative process enhances the learning capabilities of AI algorithms, improving their predictive accuracy.

CHALLENGES AND CONSIDERATIONS:

INTERPRETABILITY AND EXPLAINABILITY:

Complex AI models may lack interpretability, posing challenges in explaining how they arrive at specific predictions.

Striking a balance between accuracy and interpretability is crucial for building trust in AI-driven decision-making.

DATA QUALITY AND BIAS:

The effectiveness of AI models heavily depends on the quality and representativeness of the training data.

Biases present in historical data may be perpetuated in AI models, impacting the fairness of predictions.

ETHICAL USE OF AI:

Organizations must navigate ethical considerations, ensuring that AI is deployed responsibly and does not perpetuate discriminatory or unethical practices.

INTEGRATION WITH HUMAN DECISION-MAKERS:

AI should complement human decision-makers, with a clear understanding of where human judgment is essential. Collaboration between AI and humans is crucial to harness the strengths of both.

CHALLENGES OF COMMUNICATING AND MANAGING RISKS IN A DIGITAL AND INTERCONNECTED WORLD

In the digital and interconnected world, organizations face a myriad of challenges when it comes to communicating and managing risks. The dynamic nature of the digital landscape, coupled with increased connectivity, introduces complexities that require strategic approaches. Here are key challenges:

1. **Rapid Proliferation of Information:**

   Challenge:

   Information spreads rapidly through digital channels, including social media and online platforms.

   Misinformation and rumors can escalate quickly, creating a challenging environment for accurate risk communication.

   Strategy:

   Implement real-time monitoring and response strategies to address misinformation promptly.

   Establish official communication channels to disseminate accurate information swiftly.

2. **Complexity of Cybersecurity Risks:**

   Challenge:

   Cybersecurity risks are intricate and may not be easily comprehensible to non-technical stakeholders.

   Communicating the nuances of cyber threats and their potential impacts poses a challenge.

Strategy:

Develop clear and concise communication materials that translate technical details into understandable language.

Provide regular cybersecurity awareness training to both internal and external stakeholders.

3. **Globalization and Supply Chain Risks:**

Challenge:

Globalization has led to complex and interconnected supply chains, making organizations vulnerable to disruptions.

Communicating the intricacies of supply chain risks, especially across international borders, can be challenging.

Strategy:

Establish transparent supply chain communication channels to keep stakeholders informed about potential risks.

Conduct regular risk assessments and share the findings with relevant parties to enhance collective risk awareness.

4. **Regulatory Compliance Challenges:**

Challenge:

Adhering to diverse and evolving regulatory frameworks across different regions and industries is a complex task.

Communicating these compliance requirements to various stakeholders can be overwhelming.

Strategy:

Develop a comprehensive regulatory communication plan that outlines compliance requirements in a clear and accessible manner.

Regularly update stakeholders on changes in regulatory landscapes affecting the organization.

5. **Balancing Transparency and Confidentiality:**

Challenge:

Striking the right balance between transparency and protecting sensitive information poses a challenge.

Some risks may involve confidential data that cannot be fully disclosed.

Strategy:

Develop a risk communication protocol that outlines the level of detail to be shared based on the sensitivity of the information.

Clearly communicate the organization's commitment to transparency while respecting confidentiality constraints.

6. **Social and Environmental Risks:**

Challenge:

Social and environmental risks, such as activism and climate-related concerns, can significantly impact an organization's reputation.

Communicating the organization's stance on these issues requires a delicate approach.

Strategy:

Develop a corporate social responsibility (CSR) communication strategy that aligns with the organization's values and commitments.

Engage with stakeholders proactively on social and environmental initiatives to build trust.

7. **Managing Crisis Communication:**

Challenge:

During crises, the speed at which information is disseminated is crucial.

Coordinating an effective crisis communication strategy in real-time is challenging.

Strategy:

Establish a crisis communication team with predefined roles and responsibilities.

Conduct regular crisis drills to ensure the team's readiness and responsiveness.

2.15 STRATEGIES FOR EFFECTIVE RISK COMMUNICATION

1. **Develop a Comprehensive Communication Plan:**

Internal and External Stakeholders:

Identify key internal and external stakeholders and tailor communication strategies for each group.

Ensure that employees, customers, suppliers, and the broader community are considered in communication plans.

Multi-Channel Approach:

Utilize a mix of communication channels, including social media, email, official websites, and traditional media.

Diversifying communication channels ensures that information reaches a wider audience.

2. **Use Clear and Accessible Language:**

Avoid Jargon:

Communicate in a language that is accessible to a diverse audience, avoiding technical jargon.

Use plain language to enhance understanding and mitigate the risk of misinterpretation.

Visual Aids:

Incorporate visual aids, infographics, and charts to convey complex information more effectively.

Visual representations can enhance clarity and engagement.

3. **Establish Transparency:**

Timely and Honest Communication:

Provide timely and honest updates about risks and their potential impacts.

Transparency builds trust and demonstrates a commitment to open communication.

Acknowledge Uncertainty:

Acknowledge when there is uncertainty about certain aspects of the risk.

Clearly communicate ongoing efforts to gather more information and address uncertainties.

4. **Tailor Communication to Different Audiences:**

Customize Messaging:

Tailor risk communication messages to suit the information needs of different audience segments.

Address concerns specific to each group, demonstrating a personalized approach.

Training and Education Programs:

Implement training and education programs to enhance stakeholders' understanding of specific risks.

Informed stakeholders are better equipped to respond and collaborate in risk mitigation efforts.

5. **Engage in Two-Way Communication:**

Listen to Stakeholders:

Encourage feedback from stakeholders and listen to their concerns.

Two-way communication fosters a sense of collaboration and involvement in risk management processes.

Responsive Communication:

Respond promptly to inquiries and concerns raised by stakeholders.

Demonstrating responsiveness enhances credibility and strengthens the organization's relationship with its stakeholders.

6. **Proactive Crisis Communication Planning:**

Predefined Communication Protocols:

Establish predefined communication protocols for different types of crises.

Clearly outline the roles and responsibilities of the communication team during a crisis.

Simulations and Drills:

Conduct regular crisis communication simulations and drills to test the effectiveness of communication strategies.

Identify areas for improvement and refine communication protocols based on simulation outcomes.

7. **Leverage Technology for Communication:**

Automated Alerts:

Implement automated alert systems for immediate communication during emergencies.

Automated alerts ensure that stakeholders receive critical information promptly.

Social Media Monitoring:

Utilize social media monitoring tools to track discussions and sentiments related to the organization.

Responding to social media conversations in real-time helps manage the narrative effectively.

8. **Continuous Improvement:**

Post-Incident Analysis:

Conduct post-incident analyses to evaluate the effectiveness of risk communication strategies.

Identify lessons learned and implement improvements for future communication efforts.

Adaptation to Feedback:

Encourage stakeholders to provide feedback on the effectiveness of communication.

Use feedback to adapt communication strategies and address areas that may require improvement.

9. Collaborate with Stakeholders:

Partnerships and Collaboration:

Collaborate with industry partners, regulatory bodies, and other organizations to share information and insights.

Joint communication efforts can enhance the collective understanding of risks and foster a united approach to risk management.

Community Engagement:

Engage with the local community and seek their input on risk management initiatives.

Involving the community builds trust and ensures that local perspectives are considered in risk communication.

10. Legal and Ethical Considerations:

Legal Compliance:

Ensure that risk communication efforts adhere to legal requirements and compliance standards.

Legal compliance is essential to avoid potential liabilities and disputes.

Ethical Communication Practices:

Uphold ethical communication practices, respecting the privacy and rights of individuals and organizations.

Ethical communication builds credibility and reinforces a positive organizational reputation.

By developing comprehensive communication plans, utilizing clear and accessible language, and engaging in two-way communication, organizations can enhance their resilience and foster a culture of informed decision-making. Continuous improvement, collaboration with stakeholders, and adherence to legal and ethical standards are integral components of successful risk communication strategies in the digital age.

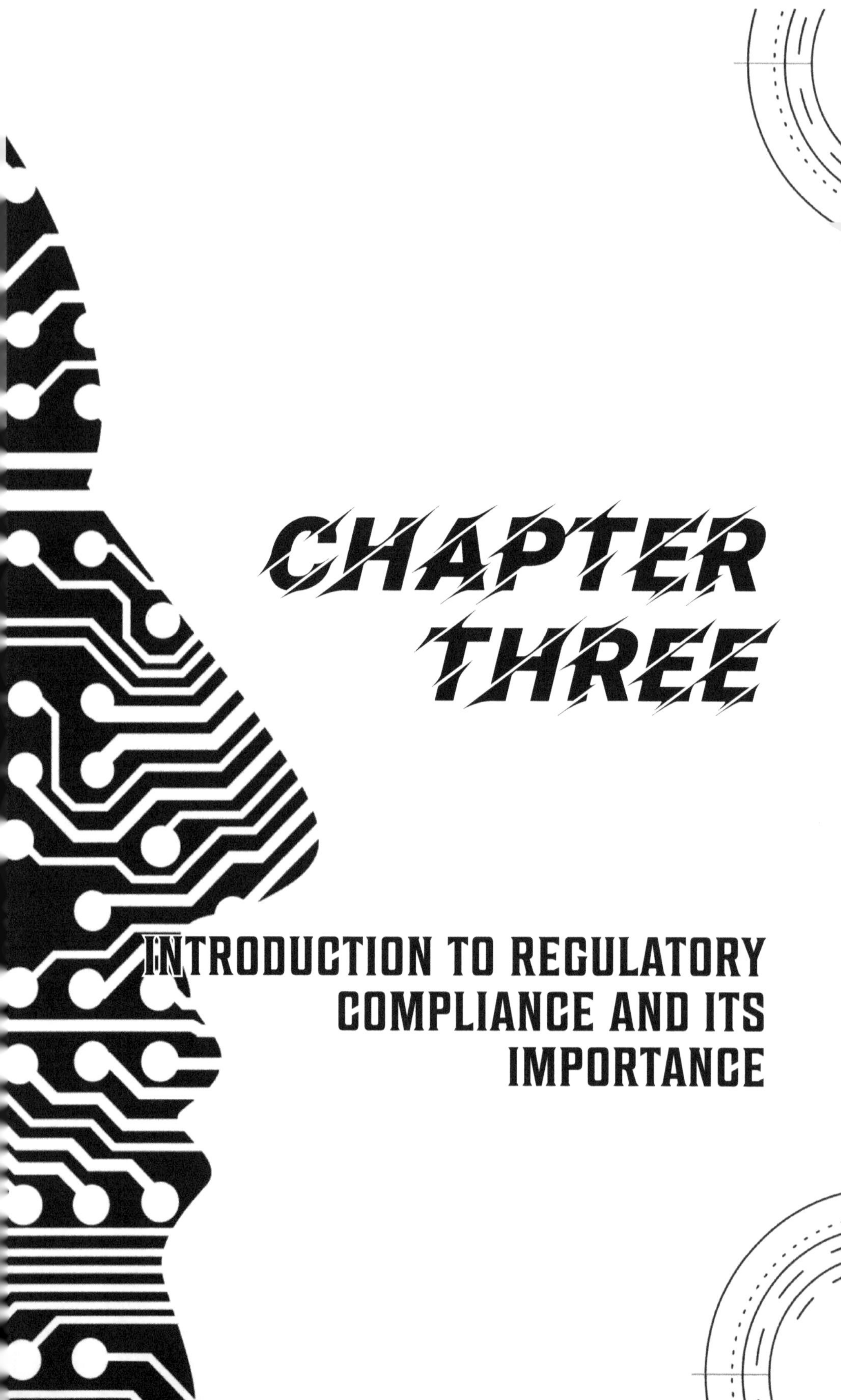

INTRODUCTION TO REGULATORY COMPLIANCE AND ITS IMPORTANCE

The previous chapter explored risk management in the digital era, shedding light on the challenges and opportunities. This chapter will further your journey into this book by providing you insights on what regulatory compliance is and why it must be given religious attention.

3.1 REGULATORY COMPLIANCE: ENSURING ETHICAL AND LEGAL BUSINESS PRACTICES

Regulatory compliance is the adherence to laws, regulations, and industry standards governing the operations of an organization. It encompasses the comprehensive set of rules and guidelines that businesses must follow to ensure ethical conduct, protect stakeholders, and maintain legal integrity. The critical role of regulatory compliance lies in establishing a framework that fosters transparency, fairness, and accountability in business practices.

DEFINING REGULATORY COMPLIANCE

At its core, regulatory compliance involves aligning business activities with the laws and regulations relevant to the industry and geographical location in which an organization operates. These regulations may cover a wide range of aspects, including financial reporting, data protection, environmental practices, employee rights, product safety, and more. Regulatory bodies, government agencies, and industry watchdogs set these standards to safeguard the interests of consumers, employees, investors, and the broader public.

KEY ELEMENTS OF REGULATORY COMPLIANCE

LAWS AND REGULATIONS:

Organizations must identify and understand the specific laws and regulations that apply to their industry and operations. This includes local, national, and international laws that govern various aspects of business conduct.

POLICIES AND PROCEDURES:

Developing and implementing policies and procedures that align with regulatory requirements is crucial. These documents serve as guidelines for employees, detailing the steps and practices necessary to maintain compliance.

MONITORING AND REPORTING:

Continuous monitoring of business activities is essential to ensure ongoing compliance. Regular reporting to regulatory authorities and internal stakeholders provides transparency and accountability.

RISK MANAGEMENT:

A robust risk management framework helps organizations identify potential compliance risks. Proactive risk assessment and mitigation strategies are integral to maintaining regulatory compliance.

DOCUMENTATION AND RECORD-KEEPING:

Thorough documentation of compliance efforts, including policies, training records, and audit reports, is vital. Proper record-keeping supports accountability and provides evidence of adherence to regulations.

TRAINING AND AWARENESS:

Employee training programs ensure that staff members are aware of regulatory requirements.

Awareness campaigns foster a culture of compliance throughout the organization.

PROTECTING STAKEHOLDER INTERESTS:

Regulatory compliance safeguards the interests of stakeholders, including customers, employees, shareholders, and the community. Adhering to ethical and legal standards builds trust and confidence among stakeholders.

ENSURING FAIR COMPETITION:

Compliance with antitrust and competition laws promotes fair business practices. Preventing monopolistic behaviors ensures a level playing field and encourages healthy competition in the market.

ETHICAL DECISION-MAKING:

Regulatory compliance guides organizations in making ethical decisions. It establishes a baseline for moral conduct, discouraging practices that could harm individuals, communities, or the environment.

FINANCIAL INTEGRITY AND TRANSPARENCY:

Compliance with financial regulations ensures the integrity and transparency of financial reporting. Accurate and transparent financial statements build investor confidence and contribute to a stable financial system.

DATA PROTECTION AND PRIVACY:

Adherence to data protection regulations safeguards the privacy and rights of individuals. Protecting sensitive information fosters trust between businesses and their customers.

ENVIRONMENTAL RESPONSIBILITY:

Compliance with environmental regulations promotes sustainable and responsible business practices. Organizations are accountable for minimizing their environmental impact and addressing ecological concerns.

EMPLOYEE RIGHTS AND WELL-BEING:

Employment laws and regulations protect the rights and well-being of employees. Compliance ensures fair labor practices, workplace safety, and ethical treatment of workers.

LEGAL LIABILITY MITIGATION:

Regulatory compliance helps mitigate legal risks and liabilities. Non-compliance can lead to legal consequences, fines, and damage to an organization's reputation.

CHALLENGES AND CONTINUOUS IMPROVEMENT:

Complexity of Regulations: The ever-evolving nature of regulations poses a challenge for organizations to stay current and adapt to changes. Continuous monitoring and updates to compliance strategies are necessary.

GLOBAL OPERATIONS:

Organizations with a global footprint face the challenge of navigating diverse regulatory landscapes. Harmonizing compliance efforts across different jurisdictions requires strategic planning.

INTEGRATION WITH CORPORATE CULTURE:

Embedding a culture of compliance within an organization requires ongoing efforts. Ensuring that employees understand and prioritize compliance is crucial for its success.

TECHNOLOGICAL ADVANCEMENTS:

The rapid pace of technological change introduces new challenges related to data security and privacy. Organizations must adapt compliance measures to address emerging technological risks.

3.1.1 THE IMPACT OF NON-COMPLIANCE ON ORGANIZATIONS: LEGAL CONSEQUENCES AND REPUTATIONAL RISKS

Non-compliance with laws, regulations, and industry standards can have severe consequences for organizations, affecting both their legal standing and reputation. The impact is multifaceted, encompassing financial penalties, legal liabilities, and damage to the organization's standing in the eyes of stakeholders. Here's an exploration of the repercussions of non-compliance:

1. Legal Consequences

Financial Penalties:

Regulatory bodies and government agencies have the authority to impose significant fines for non-compliance.

The financial impact can be substantial, especially in cases of serious violations or a pattern of non-compliance.

Legal Liabilities: Non-compliance may lead to legal actions, including lawsuits from affected parties. Organizations may face liabilities for damages, legal fees, and other costs associated with defending against legal claims.

Criminal Charges: Certain violations of laws and regulations may result in criminal charges against the organization or its executives. Individuals responsible for decision-making may face personal legal consequences, including fines and imprisonment.

License Revocation: Regulatory bodies may have the authority to revoke licenses or permits necessary for the organization to operate. License revocation can have severe implications for the continuity of business operations.

Injunctions and Cease-and-Desist Orders: Authorities can issue injunctions or cease-and-desist orders to stop specific activities that violate regulations. Non-compliance with such orders may lead to additional legal actions and penalties.

2. **Reputational Risks**

Loss of Trust and Credibility: Non-compliance damages the trust and credibility that stakeholders, including customers, investors, and employees, place in the organization. Repeated instances of non-compliance erode the organization's reputation over time.

Customer Perception: Customers are increasingly conscious of ethical business practices and may choose to disassociate from companies with a history of non-compliance. Negative perceptions can impact customer loyalty and brand loyalty.

Investor Confidence: Investors are sensitive to legal and regulatory risks that may affect the financial performance of a company. Non-compliance can lead to a loss of investor confidence, affecting stock prices and market valuation.

Supplier and Partner Relationships: Non-compliance can strain relationships with suppliers, business partners, and other stakeholders. Organizations may face difficulties in securing partnerships or maintaining collaborative ventures.

Employee Morale and Retention: Employees may feel demoralized and disengaged if they perceive the organization as operating unethically or irresponsibly. High-profile cases of non-compliance can lead to talent attrition and challenges in recruitment.

Media Scrutiny: Non-compliance often attracts media attention, resulting in negative coverage. Media scrutiny can amplify reputational damage and make it challenging for the organization to control the narrative.

3. **Operational Challenges:**

Business Disruption: Legal actions, investigations, and the fallout from non-compliance can disrupt normal business operations. Organizations may need to allocate resources to address legal challenges, diverting attention from core activities.

Increased Regulatory Scrutiny: Non-compliance may trigger heightened regulatory scrutiny, with authorities conducting more frequent audits and inspections. The organization may incur additional costs and resources to meet compliance expectations.

Strained Internal Culture: An organizational culture that tolerates or overlooks non-compliance can lead to internal strife.

Employees may become disillusioned, and ethical lapses may become embedded in the corporate culture.

4. **Long-Term Repercussions:**

Market Positioning: Repeated instances of non-compliance can result in a diminished market position. Competitors that prioritize compliance may gain a competitive advantage, impacting the long-term viability of the organization.

Regulatory Scrutiny: Organizations with a history of non-compliance may face more stringent regulatory oversight. Regulators may impose additional reporting requirements and demand more extensive compliance measures.

3.1.2   EXPLORING REGULATORY ENVIRONMENTS: A MULTIFACETED LANDSCAPE

The regulatory landscape governing businesses is a complex tapestry woven with threads of industry-specific regulations, regional mandates, and global compliance standards. Each strand contributes to the intricate fabric that organizations must navigate to ensure lawful and ethical conduct.

Let's embark on a journey through the diverse types of regulatory environments shaping the world of commerce.

1. **Industry-Specific Regulations:**

   Financial Services: In the financial realm, regulations like the Sarbanes-Oxley Act (SOX) and Dodd-Frank Wall Street Reform and Consumer Protection Act stand sentinel. They focus on financial reporting transparency, consumer protection, and the prevention of financial malfeasance.

   Healthcare: Within the healthcare sector, regulations such as the Health Insurance Portability and Accountability Act (HIPAA) safeguard patient privacy, while the Food and Drug Administration (FDA) oversees drug approval processes and healthcare provider standards.

   Energy: The energy sector adheres to regulations like those set by the Environmental Protection Agency (EPA), governing environmental impact assessments, emissions standards, and the promotion of renewable energy through mandates like Renewable Portfolio Standards (RPS).

   Telecommunications: Telecom industries navigate regulations established by entities like the Federal Communications Commission (FCC). These regulations cover spectrum allocation, net neutrality, and consumer protection within telecommunications services.

   Pharmaceuticals: In the pharmaceutical domain, compliance is dictated by regulations such as Good Manufacturing Practice (GMP) standards and guidelines from the International Council for Harmonisation of Technical Requirements for Pharmaceuticals for Human Use (ICH), ensuring adherence to rigorous drug manufacturing and clinical trial protocols.

2. **Regional Regulations:**

   European Union (EU): The EU sets the stage with regulations like the General Data Protection Regulation (GDPR) and Markets in Financial Instruments Directive (MiFID), emphasizing data protection, financial market regulation, and standardized product requirements.

United States: The U.S. regulatory landscape spans multiple domains, from Occupational Safety and Health Administration (OSHA) standards ensuring workplace safety to Environmental Protection Agency (EPA) regulations governing environmental practices.

Asia-Pacific: The Asia-Pacific region witnesses a diverse set of regulations, including the Asia-Pacific Economic Cooperation (APEC) privacy framework and individual country-specific regulations, addressing data protection, cybersecurity, and industry-specific mandates.

Latin America: In Latin America, regulations like Brazil's General Data Protection Law (LGPD) and Mexico's Federal Law for the Protection of Personal Data Held by Private Parties guide data protection, consumer rights, and industry-specific compliance.

3. **Global Compliance Standards:**

ISO Standards: The International Organization for Standardization (ISO) issues standards like ISO 9001 (Quality Management), ISO 14001 (Environmental Management), and ISO/IEC 27001 (Information Security Management), offering globally recognized benchmarks for quality, environmental sustainability, and information security.

International Labour Organization (ILO) Standards: ILO sets fundamental conventions on labor rights, emphasizing fair labor practices, workers' rights, and conducive workplace conditions.

Anti-Money Laundering (AML) and Counter-Terrorism Financing (CTF): Global compliance standards, as articulated by organizations like the Financial Action Task Force (FATF), focus on preventing money laundering, combating terrorist financing, and implementing robust customer due diligence.

Basel III: In the financial sector, the Basel III framework provides guidelines on banking regulations, capital adequacy, and effective risk management.

Global Data Protection Standards: Standards like GDPR and the Asia-Pacific Economic Cooperation Cross-Border Privacy Rules (APEC CBPR) set global benchmarks for safeguarding personal data and facilitating cross-border data transfers.

4. **Cross-Industry Compliance:**

Competition Law: Antitrust laws underpin competition law, fostering fair business practices and preventing anti-competitive behaviors.

Human Rights Standards: Guided by principles such as the United Nations Guiding Principles on Business and Human Rights, organizations adhere to standards promoting respect for human rights in their operations and supply chains.

Environmental, Social, and Governance (ESG) Standards: Frameworks like the Global Reporting Initiative (GRI) guide sustainability reporting, covering environmental impact, social responsibility, and governance practices.

5. **Technology and Cybersecurity Regulations:**

Cybersecurity Standards: Frameworks such as the NIST Cybersecurity Framework and ISO/IEC 27001 set the stage for robust cybersecurity measures, safeguarding information assets and ensuring cyber resilience.

Data Breach Notification Laws: Various regional and national laws mandate timely reporting of data breaches, reinforcing the importance of safeguarding sensitive information.

SECTORAL CHALLENGES:

1. **Industry-Specific Regulations:**

   Challenge:

   Complexity and Specialization: Different industries operate within highly specialized frameworks. Financial institutions grapple with stringent financial regulations, healthcare organizations contend with privacy laws, and energy companies must adhere to environmental standards.

   Strategy:

   Specialized Compliance Teams: Establishing dedicated compliance teams with expertise in the industry's specific regulations ensures a nuanced understanding of compliance requirements.

   Continuous Training: Regular training programs keep employees abreast of industry-specific regulatory changes and best practices.

2. **Cross-Industry Compliance:**

   Challenge:

   Interconnected Risks: Cross-industry regulations, such as competition law and environmental standards, introduce interconnected risks that demand a holistic compliance approach.

   Strategy:

   Integrated Compliance Programs: Develop integrated compliance programs that address common regulatory themes, fostering a culture of compliance that spans various industry-specific mandates.

   Collaboration Across Departments: Facilitate collaboration among different departments to ensure a comprehensive understanding of cross-industry compliance requirements.

3. **2. Geographic Challenges:**

Regional Regulations:

Challenge:

Diversity of Legal Systems: Each region has its legal nuances, and navigating diverse legal systems poses challenges for organizations with a global footprint.

Strategy:

Localized Compliance Teams: Establish compliance teams with local expertise to navigate regional regulations effectively.

Centralized Oversight: While having localized expertise, maintain centralized oversight to ensure a consistent approach to compliance across regions.

4. **Global Compliance Standards:**

Challenge:

Consistency in Adherence: Balancing adherence to global standards like ISO certifications with local regulations requires careful calibration.

Strategy:

Global Standards Framework: Develop a global compliance framework that aligns with overarching standards, providing a baseline for operations worldwide.

Tailored Approaches: Customize compliance strategies for specific regions, accounting for regional variations and legal requirements.

5. **Regulatory Technology (RegTech) Adoption:**

Challenge:

Data Privacy Concerns: Navigating diverse regulatory landscapes involves handling vast amounts of sensitive data, raising concerns about data privacy and security.

Strategy:

RegTech Solutions: Embrace Regulatory Technology (RegTech) solutions to streamline compliance processes, ensuring data security and privacy while automating routine compliance tasks.

Cybersecurity Measures: Implement robust cybersecurity measures to safeguard sensitive data and comply with data protection regulations.

6. **Continuous Monitoring and Adaptation:**

Challenge:

Evolving Regulations: Regulatory landscapes are dynamic, with laws and standards continuously evolving. Staying abreast of changes is a perpetual challenge.

Strategy:

Continuous Monitoring: Establish mechanisms for continuous monitoring of regulatory changes, leveraging technology and legal expertise to identify and adapt to evolving requirements.

Adaptive Compliance Programs: Develop agile compliance programs that can swiftly adjust to changes in regulations, ensuring organizational resilience.

7. **Collaboration and Advocacy:**

Challenge:

Advocacy for Industry Interests: In some cases, industries may need to advocate for their interests when regulations are being developed or updated.

Strategy:

Industry Associations: Join industry associations and collaborate with peers to collectively advocate for regulations that balance industry needs with societal interests.

Engage with Regulatory Bodies: Establish open lines of communication with regulatory bodies, providing input during the regulatory development process.

3.1.3   EXPLORING KEY COMPLIANCE FRAMEWORKS: ENSURING ORGANIZATIONAL INTEGRITY

Compliance frameworks are essential tools that organizations use to structure and manage their adherence to regulatory requirements, industry standards, and best practices. Here's a detailed exploration of some widely adopted compliance frameworks:

1. **ISO 27001 (Information Security Management System - ISMS):**

ISO 27001 focuses on information security management, providing a systematic approach to managing sensitive company information, ensuring its confidentiality, integrity, and availability.

Key Components: Risk Assessment and Management: Identifying and managing information security risks to protect against potential threats.

Information Security Policies: Establishing clear policies and procedures to guide information security practices.

Access Control: Defining and controlling access to information assets to prevent unauthorized use.

Incident Response and Reporting: Establishing protocols for responding to and reporting information security incidents.

Continuous Improvement: Regularly reviewing and updating information security measures to adapt to evolving threats.

Applicability:

Industry Agnostic: ISO 27001 is applicable to organizations across various industries that handle sensitive information.

2. **Sarbanes-Oxley Act (SOX):**

Purpose: Enacted to enhance corporate governance and financial reporting transparency, SOX aims to protect investors by improving the accuracy and reliability of corporate disclosures.

Key Components: Internal Controls: Establishing and maintaining effective internal controls over financial reporting.

Auditor Independence: Ensuring independence and objectivity of external auditors.

CEO and CFO Certification: Requiring CEOs and CFOs to certify the accuracy of financial statements.

Whistleblower Protections: Providing protection for employees reporting concerns about financial misconduct.

Applicability:

Publicly Traded Companies: SOX primarily applies to publicly traded companies listed on U.S. stock exchanges.

3. **GDPR (General Data Protection Regulation):**

Purpose: Enacted to protect the privacy and personal data of European Union (EU) citizens, GDPR sets standards for the collection, processing, and storage of personal information.

Key Components:

Data Subject Rights: Providing individuals with control over their personal data and defining their rights.

Data Protection Impact Assessments (DPIA): Assessing and mitigating risks associated with data processing activities.

Data Breach Notification: Requiring organizations to report data breaches promptly to relevant authorities.

Data Protection Officers (DPO): Appointing DPOs in certain cases to oversee GDPR compliance.

Applicability:

EU Organizations and Global Entities Processing EU Data: GDPR applies to organizations operating within the EU and those processing personal data of EU citizens.

4. **HIPAA (Health Insurance Portability and Accountability Act):**

Purpose: HIPAA aims to safeguard the privacy and security of protected health information (PHI) in the healthcare industry.

Key Components:

Privacy Rule: Regulating the use and disclosure of PHI, establishing patients' rights over their health information.

Security Rule: Mandating safeguards to ensure the confidentiality, integrity, and availability of electronic PHI (ePHI).

Breach Notification Rule: Requiring covered entities to notify affected individuals and regulatory authorities of data breaches.

Enforcement: Imposing penalties for non-compliance, with both civil and criminal consequences.

Applicability:

Healthcare Providers, Health Plans, and Healthcare Clearinghouses: HIPAA primarily applies to entities handling PHI in the healthcare sector.

5. **PCI DSS (Payment Card Industry Data Security Standard):**

Purpose: PCI DSS sets standards for securing payment card data to prevent data breaches and fraud in the payment card industry.

Key Components:

Build and Maintain a Secure Network: Implementing and maintaining secure network configurations and systems.

Protect Cardholder Data: Encrypting sensitive cardholder data during transmission and storage.

Maintain a Vulnerability Management Program: Regularly updating and patching systems to address vulnerabilities.

Implement Strong Access Control Measures: Restricting access to cardholder data on a need-to-know basis.

Regularly Monitor and Test Networks: Ongoing monitoring and testing of security controls and processes.

Applicability:

Entities Handling Payment Card Data: PCI DSS applies to organizations that handle, process, or store payment card information.

PRINCIPLES, CONTROLS AND BEST PRACTICES ASSOCIATED WITH THEM

1. **ISO 27001 (Information Security Management System - ISMS):**

   Principles:

   Risk-Based Approach: Identify and assess information security risks, and implement controls based on the level of risk.

   Continuous Improvement: Establish a culture of continuous improvement by regularly reviewing and enhancing the information security management system.

   Legal and Regulatory Compliance: Ensure compliance with relevant laws and regulations regarding information security.

   Controls and Best Practices:

   Access Control:

   Control: Implement role-based access controls to restrict access to information assets.

   Best Practice: Regularly review and update access permissions based on job roles.

   Information Security Policies:

   Control: Develop and enforce comprehensive information security policies.

   Best Practice: Communicate policies to all employees and provide regular training on policy changes.

   Incident Response and Reporting:

   Control: Establish an incident response plan to address and report security incidents.

   Best Practice: Conduct regular drills and exercises to ensure effective incident response.

Asset Management:

Control: Maintain an inventory of information assets and their classification.

Best Practice: Conduct regular audits to verify the accuracy of asset inventories.

Security Awareness and Training:

Control: Implement security awareness programs for employees.

Best Practice: Provide targeted training based on job roles and security responsibilities.

2. **Sarbanes-Oxley Act (SOX):**

Internal Controls:

Control: Establish and maintain effective internal controls over financial reporting.

Best Practice: Regularly assess and test internal controls to ensure effectiveness.

Auditor Independence:

Control: Ensure external auditors maintain independence and objectivity.

Best Practice: Rotate audit partners periodically to avoid conflicts of interest.

CEO and CFO Certification:

Control: Require CEOs and CFOs to certify the accuracy of financial statements.

Best Practice: Conduct regular training on certification responsibilities.

Whistleblower Protections:

Control: Establish whistleblower protection programs.

Best Practice: Communicate and promote the availability of whistleblower reporting mechanisms.

3. GDPR (General Data Protection Regulation):

Data Minimization and Purpose Limitation:

Control: Collect and process only the data necessary for the intended purpose.

Best Practice: Regularly review data processing activities to ensure alignment with purposes.

Data Subject Rights:

Control: Provide individuals with control over their personal data.

Best Practice: Establish processes for handling data subject requests promptly.

Data Protection Impact Assessments (DPIA):

Control: Conduct DPIAs for high-risk data processing activities.

Best Practice: Integrate DPIAs into project planning to identify and mitigate risks early.

Data Breach Notification:

Control: Establish procedures for prompt notification of data breaches.

Best Practice: Conduct regular drills to test the organization's ability to respond to data breaches.

4. HIPAA (Health Insurance Portability and Accountability Act):

Privacy Rule:

Control: Implement safeguards to protect the privacy of health information.

Best Practice: Train employees on the importance of patient privacy and confidentiality.

Security Rule:

Control: Implement technical safeguards to secure electronic protected health information (ePHI).

Best Practice: Regularly audit and monitor systems to detect and respond to security incidents.

Breach Notification Rule:

Control: Establish procedures for notifying affected individuals and regulatory authorities.

Best Practice: Conduct tabletop exercises to simulate response to potential breaches.

Enforcement:

Control: Enforce penalties for non-compliance, including both civil and criminal consequences.

Best Practice: Conduct regular internal audits to identify and address compliance gaps.

5. **PCI DSS (Payment Card Industry Data Security Standard):**

Build and Maintain a Secure Network:

Control: Implement secure network configurations and systems.

Best Practice: Regularly update and patch systems to address vulnerabilities.

Protect Cardholder Data:

Control: Encrypt sensitive cardholder data during transmission and storage.

Best Practice: Use tokenization to reduce the storage of actual cardholder data.

Maintain a Vulnerability Management Program:

Control: Regularly scan for and address vulnerabilities.

Best Practice: Establish a process for timely patch management and vulnerability remediation.

Implement Strong Access Control Measures:

Control: Restrict access to cardholder data on a need-to-know basis.

Best Practice: Implement multi-factor authentication for access to sensitive systems.

Regularly Monitor and Test Networks:

Control: Monitor and test security controls and processes.

Best Practice: Conduct regular penetration testing and security awareness training.

3.1.4   IMPLEMENTING A COMPLIANCE PROGRAM

Developing and implementing a comprehensive compliance program is a strategic and systematic process that involves establishing policies, procedures, and controls to ensure an organization's adherence to relevant laws, regulations, and ethical standards. Here's a step-by-step guide on how to develop and implement such a program:

1.   **Establish a Compliance Team:**

Responsibilities:

Identify and Assess Risks: Conduct risk assessments to identify areas of non-compliance or vulnerability.

Develop Policies and Procedures: Create policies and procedures based on regulatory requirements and risk assessments.

Training and Awareness: Implement training programs to educate employees about compliance policies and procedures.

2. Conduct a Risk Assessment:

Identify Compliance Risks:

Assess the organization's operations to identify areas where compliance risks may arise.

Consider industry-specific regulations, regional variations, and global compliance standards.

Prioritize Risks:

Prioritize risks based on their potential impact and likelihood of occurrence.

Focus on high-priority risks that pose the greatest threat to the organization.

3. Develop Policies and Procedures:

Draft Compliance Policies:

Develop clear, concise, and comprehensive policies that address identified risks.

Ensure alignment with relevant laws, regulations, and industry best practices.

Procedures for Implementation:

Create detailed procedures for implementing and enforcing each compliance policy.

Specify roles and responsibilities for employees at different levels of the organization.

4. Implement Training Programs:

Educate Employees:

Conduct training sessions to ensure that employees understand the importance of compliance and the specifics of the organization's policies.

Tailor training content to different roles and functions within the organization.

Regular Training Updates:

Provide ongoing training to keep employees informed about changes in regulations and compliance requirements.

Regularly assess and update training programs based on evolving risks.

5. **Establish Communication Channels:**

Internal Reporting Mechanisms:

Implement internal reporting mechanisms, such as hotlines or reporting systems, for employees to report compliance concerns.

Ensure confidentiality and protection against retaliation for whistleblowers.

External Communication:

Establish communication channels with external stakeholders, such as regulatory bodies and industry associations.

Keep stakeholders informed about the organization's commitment to compliance.

6. **Implement Monitoring and Testing:**

Regular Audits:

Conduct regular internal audits to assess the effectiveness of the compliance program.

Evaluate whether policies and procedures are being followed and identify areas for improvement.

External Audits and Assessments:

Engage external auditors or compliance experts to perform independent assessments.

Obtain certifications or compliance attestations to demonstrate adherence to industry standards.

7. Enforce Disciplinary Measures:

Establish a Disciplinary Framework:

Clearly define disciplinary measures for non-compliance.

Ensure that consequences are proportionate to the severity of violations.

Consistent Enforcement:

Enforce disciplinary measures consistently across all levels of the organization.

Communicate the consequences of non-compliance to reinforce the importance of adherence.

8. Update Policies and Procedures:

Monitor Regulatory Changes:

Stay abreast of changes in laws, regulations, and industry standards that may impact the organization's operations.

Periodically review and update policies to reflect regulatory changes.

Continuous Improvement:

Foster a culture of continuous improvement by regularly assessing the effectiveness of the compliance program.

Solicit feedback from employees and stakeholders to identify areas for enhancement.

9. Document and Recordkeeping:

Comprehensive Documentation:

Maintain thorough documentation of compliance policies, procedures, risk assessments, and training programs.

Keep records of audits, assessments, and corrective actions.

Accessible Recordkeeping:

Ensure that records are easily accessible to internal and external auditors.

Implement secure and organized recordkeeping systems.

10. **Regular Reporting to Leadership:**

Create Comprehensive Reports:

Provide regular reports to the leadership team on the state of compliance within the organization.

Include key performance indicators (KPIs) and metrics related to compliance.

Strategic Guidance:

Use compliance reports to inform strategic decision-making.

Seek leadership input for program improvements and adaptations.

11. **Respond to Incidents:**

Establish Incident Response Protocols:

Develop clear protocols for responding to compliance incidents or breaches.

Include communication plans, corrective actions, and follow-up procedures.

Continuous Learning:

Treat incidents as learning opportunities to improve the effectiveness of the compliance program.

Conduct post-incident reviews to identify root causes and preventive measures.

12. Adapt to Change:

Stay Agile:

Adapt the compliance program to changes in the organization's structure, operations, or external environment.

Continuously assess the relevance and effectiveness of the program.

Regular Reviews:

Conduct periodic reviews to ensure that the compliance program remains aligned with the organization's goals and values.

Solicit feedback from stakeholders to inform adjustments.

3.1.5   ROLE OF A COMPLIANCE OFFICER

The role of a Compliance Officer within an organization is crucial in ensuring that the business operations align with regulatory requirements, ethical standards, and internal policies. Here's an outline of the key aspects of the role:

POLICY DEVELOPMENT AND IMPLEMENTATION:

Develop and implement comprehensive compliance policies and procedures.

Ensure that policies align with relevant laws, industry standards, and the organization's values.

RISK ASSESSMENT AND MANAGEMENT:

Conduct regular risk assessments to identify potential compliance risks.

Implement risk management strategies to mitigate identified risks.

TRAINING AND AWARENESS:

Develop and deliver compliance training programs for employees at all levels.

Foster a culture of compliance by raising awareness of policies and ethical standards.

MONITORING AND AUDITING:

Establish monitoring and auditing processes to assess compliance with policies.

Conduct internal audits and assessments to identify areas for improvement.

INVESTIGATIONS AND INCIDENT RESPONSE:

Investigate compliance incidents, breaches, or reports of non-compliance.

Develop and implement incident response plans to address and mitigate issues.

COMMUNICATION AND REPORTING:

Maintain open communication channels for employees to report compliance concerns.

Regularly report on the state of compliance to leadership and relevant stakeholders.

LEGAL LIAISON:

Serve as a liaison between the organization and legal entities, ensuring legal compliance.

Stay informed about changes in laws and regulations that may impact the organization.

ETHICAL DECISION-MAKING:

Provide guidance on ethical decision-making and conduct within the organization.

Foster a culture of integrity and ethical behavior among employees.

COLLABORATION WITH DEPARTMENTS:

Collaborate with various departments to understand their unique compliance needs.

Ensure that compliance measures are integrated into departmental processes.

CONTINUOUS IMPROVEMENT:

Regularly review and update compliance policies and procedures.

Drive continuous improvement in the compliance program based on lessons learned and industry best practices.

SKILLS AND QUALIFICATIONS

Educational Background: A bachelor's degree in a relevant field (law, business, finance, etc.).

Some organizations may prefer or require advanced degrees or certifications (e.g., Certified Compliance & Ethics Professional - CCEP).

Legal Knowledge: Strong understanding of relevant laws and regulations. Ability to interpret and apply legal requirements to organizational operations.

Analytical Skills: Proficient in risk assessment and analysis. Ability to identify compliance risks and develop strategies for risk mitigation.

Communication Skills: Excellent written and verbal communication skills. Ability to communicate complex compliance issues in a clear and understandable manner.

Investigation Skills: Strong investigative skills to conduct thorough examinations of compliance incidents. Attention to detail and ability to gather and analyze evidence.

Interpersonal Skills: Ability to build relationships and collaborate with diverse teams. Tact and diplomacy in dealing with sensitive compliance matters.

Leadership and Influencing Skills: Ability to lead and influence organizational culture toward compliance. Assertiveness in enforcing compliance policies and standards.

Adaptability: Ability to adapt to changes in laws, regulations, and industry standards. Flexibility to address evolving compliance risks.

Ethical Judgment: High ethical standards and a strong sense of integrity. Ability to make ethical decisions and guide others in ethical conduct.

Project Management Skills: Effective project management skills to oversee the development and implementation of compliance initiatives. Ability to manage multiple projects simultaneously.

RESPONSIBILITIES:

Policy Development and Review: Develop, review, and update compliance policies and procedures.

Training and Education: Implement training programs for employees on compliance policies and standards.

Risk Assessment: Conduct regular risk assessments to identify compliance risks.

Monitoring and Auditing: Establish and oversee monitoring and auditing processes.

Incident Response: Develop and implement incident response plans.

Communication: Maintain communication channels for reporting compliance concerns.

Legal Liaison: Stay informed about changes in laws and regulations.

Ethical Guidance: Provide guidance on ethical decision-making.

Collaboration: Collaborate with various departments to integrate compliance measures.

Continuous Improvement: Regularly review and update compliance policies and procedures.

3.1.6 Emphasizing the Importance of a Culture of Compliance

Fostering a culture of compliance within an organization is paramount to its long-term success, reputation, and ethical standing. This culture goes beyond mere adherence to rules and regulations; it reflects a shared commitment to ethical behavior, integrity, and a proactive approach to identifying and addressing compliance risks.

Here are key reasons why cultivating a culture of compliance is crucial:

Risk Mitigation: A culture of compliance helps identify and address potential risks before they escalate. Employees become proactive in recognizing and reporting compliance concerns, minimizing the likelihood of regulatory violations.

Reputation Management: Maintaining a strong ethical culture safeguards the organization's reputation. Positive perceptions of ethical conduct contribute to customer trust, stakeholder confidence, and market credibility.

Legal and Regulatory Adherence: Employees ingrained in a compliance culture are more likely to understand and adhere to legal and regulatory requirements. This reduces the organization's exposure to legal consequences and regulatory fines.

Operational Excellence: A culture of compliance promotes efficient and effective operations. Streamlined processes, clear guidelines, and ethical decision-making contribute to overall organizational excellence.

Employee Engagement and Retention: Employees in a compliance-focused environment feel a sense of purpose and alignment with the organization's values. Higher job satisfaction and a commitment to ethical principles contribute to employee retention.

Ethical Leadership: A compliance culture starts at the top, with leaders setting the example. Ethical leadership fosters a trickle-down effect, influencing employees to emulate ethical behavior in their professional activities.

3.1.7 STRATEGIES FOR PROMOTING ETHICAL BEHAVIOR AND REGULATORY ADHERENCE

LEADERSHIP COMMITMENT:

Demonstrate strong commitment to compliance from top leadership. Leaders should prioritize compliance in their decision-making. Communicate the importance of ethical behavior and regulatory adherence consistently.

CLEAR POLICIES AND PROCEDURES:

Develop and communicate clear and accessible compliance policies and procedures. Ensure policies are easily understandable and available to all employees. Regularly update policies to reflect changes in laws and regulations.

COMPREHENSIVE TRAINING PROGRAMS:

Implement ongoing training programs on compliance. Conduct regular training sessions covering relevant laws, regulations, and ethical standards. Tailor training content to different departments and job roles.

COMMUNICATION CHANNELS FOR REPORTING CONCERNS:

Establish confidential and accessible reporting mechanisms. Implement anonymous hotlines or reporting systems. Communicate the availability of these channels and assure protection for whistleblowers.

RECOGNITION AND REWARDS FOR ETHICAL CONDUCT:

Recognize and reward ethical behavior and regulatory adherence. Implement programs that acknowledge employees who demonstrate exemplary compliance.

Integrate ethical behavior into performance evaluations and promotion considerations.

INCORPORATE COMPLIANCE INTO COMPANY VALUES:

Embed compliance into the organization's core values. Clearly articulate the importance of compliance in the company's mission and values. Reinforce these values through internal communications and leadership messaging.

Regular Audits and Assessments: Conduct regular audits to assess compliance levels. Establish internal audit processes to evaluate adherence to policies. Engage external auditors to provide independent assessments.

DISCIPLINARY CONSISTENCY:

Ensure consistent disciplinary measures for non-compliance. Clearly communicate consequences for violating compliance policies. Apply disciplinary measures consistently across all levels of the organization.

Open Lines of Communication: Encourage open communication about compliance concerns. Foster a culture where employees feel comfortable discussing compliance issues. Establish regular forums for dialogue on ethical considerations.

CONTINUOUS IMPROVEMENT AND ADAPTATION:

Embrace a culture of continuous improvement in compliance. Regularly assess and update compliance strategies based on lessons learned. Adapt the program to evolving risks and changes in the regulatory landscape

3.1.8 The Nature of Regulations: Keeping Up With The Change

THE DYNAMIC NATURE OF REGULATIONS:

Regulations are not static; they evolve in response to changes in technology, societal needs, and the global business landscape. The dynamic nature of regulations poses challenges for organizations, requiring them to stay vigilant and adaptable to remain compliant. Here's an exploration of why regulations are dynamic and the need for ongoing monitoring:

TECHNOLOGICAL ADVANCEMENTS:

Challenge: Rapid technological advancements often outpace existing regulations.

Need for Monitoring: Organizations must monitor technological developments to ensure compliance with new rules or adapt existing processes accordingly.

GLOBALIZATION:

Challenge: Expanding global operations expose organizations to diverse regulatory environments.

Need for Monitoring: Ongoing monitoring is essential to understand and comply with regulations across various jurisdictions.

CHANGING SOCIETAL EXPECTATIONS:

Challenge: Evolving societal expectations may lead to new regulations or amendments to existing ones.

Need for Monitoring: Organizations need to stay attuned to social changes that could influence regulatory developments.

EMERGING RISKS:

Challenge: New types of risks may emerge, necessitating regulatory responses.

Need for Monitoring: Continuous monitoring helps organizations identify and address emerging risks to stay ahead of regulatory requirements.

EVOLVING ECONOMIC LANDSCAPE:

Challenge: Economic shifts may prompt regulatory changes to address financial stability and consumer protection.

Need for Monitoring: Organizations must stay informed about economic trends and their potential regulatory implications.

POLITICAL AND GEOPOLITICAL FACTORS:

Challenge: Political changes and geopolitical tensions can impact regulatory frameworks.

Need for Monitoring: Organizations operating in multiple regions must monitor political developments to anticipate regulatory shifts.

3.1.8.1 STRATEGIES FOR STAYING INFORMED ABOUT REGULATORY CHANGES

Given the dynamic nature of regulations, organizations need robust strategies to stay informed about changes and updates. Here are effective strategies:

Dedicated Compliance Teams: Establish a dedicated team responsible for monitoring and interpreting regulatory changes. Assign individuals with expertise in specific regulatory areas. Ensure the team is well-connected with industry associations and regulatory bodies.

Subscription to Regulatory Updates: Subscribe to official regulatory publications and updates. Regularly check official government websites for regulatory changes. Subscribe to newsletters or updates from relevant regulatory bodies.

Utilize Regulatory Technology (RegTech): Leverage RegTech solutions for automated monitoring. Implement RegTech tools that provide real-time updates on regulatory changes. Use technology to streamline compliance processes and adapt to changes efficiently.

Engage with Industry Associations: Stay connected with industry associations and forums. Participate in industry events and conferences. Engage in discussions with peers to share insights on regulatory developments.

Legal Counsel and Consultancy: Employ legal counsel or regulatory consultants. Retain legal experts who specialize in relevant regulatory areas. Seek professional advice on interpreting and implementing regulatory changes.

Regulatory Impact Assessments: Conduct regular assessments of regulatory impact on the organization. Develop a systematic process for assessing how regulatory changes affect operations. Adjust compliance strategies based on the outcomes of impact assessments.

Internal Training Programs: Educate employees on the importance of staying informed about regulations. Conduct training sessions on regulatory awareness. Encourage employees to report potential regulatory concerns promptly.

Collaborate with Legal and Compliance Networks: Build relationships with legal and compliance networks. Join legal and compliance forums and networks. Participate in knowledge-sharing initiatives within the industry.

Monitor Regulatory Trends and Predictions: Stay informed about future regulatory trends. Follow regulatory thought leaders and publications predicting industry trends. Anticipate regulatory changes by tracking evolving global and industry-specific trends.

Regular Regulatory Compliance Audits: Conduct regular compliance audits. Integrate compliance audits into routine operational assessments. Use audit findings to identify areas requiring adjustments to meet new regulatory requirements.

3.1.9 Common Challenges in Achieving and Maintaining Compliance

Achieving and maintaining compliance is a complex and ongoing process for organizations. Several challenges can impede these efforts, ranging from the inherent complexity of regulatory environments to the continuous evolution of regulations. Here's an examination of common challenges:

COMPLEXITY OF REGULATORY ENVIRONMENTS:

Challenge: Regulatory frameworks are often intricate and subject to frequent changes.

IMPLICATIONS:

Organizations may struggle to interpret and navigate complex regulations.

Compliance efforts can be resource-intensive due to the need for specialized knowledge.

EVOLVING REGULATIONS:

Challenge: Regulations are dynamic, with constant updates and revisions.

IMPLICATIONS:

Organizations may find it challenging to keep up with the pace of regulatory changes.

Compliance strategies must be adaptable to address new requirements promptly.

DIVERSE REGULATORY LANDSCAPE:

Challenge: Organizations operating in multiple jurisdictions face diverse regulatory landscapes.

IMPLICATIONS:

Compliance teams must navigate variations in laws and standards across different regions.

Harmonizing compliance efforts globally can be complex.

LACK OF STANDARDIZATION:

Challenge: Regulatory standards may lack uniformity across industries and regions.

IMPLICATIONS:

Organizations may need to comply with multiple, sometimes conflicting, sets of regulations.

Developing a standardized approach to compliance becomes challenging.

RESOURCE CONSTRAINTS:

Challenge: Allocating resources, including personnel and technology, for compliance can be demanding.

IMPLICATIONS:

Smaller organizations may struggle to match the compliance capabilities of larger counterparts.

Resource limitations may hinder the implementation of comprehensive compliance programs.

INTERCONNECTED REGULATORY REQUIREMENTS:

Challenge: Regulations often overlap and affect multiple aspects of an organization.

IMPLICATIONS:

Achieving compliance may involve coordination between various departments.

Organizations must consider the interplay of different regulations in their compliance efforts.

RAPID TECHNOLOGICAL ADVANCEMENTS:

Challenge: Rapid changes in technology outpace existing regulations.

IMPLICATIONS:

Organizations may face challenges in adapting compliance measures to emerging technologies.

Technological innovations may introduce new compliance risks that need to be addressed.

INSUFFICIENT COMMUNICATION AND TRAINING:

Challenge: Inadequate communication and training on compliance matters.

IMPLICATIONS:

Employees may not fully understand their role in compliance, leading to unintentional violations.

Ineffective communication can hinder the implementation of compliance policies.

DATA PRIVACY AND SECURITY CONCERNS:

Challenge: Growing concerns around data privacy and security.

IMPLICATIONS:

Organizations must comply with stringent data protection regulations.

Ensuring the secure handling of data becomes critical to compliance.

VENDOR AND SUPPLY CHAIN COMPLIANCE:

Challenge: Ensuring compliance throughout the supply chain.

IMPLICATIONS:

Organizations are responsible for the compliance of their suppliers and vendors.

The lack of visibility into the compliance practices of third parties poses risks.

CHANGING BUSINESS MODELS:

Challenge: Organizations frequently evolve their business models.

IMPLICATIONS:

Changes in business operations may necessitate adjustments to compliance strategies.

Organizations must ensure that compliance measures keep pace with shifts in their business model.

CYBERSECURITY THREATS:

Challenge: The increasing frequency and sophistication of cybersecurity threats.

IMPLICATIONS:

Compliance efforts must integrate robust cybersecurity measures.

Organizations need to adapt to evolving cybersecurity regulations and standards.

ADDRESSING CHALLENGES:

To overcome these challenges, organizations should adopt a proactive and strategic approach to compliance:

Invest in Compliance Technology: Leverage RegTech solutions for automated monitoring and compliance management.

Continuous Training Programs: Implement ongoing training programs to keep employees informed about compliance requirements.

Engage with Regulatory Networks: Collaborate with industry associations and regulatory forums to stay informed about upcoming changes.

Regular Regulatory Impact Assessments: Conduct regular assessments to understand how regulatory changes impact the organization.

Implement Integrated Compliance Systems: Use integrated systems that streamline compliance efforts across different regulatory domains.

Strategic Resource Allocation: Allocate resources strategically, focusing on areas of higher compliance risk and impact.

Establish a Compliance Culture: Foster a culture of compliance from top leadership to every employee in the organization.

Periodic Compliance Audits: Conduct regular internal and external audits to identify and address compliance gaps.

Scenario Planning: Anticipate potential regulatory changes through scenario planning exercises.

Stay Informed Through Regulatory Intelligence: Utilize regulatory intelligence tools to receive real-time updates on changes in regulations.

Collaborate Across Departments: Encourage collaboration between legal, compliance, IT, and other relevant departments.

Data Protection by Design: Implement a data protection strategy that aligns with evolving data privacy regulations.

By adopting these strategies, organizations can enhance their ability to navigate the complex and evolving landscape of compliance, ensuring sustainable adherence to regulatory requirements.

3.2 COMPLIANCE AUDITS: DEFINING AND UNDERSTANDING THEIR ROLE

Compliance audits are systematic examinations conducted within an organization to assess its adherence to established regulatory frameworks, internal policies, and industry standards. These audits are comprehensive evaluations that involve reviewing processes, documentation, and practices to ensure they align with legal requirements and ethical standards. The primary purpose is to verify that the organization is operating within the prescribed boundaries and to identify areas for improvement.

3.2.1 ROLE OF COMPLIANCE AUDITS

Verification of Adherence: Confirm that the organization is following established rules and regulations. Through detailed examination, audits verify that documented policies and procedures are being consistently followed in actual practices.

Identification of Non-Compliance: Uncover instances where the organization is not in compliance. Audits help identify and document areas of non-compliance with regulatory requirements, internal policies, or industry standards.

Risk Assessment: Assess potential risks associated with non-compliance. Compliance audits evaluate the impact and likelihood of identified non-compliance, providing insights into the organization's risk landscape.

Continuous Improvement: Identify areas for enhancement in compliance processes. Audits play a crucial role in recommending improvements, fostering a culture of continuous improvement in compliance practices.

Documentation Review: Examine records and documentation for accuracy and completeness. Compliance audits ensure that documentation aligns with actual practices, helping to maintain accurate and complete records.

Employee Training Assessment: Evaluate the effectiveness of training programs. Audits assess whether employees have received and understood compliance training, ensuring that training programs effectively promote compliance awareness.

Verification of Control Measures: Confirm the effectiveness of control measures. Compliance audits assess the implementation and functionality of control mechanisms, ensuring they adequately address identified compliance risks.

Reporting and Communication: Provide clear and concise reports on compliance status. Through effective reporting, audits communicate findings to relevant stakeholders, facilitating informed decision-making.

3.2.2 IMPORTANCE OF REGULAR COMPLIANCE ASSESSMENTS

Proactive Risk Management: Regular assessments allow organizations to proactively identify and manage compliance risks before they escalate.

Adaptation to Regulatory Changes: Ongoing assessments help organizations stay abreast of changing regulations, allowing for timely adjustments to compliance measures.

Continuous Improvement Culture: Regular audits foster a culture of continuous improvement by identifying areas where processes can be enhanced for better compliance outcomes.

Prevention of Non-Compliance Consequences: Identifying non-compliance early helps prevent potential legal consequences, regulatory fines, and damage to the organization's reputation.

Employee Awareness and Training: Assessments highlight the effectiveness of employee training programs, enabling organizations to refine and tailor training content to address specific compliance gaps.

Efficient Resource Allocation: Organizations can allocate resources more efficiently by focusing on areas with higher compliance risks, guided by the findings of regular assessments.

Enhanced Organizational Resilience: A robust compliance audit program contributes to organizational resilience by ensuring that the organization can adapt to changing regulatory environments.

Stakeholder Confidence: Regular compliance assessments demonstrate a commitment to ethical conduct and regulatory adherence, fostering confidence among stakeholders, including customers, investors, and regulatory bodies.

3.2.3   Identification of Areas for Improvement

Corrective Action Planning: Develop corrective action plans based on audit findings to address non-compliance and enhance existing processes.

Process Optimization: Assess the efficiency of compliance processes and recommend optimizations to streamline operations while maintaining compliance.

Policy and Procedure Enhancements: Revise and update policies and procedures based on audit findings to ensure they align with current regulatory requirements.

Training Program Adjustments: Tailor training programs to address specific areas of weakness identified during audits, ensuring that employees receive relevant and effective compliance education.

Enhanced Monitoring and Control Measures: Strengthen monitoring and control mechanisms to better address identified compliance risks and prevent future instances of non-compliance.

Continuous Monitoring Strategies: Implement continuous monitoring strategies to provide real-time insights into compliance status and promptly identify and rectify any deviations.

Documentation Improvements: Enhance documentation practices to ensure accuracy, completeness, and alignment with regulatory requirements.

Cultural Shifts: Foster a culture of compliance and ethical behavior by addressing areas for improvement in organizational values, communication, and leadership.

CHAPTER FOUR

BUILDING A RESILIENT GOVERNANCE STRUCTURE: FOUNDATIONS AND PRINCIPLES

With GRC organizations find themselves navigating a landscape where change is the only constant, and resilience becomes synonymous with survival and success. It is within this crucible of challenges that the guiding theme of foundations and principles emerges as the bedrock of a robust governance framework.

4.1   THE IMPERATIVE OF RESILIENCE

The contemporary business environment is marked by a myriad of challenges, ranging from cybersecurity threats to global pandemics, regulatory complexities, and economic fluctuations. A governance structure that is resilient acts as a shield, enabling organizations to withstand shocks, adapt to unforeseen circumstances, and emerge stronger from disruptions. Resilience is not merely about bouncing back; it is about proactively preparing for and navigating through the ever-evolving challenges that define the modern age.

4.1.1   GUIDING THEME: FOUNDATIONS AND PRINCIPLES

At the heart of a resilient governance structure lies a well-laid foundation supported by principles that stand the test of time. This guiding theme underscores the notion that resilience is not a reactive measure but an inherent quality cultivated through a deliberate and principled approach to governance. The foundations of such a framework are built on a deep understanding of the organization's purpose, values, and long-term objectives.

4.1.2 Key Principles Underpinning Robust Governance

Ethical Leadership: A resilient governance structure begins with ethical leadership. Leaders who exemplify and uphold ethical standards set the tone for the entire organization, fostering a culture of integrity that becomes an integral part of the governance fabric.

Strategic Vision: Resilience is rooted in a strategic vision that goes beyond short-term gains. A governance framework guided by a clear and adaptive vision enables organizations to navigate uncertainties with a focus on long-term sustainability.

Risk Intelligence: Understanding and managing risks are fundamental to resilience. A robust governance structure incorporates risk intelligence, proactively identifying potential threats, and implementing strategies to mitigate and capitalize on them.

Adaptability and Innovation: Resilience requires adaptability. A governance framework that encourages a culture of innovation and adaptability positions the organization to thrive in the face of change, turning challenges into opportunities.

Stakeholder Engagement: The resilience of an organization is intertwined with its relationship with stakeholders. Effective governance involves engaging stakeholders transparently, building trust, and aligning interests to create a collective resilience against external pressures.

4.2 Understanding Governance Foundations

Understanding governance foundations is pivotal for establishing a robust and effective framework that guides organizations through the complexities of the modern age. Governance, as a fundamental aspect of organizational management, rests on foundational principles that shape its structure, purpose, and ethical underpinnings.

Let's explore these crucial governance foundations in detail:

1. **Organizational Purpose and Values:**

   Defining Identity: At the core of governance is a clear understanding of an organization's purpose and values. These serve as the North Star, guiding decision-making and actions. A governance structure anchored in the organizational identity ensures alignment with broader objectives.

2. **Leadership and Ethical Conduct:**

   Ethical Leadership: Governance foundations demand ethical leadership. Leaders set the tone for the entire organization, and their conduct influences the ethical culture. A commitment to integrity, transparency, and accountability becomes the cornerstone of governance.

3. **Roles and Responsibilities:**

   Clarity in Roles: Governance establishes clear roles and responsibilities for all stakeholders, from board members to executives and employees. Defining these roles prevents confusion, promotes accountability, and ensures that everyone contributes to the organization's success.

4. **Decision-Making Processes:**

   Transparency and Accountability: Transparent decision-making processes are integral to governance. When decision-making is transparent, stakeholders can understand and trust the rationale behind choices. Accountability mechanisms ensure that decisions align with the organization's objectives.

5. **Legal and Regulatory Compliance:**

   Adherence to Laws: Governance foundations necessitate a commitment to legal and regulatory compliance. Understanding and adhering to applicable laws and regulations is not just a best practice but a legal and ethical imperative for organizations.

6. **Stakeholder Engagement:**

    Inclusive Decision-Making: Governance extends beyond the boardroom to include stakeholders. Involving stakeholders in decision-making processes promotes inclusivity, helps in understanding diverse perspectives, and builds trust among those affected by organizational decisions.

7. **Risk Management:**

    Proactive Risk Mitigation: Governance foundations include a strategic approach to risk management. This involves identifying potential risks, assessing their impact, and implementing proactive measures to mitigate or manage these risks. A resilient governance structure acknowledges that risk is inherent and requires careful consideration.

8. **Strategic Alignment:**

    Vision and Mission Alignment: Governance foundations require alignment with the organization's vision and mission. A governance structure should facilitate the realization of strategic objectives, ensuring that every decision contributes to the organization's overarching goals.

9. **Continuous Improvement:**

    Adaptive Culture: Governance is not static; it evolves with the organization and the external environment. Foundations that prioritize continuous improvement and adaptability ensure that governance remains relevant and effective in the face of change.

4.2.1 GOVERNANCE WITHIN THE FRAMEWORK OF ORGANIZATIONAL RESILIENCE

The concept of governance within the framework of organizational resilience is intrinsically tied to the capacity of an organization to adapt, endure, and thrive in the face of uncertainties and disruptions. Governance, traditionally seen as a system of decision-making and oversight, takes on a new dimension when viewed through the lens of resilience. Let's clarify this concept and explore how resilience becomes a fundamental element in navigating uncertainties within the context of governance.

4.2.1.1 GOVERNANCE AS A PILLAR OF ORGANIZATIONAL RESILIENCE

1. **Decision-Making in Adversity:**

    *   **Clarity in Chaos:** Governance provides the structure for decision-making, even in the midst of adversity. Resilient governance ensures that there are established processes and mechanisms in place to make informed decisions when facing uncertainties.

2. **Risk Management and Anticipation:**

    *   **Proactive Adaptation:** Resilient governance involves proactive risk management. Governance structures that anticipate potential risks, assess their impact, and devise strategies for mitigation are better equipped to navigate uncertainties. This includes not only immediate risks but also those on the horizon.

3. **Adaptive Leadership:**

    *   **Dynamic Decision-Makers:** Resilience calls for adaptive leadership within the governance framework. Leaders who can pivot, innovate, and lead effectively during times of uncertainty contribute to the overall resilience of the organization.

4.2.1.2 RESILIENCE AS A FUNDAMENTAL ELEMENT

1. **Flexibility in Strategy:**

   * **Strategic Agility:** Resilience requires governance structures to be flexible in their strategic approach. This means having the ability to adapt strategic plans, change course when necessary, and seize opportunities amid uncertainties.

2. **Learning from Disruptions:**

   * **Iterative Improvement:** Resilient governance treats disruptions as learning opportunities. Rather than viewing uncertainties as setbacks, resilient organizations, guided by governance principles, engage in iterative improvements based on the lessons learned from challenges.

3. **Stakeholder Confidence:**

   * **Trust and Reputation:** Resilience contributes to stakeholder confidence. Governance structures that instill resilience foster trust among stakeholders, including employees, customers, and investors. Confidence in an organization's ability to navigate uncertainties enhances its reputation.

4. **Operational Continuity:**

   * **Business Continuity Planning:** Resilient governance incorporates robust business continuity planning. This involves ensuring that essential functions can continue during and after disruptions, minimizing downtime, and maintaining operational stability.

5. **Crisis Response:**

   * **Preparedness and Agility:** Resilient governance emphasizes crisis preparedness and response. Governance structures must be agile in managing crises, with well-defined roles, communication plans, and strategies to address unforeseen challenges promptly.

This means governance within the framework of organizational resilience represents the backbone of an organization's ability to weather storms, adapt to change, and emerge stronger from uncertainties. Resilient governance is not merely about surviving disruptions; it is about thriving in the face of adversity, guided by principles that prioritize adaptability, foresight, and strategic agility. As organizations navigate the complex and unpredictable landscapes of the modern age, the synergy between governance and resilience becomes a critical element in ensuring sustained success and growth.

4.3 THE ROLE OF LEADERSHIP IN SHAPING A RESILIENT GOVERNANCE STRUCTURE

The influence of leadership in shaping a resilient governance structure cannot be overstated. Leadership sets the tone, establishes the culture, and drives the strategic vision that determines how an organization responds to challenges and uncertainties.

Let's explore the essential leadership qualities that contribute to organizational adaptability and continuity within the framework of a resilient governance structure:

1. **Visionary Leadership:**

   Strategic Foresight: Visionary leaders have the ability to anticipate trends and foresee potential challenges. They play a crucial role in shaping a resilient governance structure by aligning it with a strategic vision that looks beyond immediate concerns and focuses on long-term adaptability.

2. **Adaptive Decision-Making:**

    Flexibility and Agility: Resilient governance requires leaders who are adaptable in their decision-making. They can pivot when necessary, make swift decisions in the face of uncertainties, and adjust strategies to align with changing circumstances.

3. **Transparent Communication:**

    Open and Honest Dialogue: Leaders who prioritize transparent communication contribute significantly to resilience. Open dialogue fosters trust, ensures that stakeholders are well-informed, and creates a culture of transparency that is crucial in times of uncertainty.

4. **Emotional Intelligence:**

    Empathy and Understanding: Emotional intelligence is paramount in resilient leadership. Leaders who understand and empathize with the emotions of their teams can navigate challenges more effectively. This quality contributes to maintaining morale and fostering a sense of unity during turbulent times.

5. **Risk Management Proficiency:**

    Proactive Risk Assessment: Leaders must be proficient in risk management. This involves not only responding to risks as they arise but also proactively assessing potential threats and putting measures in place to mitigate them. Effective risk management is integral to resilient governance.

6. **Collaboration and Team Building:**

    Cohesive Team Dynamics: Resilient governance thrives on collaboration and teamwork. Leaders who excel in team building create an environment where diverse perspectives are valued, and teams can work cohesively to address challenges collectively.

7. **Crisis Leadership:**

   Calculated Crisis Response: During crises, leaders must exhibit crisis leadership qualities. This includes maintaining composure, making well-informed decisions under pressure, and guiding the organization through the storm with a steady hand.

8. **Continuous Learning Mindset:**

   Adaptability and Growth: Resilient leaders foster a continuous learning culture. They encourage adaptability, recognize that failures are opportunities for learning, and promote a mindset of constant improvement within the organization.

9. **Business Continuity Planning:**

   Strategic Preparedness: Leaders play a key role in business continuity planning. They must lead efforts to develop and implement strategies that ensure essential functions can continue during disruptions, contributing to the overall resilience of the organization.

10. **Ethical Stewardship:**

    Integrity and Ethics: Leaders who exemplify ethical conduct contribute to the resilience of governance. Integrity builds trust, and organizations guided by ethical leaders are better equipped to navigate challenges without compromising their values.

4.4 KEY PRINCIPLES OF ADAPTABILITY AND FLEXIBILITY IN GOVERNANCE

Adaptability and flexibility are fundamental principles in governance, particularly in the context of today's rapidly changing and uncertain business landscape. These principles empower organizations to respond effectively to evolving circumstances, mitigate risks, and seize opportunities.

Let's delve into the key principles of adaptability and flexibility in governance:

1. **Dynamic Decision-Making:**

    Principle: Real-time Responsiveness

    Explanation: Governance structures that prioritize adaptability embrace real-time responsiveness. This involves the ability to make informed decisions promptly as situations unfold. Dynamic decision-making is crucial for addressing emerging risks and capitalizing on opportunities in a rapidly changing environment.

2. **Agile Strategic Planning:**

    Principle: Continuous Strategic Iteration

    Explanation: Instead of rigid, long-term plans, adaptable governance principles favor continuous strategic iteration. This involves regularly revisiting and adjusting strategic plans based on changing internal and external factors. Agile strategic planning ensures that organizational goals remain relevant in the face of evolving circumstances.

3. **Risk Anticipation and Mitigation:**

    Principle: Proactive Risk Management

    Explanation: Adaptable governance is characterized by proactive risk management. It involves identifying potential risks early, assessing their potential impact, and implementing mitigation strategies. Rather than merely reacting to risks, organizations with adaptable governance anticipate and address them before they escalate.

4. **Open Communication Channels:**

Principle: Transparent and Frequent Communication

Explanation: Transparent communication is a cornerstone of adaptability. Open channels facilitate the flow of information across the organization, ensuring that stakeholders are well-informed about changes, challenges, and strategic shifts. Frequent communication fosters a culture of trust and collaboration.

5. **Flexibility in Organizational Structure:**

Principle: Organizational Resilience

Explanation: Adaptable governance recognizes the need for organizational resilience. This involves structuring the organization in a way that allows for flexibility in roles, responsibilities, and reporting structures. Resilient organizations can quickly pivot and reallocate resources as needed.

6. **Technology Integration:**

Principle: Agile Technology Adoption

Explanation: Adaptable governance embraces the rapid adoption of technology to enhance operational efficiency. This involves integrating technologies that enable real-time data analysis, facilitate remote collaboration, and support agile decision-making processes.

7. **Continuous Learning Culture:**

Principle: Embracing a Growth Mindset

Explanation: Organizations with adaptable governance foster a continuous learning culture. This involves encouraging employees at all levels to embrace a growth mindset, learn from experiences, and adapt their approaches based on feedback and evolving best practices.

8. **Scenario Planning:**

Principle: Strategic Contingency Planning

Explanation: Adaptable governance incorporates scenario planning as a strategic tool. This involves envisioning and planning for various potential future scenarios. By considering different possibilities, organizations can better prepare for uncertainties and make more informed decisions when faced with unexpected challenges.

9. **Stakeholder Engagement:**

Principle: Listening to Stakeholder Feedback

Explanation: Adaptability in governance involves actively seeking and incorporating feedback from stakeholders. This includes customers, employees, investors, and other relevant parties. Engaging with stakeholders ensures that governance decisions align with their needs and expectations.

10. **Iterative Improvement:**

Principle: Continuous Process Enhancement

Explanation: Adaptable governance emphasizes continuous improvement of processes. This involves regularly evaluating and refining governance structures and practices based on performance assessments, lessons learned, and feedback. Iterative improvement ensures that governance remains effective and aligned with organizational goals.

4.5   AGILITY IN THE FACE OF DISRUPTION

Remaining agile in the face of unexpected disruptions is a critical capability for organizations seeking not only to survive but to thrive in today's dynamic business landscape. Agility allows organizations to respond swiftly, make informed decisions, and adapt their strategies to mitigate the impact of disruptions. Here are key strategies and practices that organizations can employ to enhance their agility in the face of unexpected disruptions:

1. **Develop a Robust Business Continuity Plan:**

    Key Strategy: Proactive Preparedness

    Explanation: Establishing a comprehensive business continuity plan ensures that organizations are prepared to manage disruptions effectively. This plan should include protocols for crisis management, communication strategies, and contingencies for maintaining essential functions during unexpected events.

2. **Foster a Culture of Agility:**

    Key Strategy: Cultural Mindset

    Explanation: Cultivate a culture that values and encourages agility. This involves fostering a mindset where employees are empowered to adapt, innovate, and contribute ideas for overcoming challenges. A culture of agility promotes quick decision-making and the ability to pivot in response to unexpected disruptions.

3. **Embrace Technology for Remote Operations:**

    Key Strategy: Digital Transformation

    Explanation: Leverage technology to enable remote operations. Cloud-based collaboration tools, virtual communication platforms, and other digital solutions empower employees to work from anywhere, ensuring business continuity during disruptions that may impact physical workplaces.

4. **Establish Cross-Functional Teams:**

Key Strategy: Collaborative Teams

Explanation: Create cross-functional teams that bring together individuals with diverse skills and expertise. These teams are better equipped to address multifaceted challenges, share insights, and collaborate efficiently in response to unexpected disruptions.

5. **Regularly Review and Update Risk Assessments:**

Key Strategy: Proactive Risk Management

Explanation: Conduct regular risk assessments to identify potential disruptions and their potential impact. This proactive approach allows organizations to implement measures to mitigate risks, ensuring a more resilient and agile response when unexpected events occur.

6. **Implement Agile Project Management:**

Key Strategy: Agile Methodologies

Explanation: Adopt agile project management methodologies, such as Scrum or Kanban. These frameworks emphasize flexibility, iterative progress, and rapid adaptation to changing circumstances, making them particularly effective in navigating unexpected disruptions.

7. **Diversify Supply Chains:**

Key Strategy: Supply Chain Resilience

Explanation: Diversify suppliers and create redundancies in the supply chain. This helps mitigate the impact of disruptions in one region or from a single supplier, allowing the organization to source critical materials or components from alternative channels.

8. **Prioritize Stakeholder Communication:**

    Key Strategy: Transparent Communication

    Explanation: Maintain open and transparent communication with stakeholders. Keeping customers, employees, investors, and other relevant parties informed during disruptions builds trust and allows the organization to manage expectations effectively.

9. **Conduct Scenario Planning Exercises:**

    Key Strategy: Preparedness Training

    Explanation: Regularly conduct scenario planning exercises to simulate potential disruptions. These exercises help organizations refine their response strategies, identify areas for improvement, and ensure that teams are well-prepared for a variety of unexpected scenarios.

10. **Encourage Employee Training and Skill Development:**

    Key Strategy: Adaptive Workforce

    Explanation: Invest in ongoing training and skill development for employees. An adaptive workforce with a diverse skill set is better equipped to handle changing roles and responsibilities in response to unexpected disruptions.

4.6 TRANSPARENT COMMUNICATION AND GOVERNANCE

Transparent communication within the governance framework is a cornerstone of effective leadership, trust-building, and organizational resilience. It ensures that information flows openly and honestly, allowing stakeholders at all levels to be well-informed, engaged, and aligned with the organization's goals. Emphasizing transparent communication is not just a best practice; it is a strategic imperative that contributes to the overall success and sustainability of an organization.

Let's delve into the importance of transparent communication and explore strategies for fostering open communication channels at all levels of the governance structure:

IMPORTANCE OF TRANSPARENT COMMUNICATION

Trust Building: Transparent communication builds trust among stakeholders. When leaders openly share information, it demonstrates authenticity and honesty, fostering a culture of trust within the organization.

Employee Engagement: Transparent communication engages employees by providing them with a clear understanding of organizational goals, strategies, and challenges. Engaged employees are more likely to be motivated, productive, and committed to the organization's success.

Risk Mitigation: Transparent communication is a crucial tool for risk mitigation. When potential risks and challenges are communicated openly, organizations can address them proactively, minimizing the impact on operations and reputation.

Informed Decision-Making: Access to accurate and timely information allows leaders at all levels to make informed decisions. Transparent communication ensures that decision-makers have a comprehensive understanding of the factors influencing organizational outcomes.

Organizational Alignment: Transparent communication helps align all stakeholders with the organization's mission, vision, and values. When everyone is on the same page, it promotes a unified and cohesive approach to achieving strategic objectives.

4.6.1 STRATEGIES FOR FOSTERING OPEN COMMUNICATION CHANNELS

Establish Clear Communication Policies: Develop and communicate clear communication policies within the governance framework. Clearly outline expectations regarding the frequency, modes, and channels of communication at different levels of the organization.

Leadership Visibility and Accessibility: Leaders should be visible and accessible to employees at all levels. This can include open-door policies, regular town hall meetings, or virtual platforms where employees can interact directly with leadership.

Utilize Technology for Accessibility: Leverage technology to facilitate communication. Use digital platforms, intranet systems, and collaboration tools to ensure that information is accessible to all employees regardless of their location within the organization.

Regularly Scheduled Updates: Establish a schedule for regular updates and communications. This can include newsletters, email updates, or other means of disseminating information consistently to keep stakeholders informed about organizational developments.

Two-Way Communication: Encourage and facilitate two-way communication. Create forums for feedback, questions, and suggestions from employees. This not only enhances transparency but also empowers employees to contribute to the decision-making process.

Training and Education: Provide training on effective communication practices. Equip employees and leaders with the skills needed to communicate transparently, including active listening, clarity in messaging, and understanding diverse communication styles.

Crisis Communication Planning: Develop a crisis communication plan. Outline procedures for communicating during times of crisis, ensuring that information is disseminated promptly, accurately, and with a focus on maintaining trust.

Promote a Culture of Openness: Foster a culture that values openness and transparency. Recognize and celebrate instances of transparent communication, and address any barriers or challenges that may hinder open communication within the organization.

Performance Metrics and Reporting: Establish clear performance metrics and reporting mechanisms. Transparently share performance data and key indicators, allowing stakeholders to assess the organization's progress and success against established goals.

Continuous Improvement: Regularly evaluate and refine communication strategies. Solicit feedback from stakeholders and adapt communication practices based on lessons learned and changing organizational needs.

4.6.2 Principle Of Integrating Risk-1nformed Decision-Making Processes

The principle of integrating risk-informed decision-making processes is crucial for organizations aiming to navigate uncertainties effectively and make informed choices that align with their strategic objectives. By incorporating risk assessments into strategic planning, governance structures can proactively identify, analyze, and manage risks, fostering a culture of resilience and adaptability. Let's explore this principle and delve into how governance structures can integrate risk assessments into strategic planning:

PRINCIPLE: INTEGRATING RISK-INFORMED DECISION-MAKING PROCESSES

1. **Proactive Risk Identification:**

    Principle: Anticipate and Identify Risks Early

    Explanation: The principle emphasizes the need to proactively identify potential risks before they escalate. Governance structures should encourage a systematic approach to risk identification, involving stakeholders at various levels to capture diverse perspectives and insights.

2. **Comprehensive Risk Analysis:**

    Principle: Thoroughly Assess and Analyze Risks

    Explanation: Before making decisions, governance structures should ensure a comprehensive analysis of identified risks. This involves assessing the likelihood and impact of each risk, considering potential interdependencies, and evaluating the organization's capacity to manage or mitigate these risks effectively.

3. **Informed Decision-Making:**

    Principle: Incorporate Risk Considerations into Decision-Making

    Explanation: The principle advocates for incorporating risk considerations directly into decision-making processes. Governance structures should ensure that decision-makers are well-informed about the potential risks associated with different options, allowing for more strategic and risk-aware decision-making.

4. **Continuous Monitoring and Adaptation:**

Principle: Monitor Risks Continuously and Adapt Strategically

Explanation: Risk-informed decision-making is an ongoing process. Governance structures should establish mechanisms for continuous monitoring of risks, allowing for timely adjustments to strategies and plans as the risk landscape evolves.

4.6.3 INCORPORATING RISK ASSESSMENTS FOR STRATEGIC PLANNING

1. **Establish a Risk Management Framework:**

Strategy: Create a Structured Approach to Risk Management

Explanation: Develop a comprehensive risk management framework within the governance structure. This includes defining roles and responsibilities, establishing risk appetite, and outlining the processes for identifying, assessing, and managing risks.

2. **Integrate Risk Assessments into Strategic Planning Processes:**

Strategy: Embed Risk Assessments in Planning Cycles

Explanation: Ensure that risk assessments are integral components of strategic planning cycles. This involves conducting risk assessments at the initiation of strategic planning and revisiting them throughout the planning period to account for changing circumstances.

3. **Scenario Planning and Sensitivity Analysis:**

   Strategy: Explore Various Risk Scenarios

   Explanation: Incorporate scenario planning and sensitivity analysis into the strategic planning process. This helps organizations explore different risk scenarios, understand potential impacts on strategic goals, and develop contingency plans for various outcomes.

4. **4. Engage Stakeholders in Risk Identification:**

   Strategy: Leverage Diverse Perspectives

   Explanation: Involve stakeholders from various levels and departments in the risk identification process. Diverse perspectives enhance the accuracy and comprehensiveness of risk assessments, providing a more nuanced understanding of potential challenges.

5. **Quantitative and Qualitative Risk Assessment:**

   Strategy: Combine Quantitative and Qualitative Approaches

   Explanation: Use a combination of quantitative and qualitative methods for risk assessment. While quantitative analysis provides numerical insights, qualitative assessments capture contextual nuances, offering a more holistic view of risks.

6. **Establish Key Risk Indicators (KRIs):**

   Strategy: Monitor Critical Risk Indicators

   Explanation: Identify and establish Key Risk Indicators (KRIs) relevant to strategic objectives. Monitoring these indicators provides early warnings of potential risks, enabling timely intervention and adjustments to strategic plans.

7. **Regular Review and Updates:**

    Strategy: Periodic Review and Revision of Risk Assessments

    Explanation: Conduct regular reviews of risk assessments and update them as needed. Periodic reassessment ensures that the organization remains aware of evolving risks and can adapt its strategies accordingly.

8. **Training and Capacity Building:**

    Strategy: Build Organizational Competency in Risk Management

    Explanation: Provide training and build organizational competency in risk management. Ensuring that employees understand risk concepts and mitigation strategies enhances the effectiveness of risk assessments across the organization.

9. **Incorporate Risk Metrics into Performance Evaluation:**

    Strategy: Link Risk Management to Performance Metrics

    Explanation: Align risk management with performance evaluation metrics. Recognize and reward teams and individuals who effectively manage and mitigate risks while achieving strategic goals.

10. **Communication of Risk Information:**

    Strategy: Transparent Communication of Risk Information

    Explanation: Ensure transparent communication of risk information throughout the organization. This includes sharing key risk findings, mitigation strategies, and the rationale behind risk-informed decisions to build a shared understanding among stakeholders.

4.7 TOOLS AND METHODOLOGIES FOR ASSESSING THE EFFECTIVENESS OF GOVERNANCE PRACTICES

Assessing the effectiveness of governance practices is crucial for organizations to ensure alignment with objectives, compliance with regulations, and the establishment of a resilient framework. Various tools and methodologies exist to evaluate governance effectiveness. Here are some widely used approaches:

1. **Governance Framework Scorecards:**

    Description: Scorecards provide a structured framework to assess governance effectiveness. Criteria are established based on key governance principles, and organizations are scored on how well they meet these criteria.

    Application: Organizations can use internally developed scorecards or adopt industry-standard frameworks, such as the Corporate Governance Scorecard or Governance Metrics International (GMI) Ratings.

2. **Governance Audits:**

    Description: Governance audits involve a comprehensive review of governance practices, policies, and procedures. External auditors or internal governance teams examine documentation, interview key stakeholders, and assess compliance with established governance standards.

    Application: Organizations can conduct periodic governance audits to identify areas for improvement and ensure alignment with legal and regulatory requirements.

3. **Self-Assessment Surveys:**

    Description: Self-assessment surveys involve distributing questionnaires or surveys to board members, executives, and other stakeholders to evaluate their perceptions of governance effectiveness. These surveys often cover aspects such as board composition, decision-making processes, and risk management.

Application: Regular self-assessment surveys can provide valuable insights into stakeholders' perspectives and help identify areas that may require attention.

4. **Balanced Scorecards:**

Description: Balanced Scorecards are strategic planning and management tools that align business activities with organizational objectives. They measure performance across various perspectives, including financial, customer, internal processes, and learning/growth.

Application: Governance effectiveness can be assessed by incorporating governance-related key performance indicators (KPIs) into the Balanced Scorecard.

5. **ISO 38500:**

Description: ISO 38500 is an international standard for corporate governance of information technology. It provides a framework for the effective and efficient use of IT resources. While specifically focusing on IT governance, its principles can be applied to broader governance practices.

Application: Organizations can use ISO 38500 as a benchmark to evaluate their IT governance practices and extend its principles to overall governance.

6. **Ethical Governance Assessment:**

Description: Ethical governance assessments evaluate the ethical dimensions of governance practices. This includes assessing the alignment of governance structures with ethical standards, transparency, and the ethical conduct of leaders.

Application: Organizations committed to ethical governance can use this assessment to ensure their practices are in line with ethical principles.

7. **Governance Risk and Compliance (GRC) Platforms:**

Description: GRC platforms are integrated solutions that help organizations manage and monitor governance, risk, and compliance activities. They provide tools for risk assessments, policy management, compliance monitoring, and reporting.

Application: Organizations can leverage GRC platforms to streamline governance processes, enhance visibility into risk management, and ensure compliance with relevant regulations.

8. **Peer Benchmarking:**

Description: Peer benchmarking involves comparing an organization's governance practices with those of industry peers or best-in-class organizations. This external benchmarking provides insights into where an organization stands relative to its peers.

Application: Organizations can use peer benchmarking to identify governance best practices and areas for improvement, fostering continuous enhancement.

9. **Board Effectiveness Assessments:**

Description: Board effectiveness assessments focus on evaluating the performance of the board of directors. This includes assessing the board's composition, diversity, decision-making processes, and its ability to fulfill its oversight responsibilities.

Application: Regular board effectiveness assessments can help boards identify strengths, weaknesses, and opportunities for improvement.

10. **Stakeholder Feedback Mechanisms:**

Description: Establishing mechanisms to gather feedback from stakeholders, including employees, customers, and investors, provides a holistic view of governance effectiveness. This can include surveys, focus groups, or direct communication channels.

Application: Incorporating stakeholder feedback helps organizations understand the impact of governance practices on different groups and identify areas for improvement.

4.8 FOUNDATIONAL ELEMENTS OF GOVERNANCE STRUCTURES

The foundational elements of governance structures are the essential building blocks that form the basis for effective governance within an organization. These elements provide the framework for decision-making, oversight, and the alignment of activities with the organization's mission and objectives. Here are the foundational elements of governance structures:

1. **Clear Organizational Purpose and Mission:**

   Description: A clear and well-defined organizational purpose and mission statement articulate the fundamental reason for the organization's existence and its intended impact on society.

   Importance: These elements provide a guiding compass for decision-making, ensuring that governance structures align activities with the organization's core purpose and values.

2. **Governance Policies and Procedures:**

   Description: Governance policies and procedures outline the rules, principles, and protocols that govern the behavior and decision-making processes of individuals and entities within the organization.

   Importance: Policies and procedures establish a framework for consistency, fairness, and accountability in governance practices, helping prevent conflicts and ensuring compliance with regulations.

3. **Board of Directors:**

   Description: The board of directors is a group of individuals elected or appointed to represent the interests of stakeholders and provide oversight, strategic guidance, and decision-making authority.

   Importance: The board plays a central role in governance, setting the direction for the organization, appointing executives, and ensuring that the organization operates ethically and in the best interest of stakeholders.

4. **Executive Leadership:**

   Description: Executive leadership consists of top-level executives, including the CEO and other key leaders, responsible for implementing the strategic vision set by the board and overseeing day-to-day operations.

   Importance: Effective executive leadership ensures the translation of governance directives into actionable plans and operational activities, fostering organizational success.

5. **Stakeholder Engagement:**

   Description: Stakeholder engagement involves actively involving individuals or groups that have an interest or stake in the organization, such as employees, customers, investors, and the community.

   Importance: Engaging stakeholders ensures that governance decisions consider diverse perspectives, builds trust, and aligns organizational activities with the needs and expectations of those affected.

6. **Transparency and Accountability:**

Description: Transparency involves openly sharing information, and accountability refers to the responsibility of individuals and entities for their actions and decisions.

Importance: Transparency and accountability are fundamental principles in governance, ensuring that stakeholders are informed, decisions are justifiable, and responsible behavior is upheld.

7. **Risk Management Framework:**

Description: A risk management framework outlines the processes, policies, and tools for identifying, assessing, and managing risks that may affect the organization's ability to achieve its objectives.

Importance: A robust risk management framework enhances organizational resilience, enabling governance structures to anticipate and mitigate potential challenges.

8. **Ethical Standards and Integrity:**

Description: Ethical standards define the moral principles that guide the behavior of individuals and the organization. Integrity involves adhering to these principles in all actions.

Importance: Upholding ethical standards and integrity is essential for maintaining trust, reputation, and the credibility of the organization within its internal and external communities.

9. **Strategic Planning and Decision-Making Processes:**

Description: Strategic planning involves setting long-term goals and objectives, and decision-making processes define how choices are made to achieve these goals.

Importance: Well-defined strategic planning and decision-making processes ensure that governance structures make informed, forward-looking decisions that align with the organization's vision.

10. Compliance and Legal Framework

Description: Compliance refers to adherence to legal requirements, regulations, and industry standards. A legal framework establishes the legal structure of the organization and its rights and responsibilities.

Importance: Compliance and a solid legal framework are essential to prevent legal issues, regulatory violations, and to ensure that the organization operates within the bounds of the law.

The foundational elements of governance structures provide the groundwork for effective organizational governance. Together, these elements create a framework that promotes transparency, accountability, ethical behavior, and strategic alignment, fostering an environment where the organization can achieve its mission and objectives while maintaining the trust and confidence of its stakeholders.

CHAPTER
FIVE

THE ROLE OF
TECHNOLOGY IN GRC:
INNOVATIONS AND
TRANSFORMATIONS

5.1   Evolution of Technology in Governance, Risk, and Compliance (GRC)

The integration of technology in Governance, Risk, and Compliance (GRC) has undergone a profound evolution, transforming how organizations approach and manage governance, mitigate risks, and ensure compliance with regulatory standards. This transformative journey is characterized by a rich historical context, key milestones, and paradigm shifts that collectively redefine the landscape of GRC.

5.1.1   Historical Context

The historical context of technology in GRC can be traced back to the late 20th century, with the digitization of business processes. Early endeavors focused on automating manual tasks, incorporating databases, and utilizing basic software solutions to streamline compliance efforts. However, the true dawn of technology in GRC emerged with the advent of the internet and subsequent digital revolution.

5.1.2   Milestones Shaping Technology Integration in GRC

Automation of Compliance Processes (1990s): The nascent stages involved automating compliance processes through rudimentary software solutions. Organizations began employing technology to manage documentation, track regulatory changes, and generate compliance reports more efficiently.

Enterprise Resource Planning (ERP) Systems (2000s): The integration of Enterprise Resource Planning (ERP) systems marked a significant leap forward. These comprehensive platforms streamlined business processes, providing a centralized hub for data management, financial reporting, and compliance tracking.

GRC Platforms and Integrated Suites (2010s): The 2010s witnessed the emergence of dedicated GRC platforms and integrated suites. These sophisticated solutions revolutionized how organizations approached GRC by providing a unified framework for risk management, compliance tracking, and governance oversight.

Advanced Analytics and Artificial Intelligence (AI) (2010s-2020s): The integration of advanced analytics and AI in the 2010s and 2020s marked a paradigm shift. Organizations began leveraging predictive analytics to identify emerging risks, enhance decision-making, and automate compliance monitoring, thereby reducing manual efforts and improving accuracy.

Blockchain Technology (2010s-2020s): The decentralized and secure nature of blockchain technology found applications in GRC, particularly in ensuring the integrity of data, enhancing transparency, and securing sensitive information, especially in industries with stringent regulatory requirements.

Cloud Computing (2010s-2020s): The adoption of cloud computing transformed the accessibility and scalability of GRC solutions. Cloud-based platforms offered real-time collaboration, remote access, and the ability to scale GRC capabilities based on organizational needs.

5.1.3 Paradigm Shifts in Technology's Role in GRC

From Reactive to Proactive Risk Management: Early GRC technology primarily facilitated reactive risk management. However, with the advent of advanced analytics and AI, organizations transitioned to proactive risk management, identifying and mitigating risks before they escalate.

Holistic GRC Integration: The evolution of GRC platforms and integrated suites signaled a shift from siloed risk, compliance, and governance efforts to a holistic and integrated approach. This allowed organizations to view GRC as an interconnected ecosystem rather than disparate functions.

Emphasis on Data Security and Privacy: With an increased focus on data security and privacy regulations, technology in GRC has evolved to prioritize secure data management, encryption, and adherence to privacy laws, ensuring organizations meet stringent compliance requirements.

User-Friendly Interfaces and Accessibility: The user experience became a focal point as technology in GRC advanced. User-friendly interfaces, intuitive dashboards, and accessibility via mobile devices became integral, facilitating widespread adoption and participation in GRC processes.

Continuous Monitoring and Reporting: Technology advancements enabled continuous monitoring of risks and compliance metrics. Real-time reporting capabilities allow organizations to adapt swiftly to changes, ensuring a timely response to emerging risks and compliance challenges.

5.1.4 Exploring the Automation of Governance Processes Facilitated by Technology

The automation of governance processes through technological advancements has reshaped how organizations manage their governance responsibilities. This shift towards automation is driven by the desire for increased efficiency, accuracy, and transparency in governance practices.

Here's an exploration of the key aspects of automation in governance processes:

DOCUMENT MANAGEMENT:

Automation: Technology facilitates the automation of document management processes, ensuring the efficient creation, distribution, and storage of crucial governance documents such as board agendas, meeting minutes, and policy documents.

Impact: Automation streamlines document workflows, reducing the risk of errors and ensuring that board members have access to up-to-date and relevant information, fostering better-informed decision-making.

COMPLIANCE TRACKING:

Automation: Compliance tracking tools use technology to monitor regulatory changes, track compliance activities, and automate the generation of compliance reports. Automated alerts notify relevant stakeholders of upcoming deadlines and changes in regulations.

Impact: This automation enhances the organization's ability to stay in compliance with evolving regulations, reducing the risk of non-compliance and associated penalties.

BOARD COMMUNICATION:

Automation: Communication tools, including secure messaging platforms and email automation, streamline communication between board members, executives, and other stakeholders. Automation ensures timely and secure delivery of important information.

Impact: Improved communication leads to more efficient decision-making processes, as board members can collaborate seamlessly and stay informed about critical updates.

MEETING MANAGEMENT:

Automation: Technology automates various aspects of meeting management, from scheduling and agenda creation to attendance tracking. Board portal solutions offer centralized platforms for managing all meeting-related activities.

Impact: Automation in meeting management saves time, enhances organization, and allows board members to focus on substantive discussions during meetings rather than logistical details.

RISK ASSESSMENT AND MONITORING:

Automation: Advanced analytics and risk management software automate the identification, assessment, and monitoring of risks. Technology enables the continuous tracking of key risk indicators and the automation of risk reporting.

Impact: Automation in risk management enhances the organization's ability to proactively identify and mitigate risks, contributing to a more resilient governance structure.

PERFORMANCE EVALUATION:

Automation: Technology facilitates the automation of performance evaluation processes for board members, executives, and the organization as a whole. Data-driven tools provide insights into governance effectiveness and individual performance.

Impact: Automated performance evaluations ensure objectivity, consistency, and the ability to identify areas for improvement, contributing to the continuous enhancement of governance practices.

5.2 IMPACT OF BOARD PORTALS AND DECISION SUPPORT SYSTEMS ON GOVERNANCE TRANSPARENCY AND DECISION-MAKING

i. **Enhanced Transparency**

Board Portals: Board portals offer a secure and centralized space for storing and accessing governance documents. This enhances transparency by providing board members with real-time access to critical information, reducing the risk of information asymmetry.

Decision Support Systems: Decision support systems leverage data analytics and visualization tools to present relevant information to board members. This transparency into data-driven insights enhances the board's understanding of key issues and opportunities.

ii. Streamlined Communication

Board Portals: Board portals facilitate secure communication channels among board members. This ensures that information is communicated efficiently, fostering collaboration and reducing the reliance on traditional communication methods.

Decision Support Systems: Decision support systems streamline the communication of complex data and insights, enabling board members to grasp information quickly and make informed decisions.

iii. Efficient Decision-Making Processes

Board Portals: Board portals streamline the preparation for meetings by providing a centralized location for documents and communication. This efficiency allows board members to come prepared, leading to more focused and productive discussions.

Decision Support Systems: Decision support systems provide data-driven insights that support the decision-making process. By presenting relevant information in a comprehensible manner, these systems empower boards to make informed and timely decisions.

iv. Security and Compliance

Board Portals: Board portals prioritize security, offering features like encryption and access controls. This ensures the confidentiality and integrity of governance-related information, contributing to compliance with data protection regulations.

Decision Support Systems: Decision support systems adhere to data security standards, ensuring the protection of sensitive information. Compliance with data privacy regulations is integral to maintaining the trust of stakeholders.

v. Remote Accessibility

Board Portals: Board portals provide remote access to governance documents, enabling board members to stay connected and engaged irrespective of their physical location. This is particularly valuable for organizations with geographically dispersed boards.

Decision Support Systems: Decision support systems with cloud-based accessibility enhance remote decision-making capabilities. Board members can access data and insights from anywhere, fostering agility in decision-making processes.

vi. Data-Driven Governance

Board Portals: Board portals contribute to data-driven governance by centralizing information and providing a platform for data storage. While not analytical in nature, they create the foundation for integrating data-driven decision support systems.

Decision Support Systems: Decision support systems leverage data analytics to provide boards with actionable insights. This data-driven approach enhances governance by enabling boards to base decisions on a comprehensive understanding of relevant information.

5.3 EXAMINING HOW TECHNOLOGY, INCLUDING PREDICTIVE ANALYTICS, ENHANCES RISK ASSESSMENT

The integration of technology, particularly predictive analytics, has revolutionized the landscape of risk assessment, enabling organizations to proactively identify, analyze, and mitigate potential risks. Here's an examination of how technology enhances risk assessment:

i. **Early Warning through Predictive Analytics**

Technology Integration: Predictive analytics leverages historical data, statistical algorithms, and machine learning to identify patterns and trends. This enables organizations to anticipate potential risks by predicting future scenarios based on current and historical data.

Impact: By providing early warnings, predictive analytics empowers organizations to take preemptive measures, preventing or mitigating risks before they escalate.

ii. **Continuous Monitoring of Key Risk Indicators (KRIs)**

Technology Integration: Automated systems and tools continuously monitor Key Risk Indicators (KRIs), which are predefined metrics that signal potential risks. These systems use technology to track and analyze KRIs in real-time.

Impact: Continuous monitoring ensures that organizations stay vigilant, allowing them to respond promptly to changes in risk profiles and enabling proactive risk management.

iii. **Scenario Planning and Simulation**

Technology Integration: Risk assessment tools incorporate scenario planning and simulation capabilities. These technologies allow organizations to simulate various risk scenarios, assess their potential impact, and develop response strategies.

Impact: By exploring different scenarios, organizations can enhance their preparedness and develop robust risk mitigation plans that are tailored to specific circumstances.

iv. Data Aggregation and Analysis

Technology Integration: Advanced data analytics tools aggregate and analyze vast amounts of structured and unstructured data from internal and external sources. This includes financial data, market trends, and relevant industry information.

Impact: Data-driven risk assessments provide a comprehensive view, enabling organizations to identify correlations, trends, and emerging risks that may not be apparent through traditional methods.

v. Customized Risk Models

Technology Integration: Technology allows organizations to create customized risk models based on their industry, operational structure, and specific risk factors. These models can be dynamically adjusted as the business environment evolves.

Impact: Customization enhances the accuracy and relevance of risk assessments, ensuring that organizations focus on the risks most pertinent to their unique circumstances.

vi. Real-Time Reporting and Dashboards

Technology Integration: Risk assessment platforms offer real-time reporting and interactive dashboards. These features provide stakeholders with instant access to critical risk information and enable dynamic visualization of risk data.

Impact: Real-time reporting enhances decision-making by providing current and actionable insights, allowing organizations to respond swiftly to changing risk landscapes.

5.4 THE CRUCIAL ROLE OF TECHNOLOGY IN CYBERSECURITY FOR EFFECTIVE RISK MITIGATION

CONTINUOUS THREAT MONITORING:

Technology's Role: Cybersecurity technologies continuously monitor network traffic, system logs, and user behaviors to detect and respond to potential threats.

Impact: This proactive monitoring allows organizations to identify cybersecurity risks in real-time, enabling rapid responses to mitigate potential breaches.

BEHAVIORAL ANALYTICS:

Technology's Role: Advanced technologies, including behavioral analytics, assess user activities to detect anomalies or suspicious behaviors that may indicate a security threat.

Impact: Behavioral analytics enhance risk mitigation by identifying potential insider threats or unauthorized access, allowing organizations to take preventive action.

MACHINE LEARNING IN THREAT DETECTION:

Technology's Role: Machine learning algorithms analyze large datasets to identify patterns associated with known and unknown cyber threats.

Impact: By leveraging machine learning, cybersecurity systems can adapt and improve their threat detection capabilities over time, staying ahead of evolving cyber threats.

INCIDENT RESPONSE AUTOMATION:

Technology's Role: Incident response automation uses technology to automate the identification, containment, eradication, and recovery phases of a cybersecurity incident.

Impact: Automation accelerates response times, reducing the impact of cybersecurity incidents and minimizing the potential damage to an organization's assets and reputation.

ENCRYPTION AND SECURE COMMUNICATION:

Technology's Role: Encryption technologies safeguard sensitive data and secure communication channels, preventing unauthorized access to critical information.

Impact: Protecting data through encryption ensures the confidentiality and integrity of information, mitigating the risk of data breaches and unauthorized access.

VULNERABILITY SCANNING AND PATCH MANAGEMENT:

Technology's Role: Automated vulnerability scanning tools identify weaknesses in systems and applications, while patch management systems automate the deployment of security updates.

Impact: Regular scanning and patching reduce the likelihood of exploitation by cyber threats, enhancing the overall resilience of the organization's cybersecurity posture.

SECURITY ANALYTICS FOR THREAT INTELLIGENCE:

Technology's Role: Security analytics platforms analyze vast amounts of data to provide actionable threat intelligence, helping organizations understand the latest cybersecurity threats.

Impact: By staying informed about emerging threats, organizations can proactively adjust their cybersecurity strategies and measures, reducing the risk of falling victim to new attack vectors.

USER AUTHENTICATION AND ACCESS CONTROLS:

Technology's Role: Technologies such as multi-factor authentication and access controls limit unauthorized access to systems and sensitive data.

Impact: Strengthening user authentication and access controls mitigates the risk of unauthorized access, protecting critical assets from compromise.

5.5 THE EMERGENCE OF E-GOVERNANCE, DIGITAL COMPLIANCE PLATFORMS, AND BLOCKCHAIN TECHNOLOGY

E-GOVERNANCE:

E-governance represents the evolution of traditional governance practices into digital realms. It involves the use of information and communication technology (ICT) to enhance the efficiency, transparency, and accessibility of government services and operations.

E-governance streamlines administrative processes, reduces bureaucracy, and improves citizen engagement. Online portals and digital services enable citizens to interact with government entities more conveniently, fostering transparency and accountability.

DIGITAL COMPLIANCE PLATFORMS:

Digital compliance platforms have emerged as comprehensive solutions for managing and ensuring compliance with regulatory requirements. These platforms leverage technology to automate compliance processes, monitor changes in regulations, and streamline reporting.

Organizations benefit from enhanced accuracy, efficiency, and real-time visibility into their compliance status. Digital compliance platforms reduce the risk of non-compliance, automate reporting, and provide audit trails for regulatory authorities.

BLOCKCHAIN TECHNOLOGY:

Blockchain is a decentralized and secure digital ledger technology. In governance and compliance, blockchain ensures the integrity, transparency, and immutability of records. It enables the creation of tamper-resistant audit trails and smart contracts.

Blockchain technology enhances trust in digital transactions, minimizes fraud, and provides a secure and transparent record of compliance-related activities. It is particularly impactful in industries with complex regulatory requirements, such as finance and healthcare.

5.6 DISCUSSING THE INTEGRATION OF ARTIFICIAL INTELLIGENCE IN RISK ANALYSIS

PREDICTIVE ANALYTICS:

Integration: Artificial Intelligence (AI) is integrated into risk analysis through predictive analytics. Machine learning algorithms analyze historical and real-time data to identify patterns and trends, predicting potential future risks.

Impact: Predictive analytics enhances risk analysis by providing early warnings, allowing organizations to proactively address emerging risks. It improves the accuracy of risk assessments and enables more informed decision-making.

AUTOMATED RISK IDENTIFICATION:

Integration: AI automates the identification of risks by continuously monitoring data sources for anomalies or deviations from expected patterns. It can analyze vast datasets more efficiently than traditional methods.

Impact: Automated risk identification accelerates the risk assessment process, ensuring timely responses to potential threats. It reduces the likelihood of overlooking critical risk factors and enhances the organization's overall risk awareness.

NATURAL LANGUAGE PROCESSING (NLP):

Integration: NLP is integrated into risk analysis tools to process and understand unstructured data, such as news articles, social media, and regulatory texts. This enables AI systems to extract relevant information for risk assessment.

Impact: NLP enhances the scope of risk analysis by incorporating insights from diverse sources. It enables organizations to stay informed about external factors that may impact risk profiles.

SCENARIO MODELING AND SIMULATION:

Integration: AI-driven scenario modeling and simulation tools use machine learning to create realistic risk scenarios. These simulations help organizations understand the potential impact of various risks on their operations.

Impact: AI-driven scenario modeling allows organizations to assess the resilience of their systems and develop effective risk mitigation strategies. It provides a dynamic approach to risk analysis that adapts to changing conditions.

5.6.1 Discussing the Use of Chatbots and Virtual Assistants in Compliance

AUTOMATED COMPLIANCE COMMUNICATION:

Chatbots are employed for automated communication in compliance processes. They assist users in understanding regulatory requirements, provide information on compliance procedures, and answer queries related to policies.

Chatbots enhance user experience by providing instant and accurate information. They ensure consistent communication and support, reducing the risk of misunderstandings or misinterpretations of compliance-related information.

INTERACTIVE COMPLIANCE TRAINING:

Virtual assistants are utilized in interactive compliance training programs. They engage users in simulated scenarios, provide real-time feedback, and offer personalized guidance on compliance best practices.

Virtual assistants make compliance training more engaging and effective. They adapt to individual learning needs, ensuring that users grasp and retain essential compliance information.

AUTOMATED COMPLIANCE AUDITS:

Chatbots and virtual assistants can automate certain aspects of compliance audits. They assist in gathering required documentation, verifying compliance status, and guiding users through audit processes.

Automation streamlines compliance audit procedures, reducing manual effort and ensuring thorough and consistent assessments. Chatbots and virtual assistants facilitate a smoother audit experience for both auditors and auditees.

REAL-TIME COMPLIANCE MONITORING:

Chatbots equipped with AI algorithms monitor real-time compliance data. They alert users to changes in regulations, upcoming deadlines, and potential compliance issues.

Real-time monitoring enhances proactive compliance management. Chatbots provide timely notifications, allowing organizations to address compliance issues promptly and avoid the risk of non-compliance.

5.6.2 Addressing Challenges Related to Data Privacy and Security

DATA ENCRYPTION:

Challenge: Safeguarding sensitive data is a critical concern. Encryption technologies, such as end-to-end encryption and data masking, help protect information both in transit and at rest.

Solution: Implement robust encryption protocols to secure data, ensuring that even if unauthorized access occurs, the information remains indecipherable.

COMPLIANCE WITH REGULATIONS

Challenge: Meeting diverse data privacy regulations poses a challenge, especially in a globalized business environment. Regulations like GDPR and CCPA require organizations to adhere to strict standards.

Solution: Develop comprehensive compliance strategies, conduct regular audits, and leverage technology to automate compliance monitoring and reporting.

IDENTITY AND ACCESS MANAGEMENT (IAM)

Challenge: Unauthorized access to sensitive information can lead to data breaches. IAM solutions help manage user identities and control access to critical systems and data.

Solution: Implement robust IAM frameworks, including multi-factor authentication and access controls, to ensure that only authorized personnel have access to sensitive data.

DATA RESIDENCY AND SOVEREIGNTY

Challenge: Data residency requirements and sovereignty concerns may conflict with global business operations. Some jurisdictions have specific regulations dictating where data can be stored.

Solution: Employ cloud solutions with data centers in compliant regions, and implement data residency policies to ensure adherence to local regulations.

DATA GOVERNANCE FRAMEWORKS:

Challenge: Ensuring data quality, integrity, and traceability is challenging without a structured data governance framework.

Solution: Develop and implement robust data governance policies, including data classification, data ownership, and data lifecycle management, to maintain control and visibility over data.

5.6.3 Discussing Cultural Shifts Needed for Successful Technology Integration

EMBRACING CHANGE:

Cultural Shift: Organizations must foster a culture that embraces change and views technology adoption as an opportunity for improvement rather than a disruption.

Impact: A culture that embraces change promotes innovation, agility, and a willingness to explore new technologies for continuous improvement.

CROSS-FUNCTIONAL COLLABORATION:

Cultural Shift: Encourage collaboration among different departments and teams, breaking down silos and fostering cross-functional cooperation.

Impact: Cross-functional collaboration ensures that technology solutions are aligned with the diverse needs of the organization, promoting holistic and integrated GRC practices.

CONTINUOUS LEARNING AND ADAPTABILITY:

Cultural Shift: Promote a culture of continuous learning and adaptability, encouraging employees to acquire new skills and stay updated on emerging technologies.

Impact: A workforce that is continuously learning and adapting is better equipped to leverage new technologies effectively, ensuring that GRC practices remain innovative and responsive to changing landscapes.

RISK-AWARE CULTURE

Cultural Shift: Cultivate a risk-aware culture where employees understand the importance of risk management and compliance in achieving organizational goals.

Impact: A risk-aware culture encourages proactive risk identification and mitigation, aligning with the organization's broader GRC objectives.

DATA-DRIVEN DECISION-MAKING:

Cultural Shift: Encourage a shift toward data-driven decision-making, where insights derived from technology and analytics inform strategic choices.

Impact: Organizations benefit from more informed and evidence-based decision-making, leading to improved GRC outcomes and a competitive advantage.

5.6.4 ANTICIPATING FUTURE TECHNOLOGICAL TRENDS SHAPING GRC

EXTENDED REALITY (XR) FOR TRAINING:

Trend: The use of XR, including virtual reality (VR) and augmented reality (AR), in training for realistic simulations and immersive learning experiences.

Impact: XR can revolutionize GRC training by providing interactive and realistic scenarios for risk management and compliance.

QUANTUM COMPUTING FOR ADVANCED ENCRYPTION:

Trend: Quantum computing advancements for more robust encryption methods, addressing the potential threat posed by quantum computers to traditional encryption.

Impact: Enhanced encryption methods contribute to improved data security, ensuring the confidentiality of sensitive information.

AI-DRIVEN PREDICTIVE GOVERNANCE:

Trend: The integration of AI for predictive governance, leveraging machine learning algorithms to anticipate regulatory changes, assess their impact, and proactively adjust compliance strategies.

Impact: AI-driven predictive governance enhances agility in compliance management, allowing organizations to stay ahead of evolving regulatory landscapes.

INTERCONNECTED GRC PLATFORMS:

Trend: Increased integration and interoperability among GRC platforms, creating interconnected ecosystems that streamline data sharing and collaboration.

Impact: Interconnected GRC platforms facilitate a holistic and unified approach to governance, risk management, and compliance, promoting efficiency and transparency.

BLOCKCHAIN FOR IMMUTABLE AUDIT TRAILS:

Trend: Wider adoption of blockchain technology for creating immutable and transparent audit trails, enhancing the integrity of compliance records.

Impact: Blockchain ensures the verifiability and authenticity of compliance-related data, reducing the risk of tampering and providing a trustworthy record.

5.6.5 NATURAL LANGUAGE PROCESSING (NLP) IN REGULATORY COMPLIANCE

Trend: The use of NLP in regulatory compliance for efficient analysis of regulatory texts, enabling organizations to quickly understand and implement compliance measures.

Impact: NLP streamlines the interpretation of complex regulatory language, aiding organizations in staying compliant.

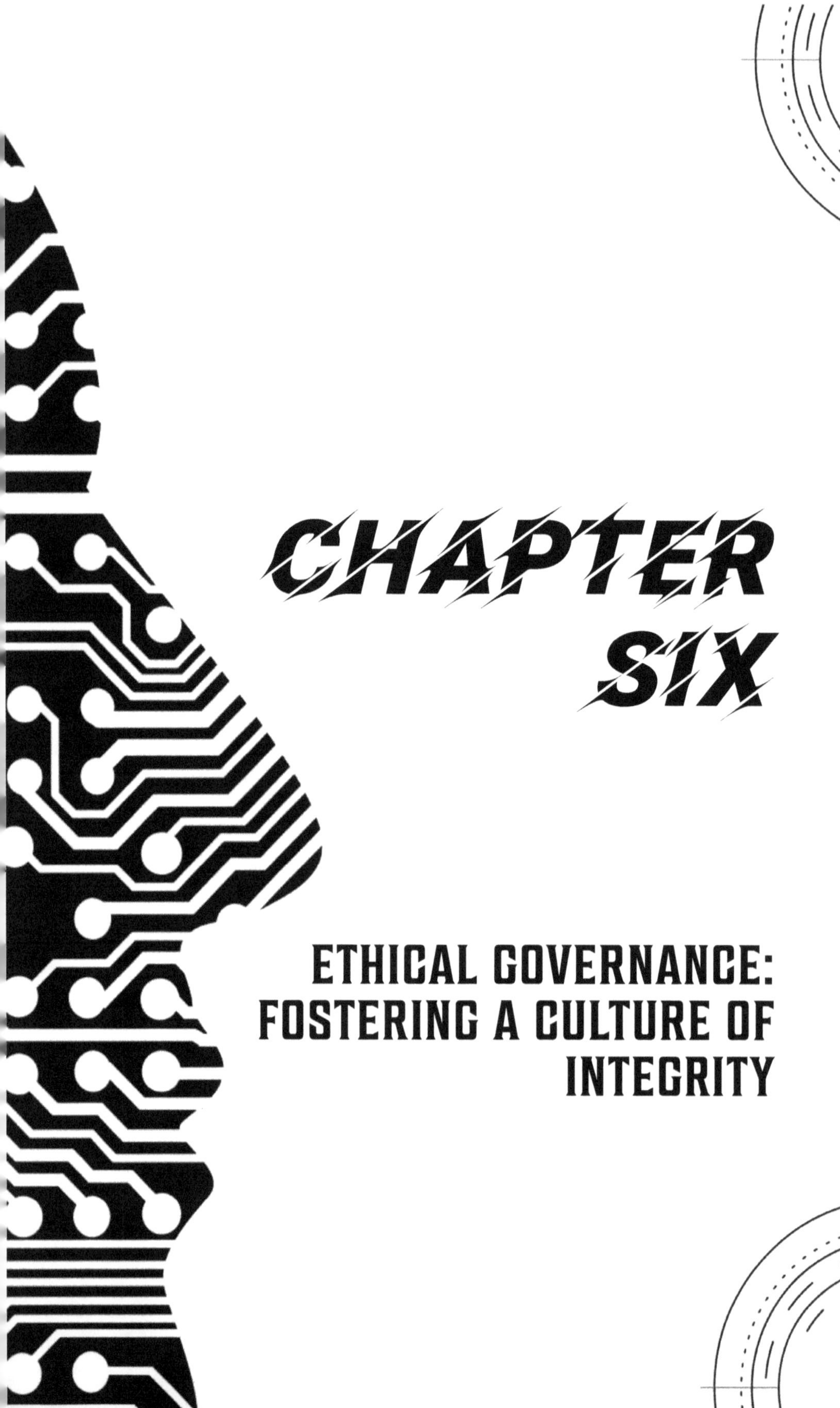

CHAPTER SIX

ETHICAL GOVERNANCE: FOSTERING A CULTURE OF INTEGRITY

After an extensive breakdown of the enormous role that technology plays in GRC, particularly in the aspect of innovations and transformations, this chapter becomes perfect to look at rudiments of ethical governance and how it can engender a culture of integrity.

FIRST, WHAT IS ETHICAL GOVERNANCE?

Ethical governance refers to the systematic and principled approach organizations take to ensure that their decision-making processes, policies, and actions align with ethical standards and values. It involves the establishment of frameworks and mechanisms that guide behavior, promote transparency, and uphold moral principles throughout all levels of an organization. Ethical governance extends beyond mere compliance with laws and regulations, emphasizing a commitment to ethical conduct, social responsibility, and the well-being of stakeholders.

WHAT IS ITS INHERENT CONNECTION TO ORGANIZATIONAL INTEGRITY?

The connection between ethical governance and organizational integrity is fundamental and symbiotic. Organizational integrity is the consistency between an organization's actions, values, and principles. Ethical governance serves as the foundation for establishing, promoting, and sustaining organizational integrity.

Key elements of this connection include:

ALIGNMENT WITH VALUES:

Ethical Governance: Establishes and reinforces ethical values and principles that guide decision-making.

Organizational Integrity: Ensures that the organization's actions and decisions are consistent with its stated values, fostering integrity.

TRANSPARENCY AND ACCOUNTABILITY:

Ethical Governance: Promotes transparency in decision-making processes and holds individuals accountable for ethical lapses.

Organizational Integrity: Transparency and accountability contribute to the perception and reality of integrity within the organization.

STAKEHOLDER TRUST:

Ethical Governance: Upholds commitments to stakeholders, including employees, customers, and the community, fostering trust.

Organizational Integrity: Trust is a cornerstone of organizational integrity, built through consistent ethical behavior and responsible decision-making.

RISK MITIGATION:

Ethical Governance: Identifies and addresses ethical risks to prevent potential harm to the organization and its stakeholders.

Organizational Integrity: Proactive risk mitigation demonstrates a commitment to organizational integrity, safeguarding against ethical breaches.

LONG-TERM REPUTATION:

Ethical Governance: Contributes to the building of a positive organizational reputation through ethical conduct.

Organizational Integrity: A positive reputation is a reflection of organizational integrity, influencing how the organization is perceived by external stakeholders.

6.1 THE PIVOTAL ROLE OF ETHICAL LEADERSHIP

Ethical leadership plays a pivotal role in setting the tone for a culture of integrity within an organization. Ethical leaders demonstrate and promote ethical behavior, fostering an environment where employees at all levels are inspired to act ethically. Key aspects of the pivotal role of ethical leadership include:

SETTING THE EXAMPLE:

Ethical leaders serve as role models, embodying the values and ethical standards they expect others to follow. Their behavior sets the example for the entire organization.

CLEAR COMMUNICATION OF VALUES:

Ethical leaders communicate the organization's values clearly and consistently. They articulate the importance of ethical conduct and the impact it has on the organization and its stakeholders.

DECISION-MAKING GUIDED BY ETHICS:

Ethical leaders make decisions guided by ethical considerations. They prioritize values over short-term gains and consider the broader impact of their choices on the organization's reputation and stakeholders.

EMPOWERING ETHICAL DECISION-MAKING:

Ethical leaders empower employees to make ethical decisions by providing guidance, resources, and support. They create an environment where ethical decision-making is valued and recognized.

ADDRESSING ETHICAL CHALLENGES:

Ethical leaders confront ethical challenges head-on. They address issues promptly, transparently, and fairly, reinforcing the organization's commitment to ethical governance and integrity.

BUILDING A CULTURE OF TRUST:

Ethical leaders build a culture of trust by demonstrating consistency, fairness, and reliability. Trust is a cornerstone of organizational integrity, and it begins with ethical leadership.

LONG-TERM PERSPECTIVE:

Ethical leaders adopt a long-term perspective, recognizing that ethical behavior contributes to sustained success and organizational resilience over time.

6.1.1 Aligning Core Values and the Organization's Mission with Ethical Principles

Core values, representing the bedrock beliefs guiding an organization, intertwine with ethical principles, ensuring that the organization's actions resonate with integrity and moral coherence. The mission, encapsulated in a succinct statement, gains profound meaning when it aligns seamlessly with ethical aspirations, signifying a commitment to principled conduct in the pursuit of overarching goals. This alignment not only shapes the organization's character but also serves as a compass for decision-making, infusing ethical considerations into the very fabric of its existence.

Integrating ethical considerations into decision-making processes becomes imperative, fostering a culture where organizational values and the mission serve as ethical touchstones. This integration transcends mere compliance, encapsulating a commitment to responsible conduct that echoes across policies, practices, and procedures. Consistency in upholding ethical principles across the organizational spectrum reinforces the authenticity of its ethical stance, laying the groundwork for trust and credibility. When employees' values harmonize with those of the organization, a synergistic blend emerges, nurturing a cohesive and ethically aligned workplace culture.

6.1.2 Significance of Transparent Communication and Stakeholder Engagement

Within the framework of ethical culture, transparent communication emerges as a linchpin, weaving threads of openness and honesty throughout the organizational tapestry. It involves the candid sharing of information with stakeholders, creating a foundation of trust and accountability. Transparent communication transcends rhetoric, embodying a commitment to keeping stakeholders informed about values, decisions, and actions. In doing so, it not only mitigates the risk of misunderstandings but also cultivates credibility, essential for fostering an ethical culture.

The significance of transparent communication extends to building trust through openness. Trust, a cornerstone of ethical culture, blossoms when stakeholders are provided with accurate and timely information. This trust, once established, becomes the bedrock upon which ethical conduct thrives. Inclusive stakeholder engagement further fortifies the ethical culture by ensuring diverse perspectives are considered. This inclusivity, reflective of ethical principles of fairness and respect, enriches decision-making processes and instills a sense of shared responsibility.

Transparent communication also acts as a conduit for accountability. Acknowledging mistakes, addressing concerns, and providing explanations exemplify an organization's commitment to ethical behavior. This accountability not only upholds the organization's ethical standards but also contributes to a culture of continuous ethical improvement. The articulation of ethical expectations through codes of conduct and policies serves as a beacon, guiding employees on the path of ethical conduct. It fosters a shared understanding of ethical standards, reducing ambiguity and promoting a culture where ethical behavior is not just expected but deeply ingrained.

Establishing mechanisms for stakeholders to provide feedback on ethical matters completes the circle of transparent communication. Actively seeking and valuing stakeholder feedback becomes a testament to the organization's commitment to openness and responsiveness. In times of crisis, transparent communication takes center stage, showcasing the organization's ethical mettle. Openly addressing challenges, taking responsibility, and outlining corrective actions during crises reinforce ethical principles and maintain stakeholder trust, even amid adversity.

6.2 INTRODUCING ETHICAL DECISION-MAKING FRAMEWORKS

Ethical decision-making frameworks serve as guiding compasses for individuals and organizations navigating the complex landscape of moral choices. These frameworks provide structured approaches to assess, analyze, and make decisions in alignment with ethical principles. Two widely recognized ethical decision-making frameworks are:

THE UTILITARIAN APPROACH:

Principle: Focuses on maximizing overall happiness or utility.

Process: Involves evaluating the consequences of different actions and choosing the one that produces the greatest net benefit.

Application: Requires considering the potential impact of decisions on all stakeholders and selecting the option that results in the greatest overall good.

THE DEONTOLOGICAL APPROACH:

Principle: Emphasizes adherence to ethical rules, duties, or principles.

Process: Involves evaluating actions based on their inherent morality rather than their outcomes.

Application: Requires following ethical principles and rules, even if the consequences may not be favorable. Upholds the importance of duty and moral obligations.

THE VIRTUE ETHICS APPROACH:

Principle: Focuses on the development of virtuous character traits.

Process: Involves considering what a virtuous person would do in a given situation.

Application: Encourages individuals to cultivate virtues such as honesty, integrity, and compassion, guiding decisions based on the development of a virtuous character.

THE RIGHTS-BASED APPROACH:

Principle: Centers on the protection of individual rights.

Process: Involves respecting and upholding the fundamental rights of individuals.

Application: Requires considering the impact of decisions on the rights and liberties of individuals and choosing actions that safeguard and respect those rights.

6.2.1   CREATION OF A COMPREHENSIVE CODE OF ETHICS

A comprehensive code of ethics is a foundational document that articulates the principles, values, and ethical standards guiding an organization's conduct. It serves as a roadmap for ethical behavior, providing clear expectations for employees and stakeholders. Key components of a comprehensive code of ethics include:

MISSION AND VALUES:

Clearly states the organization's mission and core values, emphasizing the ethical principles that underpin its identity.

ETHICAL STANDARDS AND CONDUCT:

Defines specific ethical standards and conduct expected from employees, outlining acceptable and unacceptable behaviors.

COMPLIANCE WITH LAWS AND REGULATIONS:

Emphasizes the organization's commitment to compliance with applicable laws and regulations, setting a legal and ethical baseline.

CONFLICTS OF INTEREST:

Addresses conflicts of interest and provides guidance on how employees should handle situations where personal interests may conflict with organizational interests.

STAKEHOLDER RELATIONSHIPS:

Outlines principles for maintaining ethical relationships with various stakeholders, including customers, suppliers, employees, and the community.

CONFIDENTIALITY AND PRIVACY:

Establishes guidelines for the protection of confidential information and the privacy of individuals, promoting trust and accountability.

WHISTLEBLOWING PROTECTIONS:

Includes provisions that protect whistleblowers who report unethical behavior, creating a safe environment for speaking up.

CONTINUOUS REVIEW AND UPDATES:

Acknowledges the dynamic nature of ethical challenges and commits to regular reviews and updates of the code to ensure its relevance and effectiveness.

6.2.2　IMPORTANCE OF WHISTLEBLOWING MECHANISMS IN PROMOTING ETHICAL BEHAVIOR

Whistleblowing mechanisms play a crucial role in promoting ethical behavior within organizations. These mechanisms empower employees and stakeholders to report unethical practices, misconduct, or violations of the code of ethics.

KEY ASPECTS OF THEIR IMPORTANCE INCLUDE:

Early Detection of Ethical Violations: Whistleblowing mechanisms enable the early detection of ethical violations, allowing organizations to address issues before they escalate. This proactive approach prevents potential harm to the organization and its stakeholders.

Protection for Whistleblowers: Establishing whistleblower protections fosters a culture of trust and accountability. Employees feel confident reporting concerns without fear of retaliation, creating a safe and transparent environment.

Preserving Organizational Integrity: Whistleblowing mechanisms contribute to preserving organizational integrity by addressing ethical lapses promptly. This preserves the organization's reputation and trustworthiness.

Legal and Regulatory Compliance: Having effective whistleblowing mechanisms helps organizations comply with legal and regulatory requirements. Some jurisdictions mandate the establishment of such mechanisms to ensure transparency and accountability.

Cultivating a Speak-Up Culture: Whistleblowing mechanisms contribute to cultivating a speak-up culture where employees feel encouraged to voice concerns and contribute to the organization's ethical well-being.

Internal Resolution of Issues: Whistleblowing mechanisms provide internal avenues for resolving ethical issues. This internal resolution is often more constructive and enables organizations to address concerns before they become public or escalate.

Continuous Improvement: Feedback from whistleblowers can serve as valuable input for continuous improvement in organizational policies, procedures, and ethical practices. This iterative process enhances the effectiveness of the code of ethics.

6.3 COMMON ETHICAL DILEMMAS IN GOVERNANCE

CONFLICT OF INTEREST:

Dilemma: Balancing personal interests with organizational responsibilities.

Challenge: Identifying and managing conflicts of interest to ensure decisions prioritize the organization's best interests over personal gain.

WHISTLEBLOWING AND CONFIDENTIALITY:

Dilemma: Balancing the need for transparency through whistleblowing with the obligation to maintain confidentiality.

Challenge: Establishing mechanisms that encourage reporting while safeguarding the privacy of those involved.

FAIR TREATMENT AND DISCRIMINATION:

Dilemma: Ensuring fair treatment of all individuals irrespective of background, while grappling with potential biases.

Challenge: Developing policies and practices that promote diversity, equity, and inclusion, addressing unconscious biases within the organization.

RESOURCE ALLOCATION AND STAKEHOLDER INTERESTS:

Dilemma: Allocating resources in a manner that meets stakeholder expectations while optimizing organizational objectives.

Challenge: Striking a balance between the diverse needs of stakeholders, preventing favoritism, and ensuring equitable resource distribution.

TRANSPARENCY AND INFORMATION DISCLOSURE:

Dilemma: Deciding the extent of information disclosure to stakeholders for transparency while safeguarding sensitive information.

Challenge: Establishing clear guidelines on what information can be shared, fostering open communication without compromising strategic interests.

ENVIRONMENTAL SUSTAINABILITY VS. PROFITABILITY:

Dilemma: Balancing environmental responsibility with financial goals.

Challenge: Integrating sustainable practices into governance while maintaining profitability and addressing potential conflicts between economic and ecological interests.

EMPLOYEE PRIVACY AND MONITORING:

Dilemma: Balancing the need for organizational security and performance monitoring with respecting employee privacy.

Challenge: Establishing ethical guidelines for monitoring employee activities without infringing on personal privacy rights.

CHALLENGES IN FOSTERING AN ETHICAL CULTURE

CULTURAL DIVERSITY AND INCLUSION:

Challenge: Nurturing an ethical culture that respects and includes diverse perspectives.

Approach: Implementing diversity and inclusion initiatives, promoting cultural sensitivity, and addressing bias in decision-making.

LEADERSHIP INFLUENCE AND TONE SETTING:

Challenge: Ensuring that leaders set a positive ethical tone and serve as role models.

Approach: Providing leadership training on ethical decision-making, accountability, and consistently reinforcing ethical behavior from the top.

GLOBAL OPERATIONS AND CROSS-CULTURAL CHALLENGES:

Challenge: Adapting ethical practices to different cultural contexts in global organizations.

Approach: Developing a global code of ethics that respects cultural diversity, providing cultural competency training, and ensuring consistency in ethical standards across regions.

TECHNOLOGY AND DATA ETHICS:

Challenge: Navigating ethical considerations in the use of technology and data.

Approach: Establishing clear policies on data privacy, cybersecurity, and ethical use of emerging technologies, and promoting digital literacy among employees.

SHORT-TERM PROFIT PRESSURES:

Challenge: Balancing the pressure for short-term financial gains with long-term ethical considerations.

Approach: Aligning financial goals with ethical principles, emphasizing sustainable practices, and communicating the long-term benefits of ethical decision-making.

SUPPLIER AND THIRD-PARTY ETHICS:

Challenge: Ensuring ethical behavior throughout the supply chain and in dealings with third parties.

Approach: Implementing ethical sourcing practices, conducting due diligence on third-party partners, and holding suppliers to ethical standards through contracts and audits.

RESISTANCE TO CHANGE:

Challenge: Overcoming resistance to changes in organizational culture that prioritize ethics.

Approach: Implementing change management strategies, fostering open communication, and involving employees in the process to gain buy-in and commitment to ethical values.

LEGAL AND REGULATORY COMPLIANCE:

Challenge: Navigating complex legal and regulatory environments while maintaining ethical standards.

Approach: Establishing robust compliance programs, providing regular training on legal and ethical obligations, and fostering a culture that values both compliance and ethical conduct.

BALANCING STAKEHOLDER INTERESTS:

Challenge: Juggling competing interests of various stakeholders.

Approach: Engaging stakeholders in decision-making, prioritizing transparent communication, and demonstrating a commitment to balancing diverse interests.

In addressing these challenges, organizations can develop comprehensive ethical frameworks, provide ongoing training, and foster a culture that values integrity, accountability, and continuous improvement. This multifaceted approach helps create an ethical governance environment that adapts to various dilemmas and organizational contexts.

6.3.2 INTERSECTION OF REGULATORY COMPLIANCE AND ETHICAL STANDARDS

The intersection of regulatory compliance and ethical standards represents a crucial nexus where organizations navigate the complex landscape of legal requirements and moral imperatives.

Regulatory compliance involves adhering to laws, rules, and regulations set forth by governing bodies, ensuring that an organization operates within the legal framework.

On the other hand, ethical standards encompass a broader set of principles that guide behavior, emphasizing moral values, fairness, and responsible conduct.

COMPLIANCE AS A BASELINE:

Regulatory compliance sets the baseline for organizational conduct, establishing the minimum standards that must be met to operate lawfully. It forms the foundation for ethical behavior by ensuring adherence to legal obligations.

ETHICAL STANDARDS AS ASPIRATIONS:

Ethical standards go beyond mere compliance, representing aspirational goals for organizations. They encourage behaviors that exceed the minimum requirements and align with principles of integrity, transparency, and social responsibility.

HARMONIZING COMPLIANCE AND ETHICS:

The most effective organizations harmonize regulatory compliance with ethical standards, recognizing that ethical behavior not only meets legal requirements but also contributes to long-term sustainability, stakeholder trust, and positive organizational reputation.

ADDRESSING REGULATORY GAPS WITH ETHICS:

Ethical standards act as a compass in situations where regulations may not provide explicit guidance. Organizations committed to ethical conduct proactively address gaps in regulations by establishing internal standards that prioritize ethical considerations.

NAVIGATING ETHICAL GRAY AREAS:

Ethical standards become particularly crucial in navigating ethical gray areas where the law may not provide clear guidance. In these instances, organizations must rely on a robust ethical framework to make principled decisions that align with their values.

6.4 INTRODUCING ETHICAL AUDITS AND ASSESSMENTS

To ensure that governance practices align with ethical standards, organizations employ the concept of ethical audits and assessments. These mechanisms provide a systematic and comprehensive evaluation of an organization's adherence to ethical principles, guiding continuous improvement in governance practices.

6.4.1 What are Ethical Audits?

Ethical audits involve a thorough examination of an organization's policies, procedures, and practices to assess compliance with ethical standards. These audits go beyond traditional financial audits, focusing on the alignment of actions with ethical principles.

6.4.2 Scope of Ethical Assessments

Ethical assessments encompass various facets of organizational conduct, including decision-making processes, treatment of stakeholders, transparency, environmental and social responsibility, and overall commitment to ethical behavior.

6.4.3 Key Components of Ethical Audits

Policy Evaluation: Assessing the comprehensiveness and clarity of ethical policies in place.

Decision-Making Processes: Evaluating how decisions are made and the consideration of ethical implications.

Stakeholder Engagement: Examining how the organization engages and communicates with stakeholders ethically.

Cultural Alignment: Assessing the alignment of organizational culture with ethical values.

Training and Awareness: Evaluating the effectiveness of training programs and awareness campaigns on ethical standards.

6.4.4 Benefits of Ethical Audits

Identifying Weaknesses: Ethical audits reveal weaknesses or gaps in governance practices, providing insights into areas that require improvement.

Demonstrating Commitment: Conducting ethical audits demonstrates the organization's commitment to ethical behavior and transparency.

Risk Mitigation: By proactively addressing ethical issues, organizations can mitigate the risk of legal and reputational damage.

Continuous Improvement: Ethical audits contribute to a culture of continuous improvement, fostering a commitment to ethical excellence.

6.4.5   Implementation of Ethical Audit Programs

Periodic Assessments: Ethical audits should be conducted periodically to ensure ongoing compliance and identify emerging ethical challenges.

Independent Oversight: Some organizations opt for independent third-party audits to enhance objectivity and credibility.

Feedback and Improvement Plans: Ethical audit findings should be followed by actionable improvement plans, reinforcing the organization's dedication to ethical governance.

INTEGRATION WITH REGULATORY COMPLIANCE:

Ethical audits complement regulatory compliance efforts, ensuring that organizational practices not only meet legal requirements but also align with higher ethical standards. This integration creates a robust governance framework that addresses both legal and moral imperatives.

CHAPTER
SEVEN

CASE STUDIES: ORGANIZATIONS THAT HAVE SUCCESSFULLY FOSTERED ETHICAL GOVERNANCE

CASE STUDY 1: JOHNSON & JOHNSON - THE TYLENOL CRISIS (1982):

BACKGROUND:

In 1982, Johnson & Johnson faced a crisis when seven people died after consuming Tylenol capsules laced with cyanide. The company responded swiftly, recalling 31 million bottles of Tylenol and introducing tamper-resistant packaging.

LESSONS AND INSIGHTS:

Swift and Decisive Action: Johnson & Johnson's immediate recall demonstrated the importance of swift and decisive action in the face of an ethical crisis.

Putting Safety First: Prioritizing consumer safety over short-term financial considerations reinforced the company's commitment to ethical values.

Open Communication: Transparent communication with the public, media, and authorities built trust and showcased the organization's integrity.

CASE STUDY 2: PATAGONIA - SUSTAINABLE PRACTICES (ONGOING):

BACKGROUND:

Outdoor clothing company Patagonia has been a pioneer in sustainable and ethical business practices. They emphasize transparency, fair labor practices, and environmental stewardship.

LESSONS AND INSIGHTS:

Mission-Driven Business: Integrating ethical and environmental considerations into the company's mission attracts like-minded customers and employees.

Supply Chain Transparency: Patagonia's commitment to transparency in its supply chain sets an industry standard for responsible business practices.

Educating Stakeholders: Actively educating customers about environmental issues fosters a sense of shared values and builds a community around ethical practices.

CASE STUDY 3: MICROSOFT - ACCESSIBILITY AND INCLUSIVITY (ONGOING):

BACKGROUND:

Microsoft has been a leader in promoting accessibility and inclusivity in technology. Initiatives include developing adaptive technologies and ensuring products are accessible to people with disabilities.

LESSONS AND INSIGHTS:

Inclusive Design: Prioritizing inclusive design ensures that products and services meet the needs of a diverse user base, aligning with ethical principles.

Global Impact: Microsoft's commitment to accessibility showcases the global impact ethical business practices can have on society.

Employee Engagement: Fostering a culture of inclusivity internally reinforces ethical values and enhances employee engagement.

CASE STUDY 4: GOOGLE - ETHICAL AI PRINCIPLES (ONGOING):

BACKGROUND:

Google has established ethical principles for the development and use of artificial intelligence (AI). These principles prioritize fairness, accountability, transparency, and avoiding biases in AI systems.

LESSONS AND INSIGHTS:

Responsible Innovation: Integrating ethical considerations into emerging technologies demonstrates a commitment to responsible innovation.

Stakeholder Involvement: Consulting with external stakeholders, including ethicists and social advocates, contributes to well-rounded ethical guidelines.

Long-Term Vision: Demonstrating a commitment to ethical AI aligns with a long-term vision for the responsible development of technology.

KEY TAKEAWAYS AND REINFORCEMENTS

i. Ethical Culture is proactive: Organizations that proactively integrate ethical considerations into their operations, decision-making processes, and products are better equipped to handle challenges and crises.

ii. Transparency builds trust: Open and transparent communication with stakeholders, whether in times of crisis or during day-to-day operations, is critical for building and maintaining trust.

iii. Mission-Driven values matter: Companies that embed ethical values in their mission and vision statements attract employees, customers, and partners who share those values, creating a strong ethical community.

iv. Balancing profit and purpose: Successful organizations demonstrate that ethical practices and profitability are not mutually exclusive. In fact, ethical practices often contribute to long-term financial success and brand reputation.

v. Learning from Setbacks: Johnson & Johnson's Tylenol crisis highlights the importance of learning from setbacks, adjusting practices, and reinforcing a commitment to ethical values.

vi. Innovation with Responsibility: Embracing innovation while considering the ethical implications, as seen in Google's AI principles, reinforces the idea that technological advancements should align with societal values.

These case studies underscore the enduring importance of ethical practices in ensuring organizational integrity. They showcase that ethical governance is not just a compliance requirement but a strategic imperative that contributes to long-term success, resilience, and positive societal impact.

CHAPTER EIGHT

DATA GOVERNANCE:
SAFEGUARDING INFORMATION IN
A DATA-DRIVEN WORLD

8.1 Foundational Concept of Data Governance

At its core, data governance is a comprehensive framework that outlines the policies, procedures, and practices an organization employs to manage, protect, and leverage its data assets effectively. It establishes a set of guidelines and controls to ensure that data is accurate, available, secure, and used ethically and responsibly throughout its lifecycle. Data governance is not solely an IT concern; it involves collaboration between various departments to align data practices with organizational goals and regulatory requirements.

8.1.1 Critical Role of Data Governance

DATA QUALITY MANAGEMENT:

Ensuring Accuracy: Data governance sets standards for data accuracy, completeness, and consistency. This ensures that data used for decision-making is reliable and trustworthy.

Data Profiling and Cleansing: Through data profiling and cleansing processes, data governance helps identify and rectify errors, duplicates, and inconsistencies in datasets.

DATA SECURITY AND PRIVACY:

Access Control: Data governance establishes access controls, defining who can access, modify, or delete specific data. This helps protect sensitive information and ensures compliance with privacy regulations.

Data Encryption: Implementing encryption protocols for data in transit and at rest is a key aspect of data governance, safeguarding information from unauthorized access.

COMPLIANCE MANAGEMENT:

Regulatory Alignment: Data governance ensures that data practices align with regulatory requirements such as GDPR, HIPAA, or industry-specific standards. This mitigates legal risks and penalties associated with non-compliance.

Audit Trails: Establishing audit trails and documentation mechanisms helps organizations track and report on data usage, demonstrating compliance to regulatory bodies.

DECISION-MAKING AND ANALYTICS:

Data Cataloging: Data governance includes the creation of data catalogs that provide a clear inventory of available datasets. This aids analysts and decision-makers in understanding and selecting the right data for analysis.

Master Data Management: By implementing master data management principles, data governance ensures consistency in core data elements, fostering accurate reporting and analytics.

ACCOUNTABILITY AND OWNERSHIP:

Data Stewardship: Designating data stewards responsible for specific datasets ensures accountability for data quality and compliance.

Ownership Framework: Establishing clear data ownership frameworks helps define responsibilities, making it evident who is accountable for different aspects of data management.

DATA LIFECYCLE MANAGEMENT:

Data Retention Policies: Data governance defines policies for data retention, archiving, and disposal. This ensures that outdated or unnecessary data does not clutter storage and remains in compliance with regulations.

Data Classification: Classifying data based on its sensitivity and importance helps determine appropriate storage, access controls, and lifecycle management practices.

RISK MANAGEMENT:

Identifying and Mitigating Risks: Data governance involves risk assessments to identify potential threats to data integrity and security. Mitigation strategies can then be implemented to reduce these risks.

Disaster Recovery Planning: Establishing data governance practices includes planning for disaster recovery to ensure data availability in the event of system failures, cyberattacks, or natural disasters.

ORGANIZATIONAL ALIGNMENT:

Cross-Functional Collaboration: Data governance requires collaboration across departments, fostering a culture where data is viewed as a strategic asset. This alignment ensures that data initiatives support organizational goals.

Communication and Training: Effective data governance includes communication and training programs to educate employees about data policies, fostering a shared understanding of the importance of data management.

8.1.3 INCREASING IMPORTANCE OF DATA IN CONTEMPORARY BUSINESS

In contemporary business, data has evolved from being a byproduct of operations to a strategic asset that drives decision-making, innovation, and competitive advantage. Several factors contribute to the increasing importance of data:

Digital Transformation: The shift toward digitalization has led to an exponential increase in the volume, variety, and velocity of data generated by organizations. This digital transformation is a key driver in recognizing the value of data.

Business Intelligence and Analytics: Advanced analytics and business intelligence tools enable organizations to extract actionable insights from data. This empowers decision-makers to make informed, data-driven choices that contribute to the overall success of the business.

Customer-Centricity: Businesses are leveraging data to gain a deeper understanding of customer behavior, preferences, and expectations. This customer-centric approach allows for personalized experiences, targeted marketing, and improved customer satisfaction.

Innovation and Product Development: Data plays a crucial role in fostering innovation and developing new products or services. Companies use data to identify market trends, analyze consumer feedback, and anticipate future demands, driving innovation cycles.

Operational Efficiency: Data-driven insights contribute to operational efficiency by optimizing processes, identifying bottlenecks, and streamlining workflows. This leads to cost savings and improved overall performance.

Competitive Advantage: Organizations that effectively harness data gain a competitive edge. Whether through market intelligence, supply chain optimization, or enhanced customer experiences, data-driven decision-making sets businesses apart in a rapidly evolving landscape.

Regulatory Compliance: The regulatory environment has become increasingly data-focused, with laws such as GDPR, HIPAA, and others imposing strict requirements on data handling and protection. Compliance has become a driving force in data governance strategies.

8.1.4 Challenges and Opportunities in the Data-Driven Paradigm

DATA QUALITY AND INTEGRITY:

Challenge: Ensuring data accuracy, completeness, and consistency remains a challenge. Poor data quality can lead to flawed analyses and misguided decision-making.

Opportunity: Investing in data quality management processes and technologies enhances the reliability of data, improving decision outcomes.

SECURITY AND PRIVACY CONCERNS:

Challenge: As the volume of data grows, so do security threats and privacy concerns. Protecting sensitive information from unauthorized access is an ongoing challenge.

Opportunity: Implementing robust cybersecurity measures and adhering to privacy regulations present opportunities to build trust with customers and stakeholders.

DATA GOVERNANCE COMPLEXITY:

Challenge: Establishing and maintaining effective data governance practices can be complex, especially in large organizations with diverse datasets.

Opportunity: A well-defined data governance framework provides clarity, accountability, and transparency, mitigating risks and ensuring compliance.

SKILL SHORTAGES:

Challenge: There is a shortage of skilled professionals with expertise in data analysis, machine learning, and data management.

Opportunity: Investing in employee training and development programs, as well as leveraging external expertise, can address skill shortages and build a capable workforce.

INTEGRATION OF DATA SILOS:

Challenge: Many organizations face the difficulty of integrating data from disparate sources and overcoming data silos.

Opportunity: Implementing integrated data platforms and technologies enables a unified view of data, breaking down silos and improving collaboration.

ETHICAL CONSIDERATIONS:

Challenge: The increasing reliance on data raises ethical concerns related to privacy, bias in algorithms, and the responsible use of technology.

Opportunity: Addressing ethical considerations proactively, through ethical frameworks, transparency, and responsible AI practices, can enhance the reputation and trustworthiness of organizations.

SCALE OF DATA:

Challenge: The sheer volume of data generated daily can overwhelm organizations, leading to challenges in storage, processing, and analysis.

Opportunity: Advances in cloud computing and big data technologies provide scalable solutions, allowing organizations to harness the power of large datasets efficiently.

CULTURAL SHIFT:

Challenge: Shifting organizational culture to embrace a data-driven mindset can face resistance from traditional models of decision-making.

Opportunity: Leadership commitment, communication, and fostering a culture of data literacy can drive the cultural shift needed for successful data-driven transformation.

8.2　Data Quality Maintenance

Importance of Maintaining High-Quality Data: High-quality data is foundational for organizations to make informed decisions, derive accurate insights, and maintain operational efficiency. The importance of maintaining high-quality data extends across various aspects of business operations:

Informed Decision-Making: Reliable data is essential for making informed, strategic decisions. Decision-makers rely on accurate and up-to-date information to understand market trends, customer behavior, and operational performance.

Customer Experience: High-quality data contributes to a better understanding of customer preferences and behavior. This, in turn, enables organizations to personalize interactions, offer targeted products or services, and enhance overall customer satisfaction.

Operational Efficiency: Accurate and consistent data improves operational efficiency by reducing errors, minimizing rework, and streamlining processes. It ensures that systems and applications operate with reliable inputs.

Regulatory Compliance: Many regulations, such as GDPR, HIPAA, and others, mandate the accuracy and security of data. Maintaining high-quality data is crucial for compliance, helping organizations avoid legal issues and penalties.

Effective Analytics: Data quality directly impacts the effectiveness of analytics initiatives. Reliable data is essential for generating meaningful insights and reports, supporting data-driven decision-making across the organization.

Cost Savings: Poor data quality can lead to costly errors and inefficiencies. By investing in data quality, organizations can avoid the financial repercussions of incorrect decisions, operational disruptions, and customer dissatisfaction.

8.2.1 STRATEGIES FOR DATA CLEANSING, VALIDATION, AND ONGOING QUALITY ASSURANCE

DATA CLEANSING:

Remove Duplicate Records: Identify and eliminate duplicate records to ensure data consistency and accuracy.

Standardize Data Formats: Standardizing formats for names, addresses, and other data elements improves consistency and facilitates analysis.

Correcting Errors: Regularly review and correct errors in data fields, such as misspellings or inaccuracies.

DATA VALIDATION:

Automated Validation Rules: Implement automated validation rules to ensure that data entered into systems meets predefined criteria.

Cross-Verification: Cross-verify data against external sources or databases to validate its accuracy.

Real-Time Validation: Conduct real-time validation during data entry to prevent the entry of incorrect or incomplete information.

ONGOING QUALITY ASSURANCE:

Regular Audits: Conduct regular data quality audits to identify and address issues proactively.

Data Profiling: Use data profiling tools to analyze the structure and content of datasets, identifying anomalies and patterns.

Data Quality Metrics: Establish key data quality metrics and monitor them regularly to track improvements and identify areas for enhancement.

DATA GOVERNANCE FRAMEWORK:

Data Ownership: Assign data ownership responsibilities to individuals or teams, ensuring accountability for data quality.

Data Policies and Standards: Establish clear data policies and standards to guide data quality efforts across the organization.

TRAINING AND AWARENESS:

Employee Training: Provide training to employees on the importance of data quality and the correct methods for data entry and maintenance.

Data Literacy Programs: Foster a culture of data literacy, ensuring that employees understand the impact of data quality on business outcomes.

AUTOMATED DATA QUALITY TOOLS:

Data Quality Software: Invest in data quality tools that automate the identification and correction of data errors.

Data Profiling Tools: Use data profiling tools to gain insights into data quality issues and identify areas for improvement.

FEEDBACK LOOPS:

User Feedback: Encourage users to provide feedback on data quality issues they encounter, creating a feedback loop for continuous improvement.

Continuous Monitoring: Implement continuous monitoring mechanisms to identify and address data quality issues as they arise.

SCALABLE INFRASTRUCTURE:

Scalable Architecture: Ensure that the infrastructure supporting data storage and processing is scalable to accommodate growing datasets while maintaining data quality standards.

DATA QUALITY SCORECARDS:

Scorecard Metrics: Develop data quality scorecards that provide a visual representation of key metrics, making it easier to track progress and identify areas needing attention.

COLLABORATION ACROSS DEPARTMENTS:

Cross-Functional Collaboration: Foster collaboration between departments to ensure that data quality standards are consistently applied throughout the organization.

8.3 IMPORTANCE OF DATA SECURITY AND PRIVACY

Data security and privacy are paramount in the digital age, where the collection, storage, and processing of vast amounts of sensitive information have become integral to business operations. The importance of safeguarding data can be highlighted by several critical factors:

TRUST AND REPUTATION:

Data breaches and privacy violations can severely damage an organization's reputation and erode the trust of customers, partners, and stakeholders. Maintaining trust is essential for long-term success.

LEGAL AND REGULATORY COMPLIANCE:

Adhering to data protection regulations is not just a best practice; it is a legal requirement. Non-compliance can result in severe penalties, fines, and legal consequences that can impact the financial stability of an organization.

CUSTOMER EXPECTATIONS:

With increasing awareness of privacy issues, customers expect organizations to handle their data responsibly. Failing to meet these expectations can lead to customer dissatisfaction and loss of business.

BUSINESS CONTINUITY:

A data breach can disrupt normal business operations, leading to financial losses, operational setbacks, and a decline in customer confidence. Ensuring data security is crucial for maintaining business continuity.

INTELLECTUAL PROPERTY PROTECTION:

Businesses often possess proprietary information, intellectual property, and trade secrets. Failure to secure this sensitive data can result in the loss of competitive advantages and innovation.

GLOBAL INTERCONNECTEDNESS:

In a globally interconnected business environment, data flows across borders. Adhering to international data protection standards is crucial for conducting business on a global scale and fostering international partnerships.

8.4 BEST PRACTICES FOR SAFEGUARDING SENSITIVE INFORMATION

DATA ENCRYPTION:

Implement encryption for data at rest and in transit to protect it from unauthorized access. This includes encrypting sensitive files, databases, and communications.

ACCESS CONTROLS:

Enforce strict access controls to ensure that only authorized personnel have access to sensitive information. Use role-based access controls to limit permissions based on job responsibilities.

REGULAR SECURITY AUDITS:

Conduct regular security audits to identify vulnerabilities and assess the effectiveness of security measures. This includes penetration testing, vulnerability assessments, and monitoring for unusual activities.

DATA MINIMIZATION:

Adopt a data minimization strategy by only collecting and retaining the data necessary for business operations. Avoid unnecessary data storage to reduce the risk in the event of a breach.

EMPLOYEE TRAINING:

Provide comprehensive training to employees on data security best practices, including recognizing phishing attempts, using secure passwords, and understanding the importance of safeguarding sensitive information.

INCIDENT RESPONSE PLAN:

Develop and regularly update an incident response plan to outline the steps to be taken in the event of a data breach. This includes communication protocols, legal obligations, and strategies for mitigating damage.

DATA BACKUPS:

Implement regular and secure data backups to ensure that, in the event of data loss or a ransomware attack, critical information can be restored without compromising integrity.

DATA CLASSIFICATION:

Classify data based on its sensitivity and establish different levels of protection accordingly. This helps prioritize security measures for the most critical information.

PRIVACY BY DESIGN:

Integrate privacy considerations into the design of systems and processes from the outset. By adopting a "privacy by design" approach, organizations can minimize the risk of privacy breaches.

VENDOR SECURITY:

Ensure that third-party vendors and partners adhere to high-security standards, especially if they have access to your organization's data. Include security assessments in vendor due diligence processes.

DATA PROTECTION IMPACT ASSESSMENTS (DPIA):

Conduct DPIAs to assess and mitigate the risks associated with processing personal data, especially when introducing new processes or technologies that involve sensitive information.

LEGAL COMPLIANCE:

Stay informed about and comply with data protection laws applicable to your organization, such as GDPR, HIPAA, or other regional regulations. This includes obtaining necessary consents and notifying authorities of data breaches as required.

REGULAR UPDATES AND PATCHING:

Keep software, systems, and applications up to date with the latest security patches to address vulnerabilities and protect against known threats.

SECURE DEVELOPMENT PRACTICES:

Follow secure coding practices during software development to minimize the risk of introducing vulnerabilities. Conduct regular code reviews and security testing.

TRANSPARENT PRIVACY POLICIES:

Clearly communicate your organization's privacy policies to customers and stakeholders. Provide transparent information about data collection practices, purposes, and rights.

By adhering to these best practices, organizations can establish a robust data security and privacy framework that not only safeguards sensitive information but also demonstrates a commitment to ethical data handling and legal compliance.

CHAPTER NINE

DATA LIFECYCLE MANAGEMENT

9.0 Introduction to Data Lifecycle Management

Data Lifecycle Management (DLM) is a strategic approach to managing the entire lifespan of data within an organization, from its creation or acquisition to its eventual archival or disposal. This framework recognizes that data has varying levels of importance and relevance at different stages of its lifecycle. By implementing effective data lifecycle management strategies, organizations can optimize the use of data, ensure its quality, and meet compliance requirements.

9.1 Strategies for Handling Data Across its Lifecycle

DATA CLASSIFICATION:

Strategy: Classify data based on its sensitivity, importance, and regulatory requirements. This helps prioritize resources for the protection and management of critical data.

DATA CREATION AND ACQUISITION:

Strategy: Establish clear processes for data creation and acquisition, ensuring that new data adheres to quality standards and is appropriately classified. Implement automated metadata tagging to provide context to newly generated data.

DATA STORAGE AND ORGANIZATION:

Strategy: Choose storage solutions based on the specific needs of data types. Implement organized folder structures, data catalogs, and metadata management to enhance accessibility and facilitate efficient retrieval.

DATA USAGE AND ANALYSIS:

Strategy: Define access controls and permissions to regulate data usage. Monitor data access patterns to identify trends and ensure that data is being utilized effectively for analytics and decision-making.

DATA SHARING AND COLLABORATION:

Strategy: Facilitate secure data sharing and collaboration by implementing collaboration tools and platforms. Enforce access controls to restrict data access to authorized individuals or teams.

DATA QUALITY MANAGEMENT:

Strategy: Implement data quality checks and cleansing processes regularly. Proactively address data quality issues to ensure that decision-makers rely on accurate and reliable information.

DATA ARCHIVING:

Strategy: Establish criteria for archiving data based on relevance and regulatory requirements. Move less frequently accessed data to cost-effective, long-term storage solutions while maintaining accessibility.

DATA RETENTION POLICIES:

Strategy: Define clear data retention policies that align with regulatory requirements and business needs. Periodically review and update these policies to ensure they remain current and effective.

DATA SECURITY:

Strategy: Implement robust security measures throughout the data lifecycle. This includes encryption, access controls, regular security audits, and monitoring for anomalous activities to protect data from unauthorized access or breaches.

COMPLIANCE MONITORING:

Strategy: Regularly monitor changes in data protection and privacy regulations. Ensure that data management practices align with evolving compliance requirements and conduct periodic audits to verify compliance.

DATA DISPOSAL AND DELETION:

Strategy: Establish secure processes for data disposal and deletion when it reaches the end of its useful life. Ensure that sensitive data is irreversibly deleted to minimize the risk of data breaches.

AUDIT TRAILS AND DOCUMENTATION:

Strategy: Maintain comprehensive audit trails that document data activities throughout its lifecycle. This documentation is crucial for demonstrating compliance, investigating incidents, and conducting internal reviews.

AUTOMATED DATA LIFECYCLE MANAGEMENT TOOLS:

Strategy: Implement automated tools for data lifecycle management to streamline processes, enforce policies consistently, and reduce the manual effort involved in managing data across its various stages.

DATA GOVERNANCE FRAMEWORK:

Strategy: Integrate data lifecycle management into the overall data governance framework. Establish roles and responsibilities for data stewards and administrators to oversee the proper execution of data lifecycle processes.

USER TRAINING AND AWARENESS:

Strategy: Conduct training programs to educate employees on the importance of proper data handling practices and compliance requirements. Foster a culture of data literacy and responsibility.

By adopting these strategies, organizations can ensure that data is managed effectively throughout its lifecycle, maintaining its relevance, quality, and compliance with regulatory standards. This holistic approach to data lifecycle management contributes to optimized data utilization, reduced risks, and efficient adherence to legal and industry-specific requirements.

9.2   IMPORTANCE OF DATA STANDARDS AND CLASSIFICATION

Data standards and classification play a pivotal role in the realm of data management, offering a structured framework for organizing and interpreting information. The importance of these practices extends across various aspects of data governance, ensuring consistency, interoperability, and effective management of data assets.

CONSISTENCY:

Data Structure: Standards define a consistent structure for data elements, ensuring uniformity in how data is formatted, named, and stored. This consistency simplifies data management, analysis, and interpretation.

Naming Conventions: Standardized naming conventions reduce ambiguity and enhance clarity, making it easier for users to understand the meaning of data attributes.

INTEROPERABILITY:

Integration of Systems: Data standards facilitate the seamless integration of systems and applications. When different systems adhere to the same standards, data can flow between them without compatibility issues.

Data Exchange: Standardized data formats enable efficient and error-free exchange of information between organizations, applications, and platforms, fostering interoperability.

EFFECTIVE DATA GOVERNANCE:

Data Quality: Classification standards contribute to data quality by providing a systematic approach to identifying, organizing, and managing data. This, in turn, supports data governance initiatives.

Compliance: Standards aid in compliance with regulatory requirements. By classifying data according to regulatory standards, organizations can ensure that sensitive information is handled appropriately and legal obligations are met.

EFFICIENT DATA MANAGEMENT:

Data Retrieval: Standardized classification simplifies data retrieval processes. Users can quickly locate and access relevant information when data is consistently organized and classified.

Data Storage: Standardized practices optimize data storage by eliminating redundancies and ensuring that data is stored in a structured manner, improving overall efficiency.

FACILITATING DATA ANALYSIS:

Analytics and Reporting: Data standards enhance the accuracy and reliability of analytics and reporting. When data is classified and structured consistently, it becomes easier to perform meaningful analyses and generate reliable reports.

Data Modeling: Standardized classification supports effective data modeling, enabling organizations to create robust data models that accurately represent their business processes.

DECISION-MAKING:

Informed Decision-Making: Consistent data standards contribute to more informed decision-making. Decision-makers can rely on standardized, high-quality data to make strategic choices with confidence.

Risk Management: Standardization aids in risk management by ensuring that data used for decision-making is accurate, complete, and aligned with organizational goals.

DATA SECURITY:

Access Controls: Classification standards support the implementation of access controls. By categorizing data based on sensitivity, organizations can enforce access restrictions to protect confidential information.

Security Policies: Data standards contribute to the formulation and implementation of security policies, guiding organizations in safeguarding their data assets.

ADAPTABILITY AND SCALABILITY:

Adaptation to Change: Standardized practices make data systems more adaptable to changes. When new data sources or technologies are introduced, adherence to standards ensures a smoother integration process.

Scalability: Organizations can scale their data management processes more effectively when standards are in place. Standardized approaches support growth without compromising data quality.

DATA COLLABORATION:

Cross-Organizational Collaboration: Common data standards facilitate collaboration between organizations. When working with partners, suppliers, or other stakeholders, standardized practices ensure that data is exchanged seamlessly.

9.3 PROMINENT DATA GOVERNANCE FRAMEWORKS

Several data governance frameworks have been developed to provide structured approaches for organizations looking to implement effective data governance practices. One notable framework is the Data Management Body of Knowledge (DAMA-DMBOK).

1. **DAMA-DMBOK (Data Management Body of Knowledge):**

   DAMA-DMBOK is a comprehensive framework developed by the Data Management Association International (DAMA). It offers a standardized set of principles, practices, and guidelines for effective data management and governance.

   The framework is structured around a "Body of Knowledge" that covers various aspects of data management, including data governance, data architecture, data modeling, data quality, and more.

Key Components:

Data Governance:

Defines the roles, responsibilities, and processes for effective data governance.

Emphasizes the importance of establishing a data governance framework to ensure accountability and transparency in data management.

Data Architecture:

Provides guidance on designing and managing the architecture of data assets within an organization.

Covers data modeling, metadata management, and the alignment of data architecture with business goals.

Data Modeling and Design:

Offers best practices for creating logical and physical data models.

Focuses on ensuring that data models accurately represent the business requirements and support data governance objectives.

Data Quality Management:

Outlines strategies and methodologies for assessing and improving the quality of organizational data.

Includes guidelines for establishing data quality standards, monitoring data quality, and implementing corrective actions.

Reference and Master Data Management:

Addresses the management of reference data and master data to ensure consistency and integrity across the organization.

Provides guidance on establishing master data management practices and processes.

Data Warehousing and Business Intelligence:

Offers principles for designing and managing data warehouses and supporting business intelligence initiatives.

Emphasizes the importance of aligning data warehousing efforts with overall data governance objectives.

Data Security Management:

Focuses on safeguarding data assets through the implementation of security measures.

Addresses aspects of data privacy, access controls, and security policies within a data governance context.

2. **CDMP (Certified Data Management Professional):**

The Certified Data Management Professional (CDMP) is a certification program and framework developed by DAMA. While DAMA-DMBOK provides the broader framework, CDMP offers a certification path for data management professionals.

Key Components:

Data Governance and Stewardship:

Covers the principles of data governance, including roles and responsibilities of data stewards.

Focuses on the establishment of data governance programs within organizations.

Data Architecture and Modeling:

Addresses the design and implementation of data architectures.

Emphasizes the importance of data modeling and its role in supporting data governance and management.

Data Quality:

Examines strategies for assessing and improving data quality.

Covers data profiling, data cleansing, and the establishment of data quality frameworks.

Data Warehousing:

Provides insights into the principles of data warehousing.

Covers topics such as data warehouse design, ETL (Extract, Transform, Load) processes, and aligning data warehousing efforts with organizational goals.

3. **IBM Data Governance Council Framework:**

IBM's Data Governance Council Framework is designed to help organizations establish and mature their data governance programs.

It provides a holistic approach to data governance, emphasizing collaboration, communication, and accountability.

Key Components:

Data Governance Principles:

Defines a set of principles to guide the development and implementation of data governance practices.

Focuses on principles such as accountability, transparency, and stakeholder engagement.

Governance Structures and Roles:

Outlines the organizational structures and roles needed for effective data governance.

Includes the definition of roles such as data stewards, data owners, and executive sponsors.

Policy and Standards:

Emphasizes the importance of establishing data policies and standards.

Provides guidance on developing, communicating, and enforcing data governance policies.

Measurement and Metrics:

Highlights the need for measuring the effectiveness of data governance initiatives.

Covers the development of key performance indicators (KPIs) and metrics to assess progress and impact.

9.3.1 HOW THESE FRAMEWORKS PROVIDE STRUCTURED APPROACHES

COMPREHENSIVE COVERAGE:

Each framework provides a comprehensive set of guidelines covering various aspects of data governance, ensuring that organizations have a holistic approach to managing their data.

STRUCTURED PROCESSES:

These frameworks introduce structured processes and methodologies for implementing data governance practices. This includes defining roles, establishing policies, and developing measurable metrics.

BEST PRACTICES:

The frameworks incorporate industry best practices, drawing from the collective knowledge and experience of data management professionals. This ensures that organizations adopt proven methods for effective data governance.

ALIGNMENT WITH BUSINESS GOALS:

The frameworks emphasize the alignment of data governance efforts with overall business goals. This ensures that data management practices support organizational objectives and contribute to strategic success.

CERTIFICATION PROGRAMS:

Certification programs associated with these frameworks, such as the CDMP, provide a structured path for professionals to enhance their skills and knowledge in data management, contributing to the overall success of data governance initiatives.

9.3.2　PRACTICAL STRATEGIES FOR IMPLEMENTING A DATA GOVERNANCE FRAMEWORK

Implementing a data governance framework requires careful planning, collaboration, and a systematic approach. Here are practical strategies for organizations to consider when embarking on the journey of implementing a data governance framework:

Define Clear Objectives and Scope: Clearly articulate the objectives of the data governance initiative. Identify the scope by specifying which data assets, processes, and business areas will be covered. This clarity ensures that the efforts remain focused and achievable.

Establish Executive Sponsorship: Secure support and sponsorship from executives who understand the strategic value of data governance. Executive buy-in is critical for securing resources, overcoming resistance, and fostering a culture of data accountability.

Build a Cross-Functional Data Governance Team: Form a cross-functional team with representatives from various departments, including IT, data management, legal, compliance, and business units. This diverse team ensures that different perspectives are considered during the implementation.

Define Roles and Responsibilities: Clearly define roles and responsibilities for key data governance positions, such as data stewards, data owners, and executive sponsors. Ensure that individuals understand their roles in managing and safeguarding data.

Develop Data Governance Policies and Standards: Establish comprehensive data governance policies and standards that align with organizational objectives and regulatory requirements. These policies should cover data quality, privacy, security, and compliance.

Create a Data Governance Framework Roadmap: Develop a roadmap that outlines the stages of the data governance implementation. This roadmap should include key milestones, timelines, and deliverables. A phased approach allows for manageable implementation and continuous improvement.

Conduct a Data Assessment: Perform a thorough assessment of existing data assets, processes, and governance practices. Identify strengths, weaknesses, and areas for improvement. This assessment informs the development of targeted governance strategies.

Prioritize Data Assets: Prioritize data assets based on their strategic importance and sensitivity. Focus initial efforts on the most critical data elements and processes to demonstrate quick wins and build momentum.

Implement Data Quality Measures: Implement data quality measures to assess and improve the accuracy, completeness, and consistency of data. Define data quality metrics and incorporate them into regular monitoring processes.

Establish Communication and Training Programs: Develop communication and training programs to raise awareness and build a data-centric culture. Regularly communicate the benefits of data governance and provide training to employees on their roles in supporting data quality and security.

Select Appropriate Data Governance Tools: Choose tools that support data governance functions such as metadata management, data lineage tracking, and policy enforcement. These tools can enhance visibility into data processes and facilitate governance activities.

Implement Data Governance Metrics and Key Performance Indicators (KPIs): Define metrics and KPIs to measure the success of data governance initiatives. Track progress against these indicators and use the insights gained to refine strategies and address emerging challenges.

9.3.3 Considerations for Tailoring Frameworks to Fit Unique Needs

i. Organizational Culture: Consider the existing organizational culture and adapt the framework to align with it. A data governance program that reflects and respects the organizational culture is more likely to gain acceptance and support.

ii. Size and Complexity: Tailor the framework to the size and complexity of the organization. Smaller organizations may require a more streamlined approach, while larger enterprises may need a more robust and scalable framework.

iii. Regulatory Environment: Consider the regulatory environment in which the organization operates. Tailor data governance policies and practices to comply with industry-specific regulations and legal requirements.

iv. Business Objectives: Align data governance initiatives with the broader business objectives of the organization. Ensure that data governance efforts contribute directly to achieving strategic goals and improving overall business performance.

v. Resource Availability: Assess the availability of resources, including personnel, technology, and budget. Tailor the implementation plan to leverage existing resources efficiently and seek incremental improvements based on resource availability.

vi. Data Sensitivity: Recognize the varying levels of sensitivity of different data assets. Tailor security and privacy measures to the specific requirements of each data category, ensuring that sensitive data receives the highest level of protection.

vii. Industry Best Practices: Stay informed about industry best practices and emerging trends in data governance. Tailor the framework to incorporate innovations and lessons learned from similar organizations within the industry.

viii. Flexibility and Scalability: Design the framework with flexibility and scalability in mind. Ensure that the framework can evolve to accommodate changes in the organization's size, structure, and business objectives over time.

ix. Engage Stakeholders: Actively engage stakeholders throughout the tailoring process. Solicit feedback from key departments, leadership, and end-users to ensure that the adapted framework meets their specific needs and addresses their concerns.

x. Continuous Improvement: Establish a culture of continuous improvement within the data governance program. Regularly review and update the framework based on lessons learned, evolving organizational needs, and changes in the external environment.

9.3.4 EXPLORING THE REGULATORY LANDSCAPE GOVERNING DATA PRACTICES

The regulatory landscape governing data practices is multifaceted and varies across regions and industries. Several regulations aim to protect the privacy, security, and ethical use of personal and sensitive information. Key regulations include:

General Data Protection Regulation (GDPR): Enforced by the European Union (EU), GDPR focuses on protecting the privacy and rights of individuals. It establishes rules for the processing and handling of personal data, emphasizing transparency, consent, and data subject rights.

Health Insurance Portability and Accountability Act (HIPAA): HIPAA, in the United States, safeguards the privacy and security of individuals' health information. It sets standards for the protection of electronic health records (EHR) and outlines rules for healthcare providers, insurers, and business associates.

California Consumer Privacy Act (CCPA): CCPA, applicable in California, grants consumers control over their personal information held by businesses. It includes provisions for transparency, access, deletion, and the right to opt-out of the sale of personal information.

Sarbanes-Oxley Act (SOX): SOX, enacted in the U.S., focuses on financial reporting and corporate governance. While not specifically about data privacy, it requires controls over financial information systems, which often involve sensitive data.

Payment Card Industry Data Security Standard (PCI DSS): P C I DSS is a global standard for protecting credit cardholder data. It applies to organizations that handle payment card information and aims to secure payment card transactions against breaches and fraud.

Children's Online Privacy Protection Act (COPPA): COPPA, in the U.S., protects the online privacy of children under 13. It requires operators of websites or online services directed at children to obtain parental consent before collecting personal information from minors.

9.4 How Data Governance Aligns with and Supports Compliance

Data governance plays a crucial role in ensuring compliance with these regulations by establishing processes, controls, and accountability mechanisms.

Here's how data governance aligns with and supports compliance:

a. *Data Mapping and Inventory:* Data governance involves creating data maps and inventories, identifying the types of data collected and processed. This aligns with GDPR's requirement for data mapping and understanding the flow of personal data within an organization.

b. *Consent Management:* Data governance frameworks often include processes for obtaining and managing consent. This aligns with GDPR, which requires organizations to obtain clear and explicit consent from individuals before processing their personal data.

c. *Data Protection Impact Assessments (DPIA):* DPIA is a GDPR requirement for assessing and mitigating risks associated with data processing activities. Data governance supports this by integrating DPIA processes into data management practices, ensuring that privacy risks are systematically evaluated.

d. *Access Controls and Data Security:* Data governance establishes access controls and security measures, aligning with GDPR, HIPAA, and other regulations that mandate safeguarding sensitive information. This includes encryption, secure storage, and mechanisms to prevent unauthorized access.

e. *Data Quality and Accuracy:* Ensuring data quality and accuracy is a fundamental aspect of data governance. This is crucial for complying with regulations like GDPR, which emphasize the right of individuals to have accurate personal data.

f. *Data Subject Rights:* GDPR grants individuals certain rights over their personal data. Data governance ensures that organizations have processes in place to honor these rights, including the right to access, rectify, and erase personal data.

g. *Incident Response and Breach Notification:* Data governance frameworks include incident response plans and breach notification procedures. This aligns with regulations like GDPR, which require organizations to promptly notify authorities and affected individuals in the event of a data breach.

h. *Documentation and Accountability:* Data governance emphasizes documentation and accountability, ensuring that organizations can demonstrate compliance with data protection regulations. This aligns with the documentation requirements of various privacy laws.

i. *Training and Awareness:* Data governance programs often include training initiatives to raise awareness about data privacy and security. This supports compliance by ensuring that employees understand their roles in safeguarding sensitive information.

j. *Data Retention and Deletion:* Many regulations, including GDPR and CCPA, have requirements related to data retention and deletion. Data governance establishes policies and procedures for managing the lifecycle of data, aligning with these regulatory requirements.

k. *Cross-Border Data Transfers:* GDPR places restrictions on the transfer of personal data outside the EU. Data governance supports compliance by implementing mechanisms, such as standard contractual clauses, to ensure lawful cross-border data transfers.

l. Vendor Management: Regulations often extend responsibilities to third-party vendors (processors). Data governance includes vendor management practices to ensure that external partners comply with data protection requirements.

8.5 LEGAL AND ETHICAL IMPLICATIONS OF DATA GOVERNANCE

Data governance involves the establishment of policies, procedures, and controls to ensure the effective and responsible management of data within an organization. Both legal and ethical considerations play a significant role in shaping data governance practices.

LEGAL IMPLICATIONS:

Compliance with Data Protection Laws: Legal implications primarily revolve around compliance with data protection laws such as the General Data Protection Regulation (GDPR), the California Consumer Privacy Act (CCPA), and others. Organizations must adhere to the specific requirements outlined in these regulations to protect individuals' privacy rights.

Data Breach Notification Requirements: Many jurisdictions have laws mandating the timely and transparent notification of data breaches. Organizations are legally obligated to inform affected individuals and, in some cases, regulatory authorities, when a breach occurs.

Data Retention and Deletion Obligations: Data governance practices must align with legal requirements related to data retention and deletion. Laws such as GDPR and CCPA specify how long organizations can retain certain types of data and when they must delete it.

Cross-Border Data Transfer Restrictions: Legal considerations come into play when organizations transfer personal data across borders. Data protection laws, like GDPR, impose restrictions on such transfers, requiring organizations to implement safeguards to protect the data.

Consumer Rights Enforcement: Data governance practices must support the enforcement of consumer rights mandated by data protection laws. Individuals have rights to access their data, rectify inaccuracies, and request the deletion of their information.

ETHICAL IMPLICATIONS:

Respect for Individual Privacy: Ethical considerations in data governance emphasize respect for individual privacy. Organizations should go beyond legal requirements and consider the ethical implications of data collection, processing, and sharing.

Transparency and Informed Consent: Ethical data governance involves being transparent about data practices and obtaining informed consent from individuals before collecting or processing their data. This ensures that individuals are aware of how their information will be used.

Fair and Non-Discriminatory Practices: Ethical data governance requires organizations to adopt fair and non-discriminatory practices. This includes avoiding bias in data algorithms and ensuring that data-driven decisions do not disproportionately impact certain groups.

Data Accuracy and Integrity: Maintaining the accuracy and integrity of data is an ethical responsibility. Organizations should take measures to ensure that the data they collect and use is accurate, up-to-date, and reliable.

Security and Protection Against Misuse: Ethical data governance involves implementing robust security measures to protect data against unauthorized access and misuse. Organizations have an ethical duty to safeguard sensitive information from breaches and cyber threats.

9.5.1 CONSEQUENCES OF NON-COMPLIANCE AND ETHICAL LAPSES

Legal Penalties and Fines: Non-compliance with data protection laws can result in severe legal consequences, including fines and penalties. Regulators have the authority to impose significant financial sanctions on organizations that fail to meet legal obligations.

Reputational Damage: Ethical lapses and non-compliance can lead to reputational damage. News of data breaches, privacy violations, or unethical data practices can erode public trust and negatively impact an organization's brand and reputation.

Loss of Customer Trust: Failure to uphold ethical standards and legal requirements can lead to a loss of customer trust. Customers are increasingly concerned about how organizations handle their data, and breaches of trust can result in a decline in customer loyalty.

Litigation and Lawsuits: Individuals affected by data breaches or unethical data practices may pursue legal action against the organization. This can result in costly litigation, settlements, and damage to the organization's financial standing.

Operational Disruptions: Dealing with the aftermath of a data breach or legal action can cause operational disruptions. Organizations may need to divert resources to address the incident, implement corrective measures, and navigate regulatory investigations.

Regulatory Scrutiny and Audits: Non-compliance with data protection laws may lead to regulatory scrutiny and audits. Regulatory authorities have the power to investigate organizations suspected of violating data protection regulations, leading to further legal consequences.

Exclusion from Business Opportunities: Companies that have a history of non-compliance or ethical lapses may face exclusion from business opportunities, partnerships, or contracts. Business partners and clients may be hesitant to engage with organizations with a tarnished track record.

Employee Consequences: Ethical lapses can also have internal consequences, affecting employee morale and trust. Employees may lose confidence in the organization's commitment to ethical practices, leading to decreased job satisfaction and potential talent attrition.

9.6 Common Challenges In Implementing And Maintaining Effective Data Governance

Implementing and maintaining effective data governance can be a complex undertaking, and organizations often face common challenges. Addressing these challenges requires a strategic approach and a commitment to building a strong data governance framework. Here are common challenges and strategies for overcoming them:

1. **Lack of Executive Support:**

   Challenge: Data governance initiatives may struggle without visible support from top-level executives who provide the necessary resources and prioritize the program.

   Strategy:

   Engage Executive Stakeholders: Clearly communicate the business value of data governance, emphasizing its impact on strategic objectives, compliance, and risk mitigation.

   Establish an Executive Steering Committee: Form a committee of key executives to champion data governance initiatives, ensuring their active involvement and support.

2. **Insufficient Resources:**

   Challenge: Limited budget, manpower, and technology resources can hinder the effective implementation of data governance practices.

Strategy:

Prioritize and Phase Implementation: Identify critical areas and start with a phased approach, prioritizing initiatives based on their impact on business objectives and regulatory compliance.

Leverage Existing Resources: Maximize the use of existing tools, technologies, and human resources before considering additional investments.

3. **Resistance to Change:**

Challenge: Employees may resist adopting new data governance processes and responsibilities due to fear, uncertainty, or a lack of understanding.

Strategy:

Communicate Benefits Clearly: Clearly articulate the benefits of data governance for individuals and the organization, emphasizing improved data quality, decision-making, and compliance.

Provide Training and Support: Offer training programs to build awareness and skills. Create a support system to address concerns and provide guidance as employees adapt to new processes.

4. **Data Silos and Fragmentation:**

Challenge: Data scattered across siloed departments and systems can hinder a unified approach to data governance.

Strategy:

Establish Cross-Functional Teams: Form cross-functional teams with representatives from different departments to collaborate on data governance initiatives.

Implement Master Data Management (MDM): Use MDM practices to create a centralized and consistent view of critical data across the organization.

5. **Lack of Data Quality:**

   Challenge: Poor data quality can undermine the effectiveness of data governance efforts, leading to inaccurate analyses and decision-making.

   Strategy:

   Implement Data Quality Management: Integrate data quality management practices into data governance, including data profiling, cleansing, and ongoing monitoring.

   Define Data Quality Metrics: Establish clear metrics for data quality and regularly assess and report on the quality of key data elements.

6. **Inadequate Data Security Measures:**

   Challenge: Insufficient data security measures can expose organizations to the risk of breaches and compromise sensitive information.

   Strategy:

   Implement Robust Security Policies: Develop and enforce comprehensive security policies, encompassing access controls, encryption, and measures to protect against internal and external threats.

   Regular Security Audits: Conduct regular security audits to identify vulnerabilities and ensure compliance with industry standards and regulations.

7. **Undefined Data Governance Framework:**

   Challenge: Lack of a clear and comprehensive data governance framework can result in ad-hoc practices and inconsistent governance.

Strategy:

Develop a Data Governance Framework: Establish a well-defined and documented data governance framework that includes policies, procedures, roles, and responsibilities.

Align with Business Goals: Ensure that the data governance framework aligns with the organization's overall business goals and objectives.

8. **Limited Data Governance Awareness:**

   Challenge: Many employees may not fully understand the importance and relevance of data governance to their roles.

   Strategy:

   Educate and Communicate: Conduct awareness campaigns to educate employees about the value of data governance and how it contributes to their daily tasks and the organization's success.

   Regular Communication: Maintain ongoing communication channels to keep employees informed about data governance initiatives, achievements, and updates.

9. **Changing Regulatory Landscape:**

   Challenge: Evolving data protection and privacy regulations can pose challenges in maintaining compliance.

   Strategy:

   Regular Regulatory Monitoring: Stay informed about changes in the regulatory landscape and proactively adapt data governance practices to ensure ongoing compliance.

   Legal Consultation: Engage legal experts to provide guidance on interpreting and implementing regulatory requirements within the data governance framework.

10. Lack of Metrics for Success:

Challenge: Without defined metrics, it becomes challenging to measure the success and effectiveness of data governance initiatives.

Strategy:

Establish Key Performance Indicators (KPIs): Define and track key performance indicators that align with the goals of data governance, such as improved data quality, reduced time to data access, and increased compliance.

Regular Assessments: Conduct regular assessments to evaluate the impact of data governance on organizational objectives and adjust strategies as needed.

By addressing these challenges with a strategic and proactive approach, organizations can build and maintain an effective data governance program that enhances data quality, compliance, and overall organizational success. Continuous improvement and adaptation are key to ensuring that data governance practices remain aligned with business goals and the evolving data landscape.

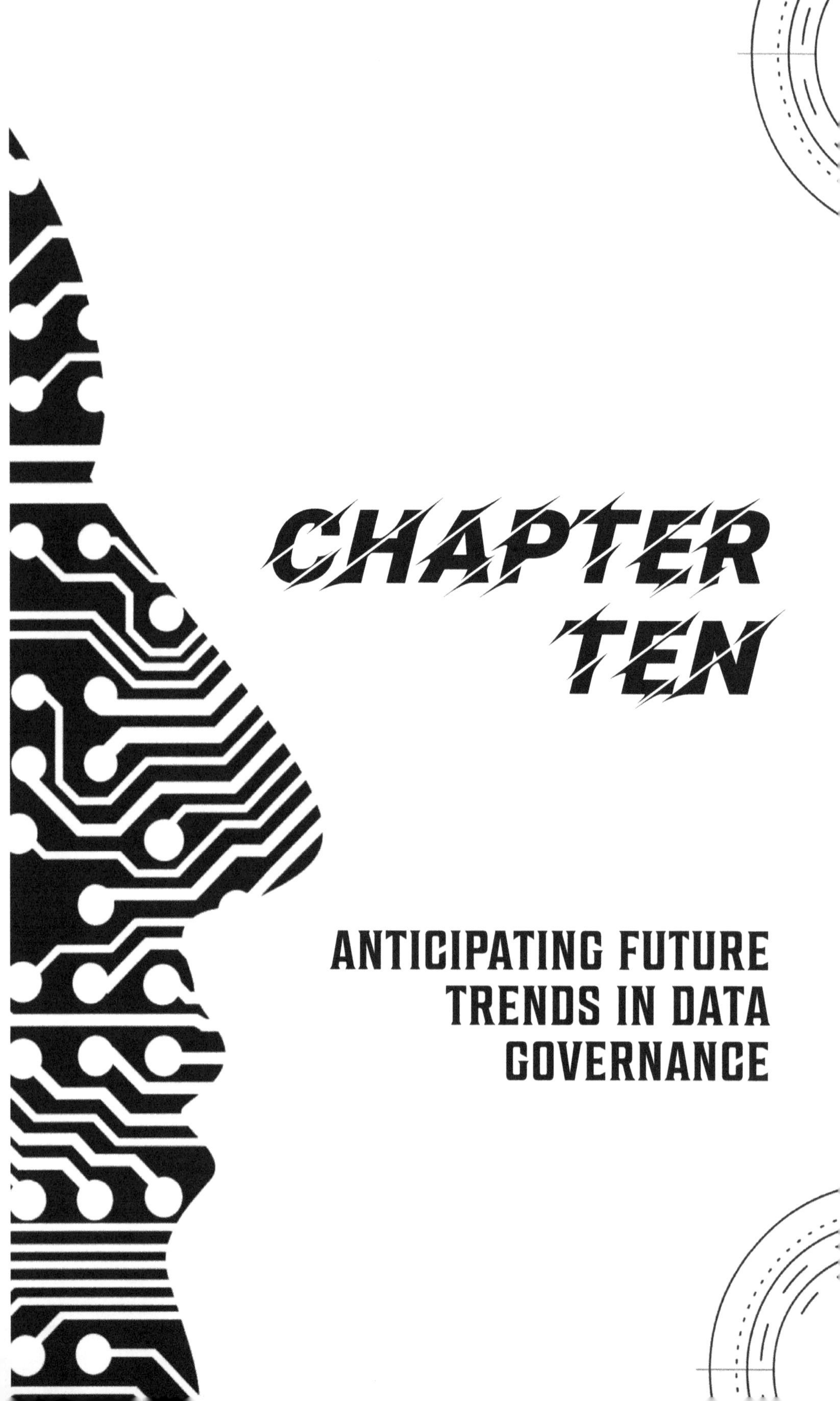

CHAPTER TEN

ANTICIPATING FUTURE TRENDS IN DATA GOVERNANCE

The landscape of data governance continues to evolve, driven by technological advancements, regulatory changes, and shifting organizational priorities.

Several future trends are expected to shape the evolution of data governance:

1. **Artificial Intelligence (AI) and Machine Learning (ML) Integration:**

    The integration of AI and ML into data governance processes will enable automated decision-making, anomaly detection, and predictive analytics.

    Impact: Organizations will leverage AI and ML algorithms to enhance data quality, automate governance tasks, and proactively identify potential risks and opportunities.

2. **Blockchain for Enhanced Data Security:**

    Trend: The adoption of blockchain technology will increase to ensure secure and transparent data transactions, particularly in industries requiring immutable and auditable data records.

    Impact: Blockchain can provide a decentralized and tamper-proof ledger, enhancing data security, transparency, and integrity within the data governance framework.

3. **Data Privacy and Ethical AI Regulations:**

    Trend: Increasing regulatory focus on data privacy and ethical AI will shape data governance practices, with more stringent requirements for responsible data handling.

    Impact: Organizations will need to align data governance frameworks with evolving privacy regulations, emphasizing ethical considerations in AI and ML applications.

4. **Automated Metadata Management:**

    Trend: The automation of metadata management processes will become more prevalent, streamlining the identification, classification, and management of data assets.

    Impact: Automated metadata management will enhance data lineage tracking, improve data discovery, and support compliance efforts within the data governance framework.

5. **Cloud-Centric Data Governance:**

    Trend: Increased reliance on cloud services will drive the development of cloud-centric data governance strategies to manage and govern data across distributed environments.

    Impact: Organizations will need to implement robust cloud-based data governance solutions, addressing challenges related to data sovereignty, integration, and security in the cloud.

6. **Extended Collaboration with Data Ecosystems:**

    Trend: Data governance will extend beyond organizational boundaries, fostering collaboration within broader data ecosystems that include partners, suppliers, and other stakeholders.

    Impact: Organizations will need to develop interoperable data governance frameworks that accommodate collaborative data initiatives while ensuring security and compliance.

7. Explainable AI and Transparent Decision-Making:

Trend: There will be a growing emphasis on making AI and ML algorithms more interpretable and transparent, aligning with the need for accountable and understandable decision-making.

Impact: Data governance frameworks will incorporate measures to ensure explainability and transparency in AI-driven decisions, particularly in industries with regulatory requirements.

8. Focus on Data Ethics and Responsible AI:

Trend: The integration of ethical considerations into data governance practices will become more pronounced, emphasizing responsible AI and the ethical use of data.

Impact: Organizations will establish guidelines and frameworks within their data governance practices to ensure ethical data handling, protecting individuals' rights and minimizing biases.

9. Quantum-Safe Cryptography:

Trend: As quantum computing advances, there will be an increased focus on quantum-safe cryptography to protect sensitive data from potential threats posed by quantum computers.

Impact: Data governance frameworks will need to evolve to incorporate quantum-resistant encryption methods to ensure the long-term security of data.

10. Data Democratization and Self-Service Analytics:

Trend: The trend towards data democratization will continue, empowering users with self-service analytics capabilities while requiring robust governance to maintain data quality and security.

Impact: Data governance practices will need to strike a balance between enabling data access and ensuring responsible use, fostering a culture of data-driven decision-making across the organization.

11. Integration of Robotic Process Automation (RPA):

Trend: The integration of RPA with data governance will automate routine data management tasks, improving efficiency and reducing errors.

Impact: Organizations will leverage RPA to streamline data governance workflows, allowing human resources to focus on more strategic aspects of data management.

12. Real-Time Data Governance:

Trend: The shift towards real-time data governance will enable organizations to respond promptly to changing data conditions, ensuring agility and proactive risk management.

Impact: Data governance frameworks will incorporate real-time monitoring, analytics, and decision-making capabilities, allowing organizations to adapt quickly to dynamic data environments.

As data governance continues to evolve, organizations must stay adaptable and responsive to these emerging trends. Integrating these advancements into data governance frameworks will be crucial for ensuring compliance, enhancing data quality, and leveraging the full potential of data as a strategic asset.

CHAPTER
ELEVEN
STAKEHOLDER ENGAGEMENT:
COLLABORATIVE
APPROACHES
TO GRC

T he active participation of stakeholders is fundamental to the success of an organization's strategic initiatives, risk management, and compliance efforts. Stakeholder engagement forms the cornerstone of a collaborative and holistic approach to GRC, fostering transparency, accountability, and effective decision-making across all levels of an organization.

11.1 THE COLLABORATIVE NATURE OF EFFECTIVE GRC PRACTICES

HOLISTIC RISK MANAGEMENT:

Importance: Stakeholder engagement ensures that risk management is a collective effort involving individuals from various departments, each bringing unique insights and expertise.

Collaborative Nature: Through collaboration, organizations can identify, assess, and mitigate risks comprehensively, leveraging the collective intelligence of stakeholders to create a robust risk management framework.

STRATEGIC ALIGNMENT:

Importance: Stakeholder engagement aligns GRC practices with the organization's strategic objectives, ensuring that risk and compliance efforts contribute directly to the achievement of business goals.

Collaborative Nature: Collaboration with stakeholders allows GRC professionals to gain a deeper understanding of the organization's strategic direction, enabling the tailoring of GRC practices to support and enhance the achievement of strategic objectives.

REGULATORY COMPLIANCE:

Importance: Engaging stakeholders is crucial for staying abreast of regulatory changes and ensuring that the organization remains compliant with evolving legal requirements.

Collaborative Nature: Collaboration enables the establishment of cross-functional teams to interpret, implement, and monitor compliance with regulations, fostering a shared responsibility for adherence to legal standards.

ETHICAL DECISION-MAKING:

Importance: Stakeholder engagement supports the ethical dimension of GRC, promoting a culture of integrity and responsible decision-making.

Collaborative Nature: A collaborative approach ensures that ethical considerations are collectively addressed, fostering a shared commitment to ethical behavior and principled decision-making.

EFFECTIVE COMMUNICATION:

Importance: Stakeholder engagement enhances communication channels, ensuring that relevant information regarding governance, risk, and compliance is effectively disseminated throughout the organization.

Collaborative Nature: Through collaboration, organizations can establish open communication lines, facilitating the exchange of information, insights, and feedback among stakeholders, leading to informed decision-making.

ADAPTIVE GOVERNANCE STRUCTURES:

Importance: Engaging stakeholders allows organizations to adapt governance structures to changing internal and external environments.

Collaborative Nature: Collaboration supports the development of flexible governance frameworks that can quickly respond to emerging risks, market shifts, and regulatory changes, ensuring organizational resilience.

RISK CULTURE AND AWARENESS:

Importance: Stakeholder engagement contributes to the cultivation of a risk-aware culture throughout the organization, where employees at all levels understand and actively participate in risk management efforts.

Collaborative Nature: Collaboration fosters the integration of risk awareness into the organizational culture, with stakeholders collectively working towards embedding risk management practices into day-to-day operations.

INNOVATION AND CONTINUOUS IMPROVEMENT:

Importance: Engaging stakeholders stimulates innovation in GRC practices, fostering a culture of continuous improvement.

Collaborative Nature: Through collaboration, organizations can harness the diverse perspectives of stakeholders to innovate GRC processes, driving efficiency, effectiveness, and adaptability.

11.2 IDENTIFICATION AND CLASSIFICATION OF KEY STAKEHOLDERS IN GRC

Identifying and classifying key stakeholders is crucial for effective engagement and collaboration. The key stakeholders in GRC can be broadly categorized as follows:

EXECUTIVE LEADERSHIP:

Role: Executives, including the CEO, CFO, and other C-suite members, provide strategic direction and oversight for GRC initiatives.

Interest: Strategic alignment of GRC with organizational goals, risk mitigation for financial stability, and ensuring compliance.

BOARD OF DIRECTORS:

Role: The Board provides governance oversight, approves risk management strategies, and ensures compliance with legal and ethical standards.

Interest: Ensuring effective governance, monitoring risk exposure, and safeguarding the organization's reputation.

COMPLIANCE OFFICERS:

Role: Compliance officers are responsible for ensuring that the organization adheres to relevant laws and regulations.

Interest: Mitigating legal risks, maintaining regulatory compliance, and avoiding penalties or reputational damage.

RISK MANAGEMENT TEAM:

Role: Risk managers identify, assess, and mitigate risks to protect the organization's assets and interests.

Interest: Identifying and managing risks, optimizing risk-return profiles, and ensuring organizational resilience.

INTERNAL AUDIT TEAM:

Role: Internal auditors provide independent assessments of internal controls, risk management, and compliance activities.

Interest: Ensuring the effectiveness of internal controls, identifying areas for improvement, and validating compliance efforts.

LEGAL COUNSEL:

Role: Legal advisors provide legal guidance to ensure that the organization operates within the bounds of the law.

Interest: Avoiding legal disputes, ensuring legal compliance, and protecting the organization from legal liabilities.

IT AND CYBERSECURITY TEAMS:

Role: IT and cybersecurity teams manage technology-related risks and safeguard the organization's digital assets.

Interest: Protecting data integrity and confidentiality, ensuring cybersecurity resilience, and preventing data breaches.

HUMAN RESOURCES:

Role: HR professionals contribute to GRC by managing employee-related risks, ensuring ethical behavior, and promoting a positive organizational culture.

Interest: Employee well-being, ethical conduct, and alignment of HR practices with GRC objectives.

OPERATIONS AND BUSINESS UNITS:

Role: Operational teams are involved in day-to-day business activities and are critical for implementing GRC practices at the operational level.

Interest: Operational efficiency, risk mitigation in daily activities, and alignment with strategic goals.

EXTERNAL AUDITORS:

Role: External auditors provide an independent assessment of financial statements and internal controls.

Interest: Ensuring financial transparency, validating internal controls, and providing assurance to external stakeholders.

CUSTOMERS AND CLIENTS:

Role: Customers and clients are external stakeholders who may have expectations related to product/service quality, ethical business practices, and data security.

Interest: Product/service quality, ethical conduct, and protection of their data and privacy.

INVESTORS AND SHAREHOLDERS:

Role: Investors and shareholders have a financial interest in the organization and seek transparency, ethical practices, and sustainable growth.

Interest: Financial performance, ethical conduct, and transparency in governance and risk management.

11.3 DIVERSE INTERESTS AND EXPECTATIONS OF STAKEHOLDERS

Stakeholders in GRC have diverse interests and expectations shaped by their roles, responsibilities, and relationships with the organization. Understanding these diverse interests is essential for effective stakeholder engagement. Some examples of diverse interests and expectations include:

EXECUTIVE LEADERSHIP:

Interest: Strategic alignment, financial stability, and long-term sustainability.

Expectations: Effective risk management, compliance with laws and regulations, and transparent reporting.

BOARD OF DIRECTORS:

Interest: Effective governance, risk oversight, and protection of shareholder value.

Expectations: Regular updates on risk exposure, adherence to compliance standards, and proactive risk mitigation.

COMPLIANCE OFFICERS:

Interest: Legal risk mitigation, adherence to compliance standards, and ethical conduct.

Expectations: Robust compliance programs, timely reporting, and proactive identification and resolution of compliance issues.

RISK MANAGEMENT TEAM:

Interest: Identifying and managing risks, optimizing risk-return profiles.

Expectations: Accurate risk assessments, proactive risk mitigation strategies, and alignment of risk management with strategic goals.

INTERNAL AUDIT TEAM:

Interest: Effectiveness of internal controls, risk management, and compliance activities.

Expectations: Independent and objective assessments, identification of control weaknesses, and recommendations for improvement.

LEGAL COUNSEL:

Interest: Legal risk mitigation, adherence to laws and regulations.

Expectations: Legal compliance, timely legal advice, and proactive risk management to prevent legal issues.

IT AND CYBERSECURITY TEAMS:

Interest: Data security, cybersecurity resilience, and protection against cyber threats.

Expectations: Robust cybersecurity measures, timely response to threats, and adherence to data protection standards.

HUMAN RESOURCES:

Interest: Employee well-being, ethical behavior, and positive organizational culture.

Expectations: Ethical conduct, compliance with HR laws, and integration of GRC principles into HR practices.

OPERATIONS AND BUSINESS UNITS:

Interest: Operational efficiency, risk mitigation in daily activities.

Expectations: Alignment of GRC practices with operational goals, proactive risk management, and integration of GRC into daily workflows.

EXTERNAL AUDITORS:

Interest: Financial transparency, validation of internal controls.

Expectations: Reliable financial reporting, adherence to accounting standards, and cooperation in audit processes.

CUSTOMERS AND CLIENTS:

Interest: Product/service quality, ethical conduct, and data security.

Expectations: Ethical business practices, transparent communication, and protection of their data and privacy.

INVESTORS AND SHAREHOLDERS:

Interest: Financial performance, ethical conduct, and sustainable growth.

Expectations: Transparent reporting, risk disclosure, and strategic initiatives that enhance shareholder value.

Understanding and addressing the diverse interests and expectations of stakeholders in GRC is vital for building trust, fostering collaboration, and achieving shared organizational objectives. By actively engaging with stakeholders, organizations can navigate complexities, enhance decision-making processes, and cultivate a culture of accountability and transparency in GRC practices.

11.4 Establishing the Link between Stakeholder Engagement and Successful GRC Outcomes

Stakeholder engagement is integral to the success of Governance, Risk, and Compliance (GRC) outcomes.

The collaborative involvement of stakeholders significantly impacts risk mitigation and compliance efforts in the following ways:

HOLISTIC RISK MANAGEMENT:

Impact: Stakeholder engagement ensures a comprehensive understanding of potential risks across the organization.

Outcome: Holistic risk identification allows for more accurate risk assessments, enhancing preparedness to address a broad range of risks.

STRATEGIC ALIGNMENT OF GRC INITIATIVES:

Impact: Engaging stakeholders aligns GRC initiatives with the organization's strategic goals.

Outcome: Strategically aligned GRC practices become integral to the organization's success and sustainability.

PROACTIVE COMPLIANCE MANAGEMENT:

Impact: Stakeholders actively collaborate in interpreting and implementing compliance requirements.

Outcome: Proactive engagement reduces the risk of non-compliance, enabling organizations to anticipate regulatory changes and adjust their strategies accordingly.

EARLY DETECTION OF EMERGING RISKS:

Impact: Collaborative stakeholder engagement facilitates real-time insights into industry trends and emerging risks.

Outcome: Early detection of emerging risks allows for timely adjustments to risk management strategies and proactive mitigation planning.

TRANSPARENT COMMUNICATION CHANNELS:

Impact: Open communication channels established through stakeholder engagement ensure effective information dissemination.

Outcome: Transparent communication fosters a culture of awareness, accountability, and shared responsibility, enhancing the organization's ability to address challenges collectively.

ADAPTIVE GOVERNANCE STRUCTURES:

Impact: Stakeholders provide input for the development of flexible governance frameworks.

Outcome: Adaptive governance structures, influenced by stakeholder collaboration, enable organizations to respond promptly to evolving risks and market dynamics.

EFFICIENT RISK MITIGATION STRATEGIES:

Impact: Stakeholders actively contribute to the development of efficient risk mitigation strategies.

Outcome: Informed by diverse perspectives, risk mitigation strategies become more effective, addressing potential risks before they escalate.

CULTURAL INTEGRATION OF GRC PRACTICES:

Impact: Stakeholder engagement fosters shared ownership and responsibility for GRC practices.

Outcome: Culturally integrated GRC practices encourage active participation in risk management and compliance efforts at all organizational levels.

ENHANCED PROBLEM-SOLVING CAPABILITIES:

Impact: Diverse stakeholder perspectives enrich problem-solving discussions.

Outcome: Collaborative problem-solving enhances the organization's ability to navigate uncertainties and implement effective solutions.

INTEGRATED COMPLIANCE AND RISK STRATEGIES:

Impact: Collaboration with stakeholders allows for the integration of compliance and risk management strategies.

Outcome: Integrated strategies align compliance efforts with risk management objectives, creating a cohesive and effective GRC framework

11.4.1 BENEFITS OF EFFECTIVE STAKEHOLDER ENGAGEMENT IN GRC

IMPROVED RISK IDENTIFICATION AND MANAGEMENT:

Benefit: Stakeholder engagement facilitates a diverse and comprehensive understanding of potential risks.

Outcome: Improved risk identification enables organizations to proactively assess, prioritize, and effectively manage risks, reducing the likelihood of unexpected disruptions.

ENHANCED COMPLIANCE AND REGULATORY ADHERENCE:

Benefit: Collaborative engagement with stakeholders ensures a thorough understanding of compliance requirements.

Outcome: Enhanced compliance awareness and adherence result in proactive measures to meet regulatory standards, reducing the risk of non-compliance and associated consequences.

STRENGTHENED ORGANIZATIONAL RESILIENCE:

Benefit: Stakeholder involvement contributes to the development of adaptive governance structures.

Outcome: Strengthened organizational resilience allows the organization to navigate challenges, adapt to changing circumstances, and maintain continuity in the face of uncertainties.

INCREASED TRANSPARENCY AND ACCOUNTABILITY:

Benefit: Open communication channels established through stakeholder engagement foster transparency.

Outcome: Increased transparency enhances accountability, as stakeholders are informed about GRC practices, decisions, and outcomes, fostering a culture of trust and responsibility.

PROACTIVE PROBLEM-SOLVING AND DECISION-MAKING:

Benefit: Diverse stakeholder perspectives enrich problem-solving discussions.

Outcome: Proactive problem-solving and decision-making, informed by stakeholder insights, lead to effective and timely responses to challenges, reducing the impact of potential issues.

CULTURAL INTEGRATION OF GRC PRACTICES:

Benefit: Stakeholder engagement fosters a sense of shared ownership for GRC practices.

Outcome: Culturally integrated GRC practices encourage active participation at all organizational levels, creating a unified approach to risk management, compliance, and governance.

OPTIMIZED RESOURCE ALLOCATION:

Benefit: Collaboration with stakeholders aids in prioritizing risks and compliance efforts.

Outcome: Optimized resource allocation ensures that resources are directed towards the most critical areas, maximizing the effectiveness of risk mitigation and compliance initiatives.

INCREASED EMPLOYEE ENGAGEMENT AND COMMITMENT:

Benefit: Involving employees as stakeholders enhances engagement and commitment.

Outcome: Engaged employees are more likely to adhere to GRC policies, report risks, and actively contribute to the organization's overall risk management and compliance efforts.

INNOVATION AND CONTINUOUS IMPROVEMENT:

Benefit: Stakeholder engagement stimulates innovative thinking in GRC practices.

Outcome: Continuous improvement in GRC strategies, driven by stakeholder insights, ensures that the organization remains adaptive, responsive, and innovative in its approach to governance and risk management.

POSITIVE REPUTATION AND STAKEHOLDER TRUST:

Benefit: Transparent communication builds a positive organizational reputation.

Outcome: Positive reputation and stakeholder trust are vital assets, contributing to the organization's credibility, attracting investors, and fostering long-term relationships with key stakeholders.

ALIGNMENT WITH ORGANIZATIONAL VALUES:

Benefit: Stakeholder engagement ensures alignment with organizational values and mission.

Outcome: GRC practices that reflect organizational values create a consistent and ethical framework, contributing to a positive organizational culture.

STRATEGIC PLANNING AND ALIGNMENT:

Benefit: Collaborative engagement allows for strategic alignment of GRC initiatives.

Outcome: GRC practices aligned with strategic goals support the organization's overall objectives, contributing to sustained growth and success.

Effective stakeholder engagement in GRC, therefore, yields a multitude of benefits that extend beyond risk identification and compliance, fostering a resilient, transparent, and adaptive organizational culture.

11.4.2 STRATEGIES FOR STAKEHOLDER ENGAGEMENT IN GRC

Effective stakeholder engagement in Governance, Risk, and Compliance (GRC) is essential for building a collaborative and informed approach to organizational governance.

Here are several strategies for fostering meaningful stakeholder engagement in the realm of GRC:

i.   Identify Key Stakeholders: In order to initiate a robust stakeholder engagement strategy, it is imperative to first identify the key individuals or groups with a vested interest in GRC processes. A comprehensive stakeholder analysis involving surveys, interviews, and workshops can help in pinpointing those crucial stakeholders.

ii. Establish Clear Communication Channels: Creating transparent and accessible communication channels is vital for keeping stakeholders informed. Regular newsletters, town hall meetings, and online platforms can serve as effective tools for sharing updates, developments, and key information related to GRC practices.

iii. Tailor Communication to Stakeholder Needs: Recognizing the diversity in stakeholder preferences and needs is crucial. A strategic approach involves customizing communication methods to resonate with different stakeholder groups. This ensures that information is delivered in a format that is both accessible and relevant.

iv. Hold Regular Engagement Sessions: Scheduling routine engagement sessions provides a structured platform for stakeholders to voice their feedback and concerns. Workshops, webinars, and forums serve as effective mediums for facilitating active participation and discussion on various GRC initiatives.

v.   Involve Stakeholders in Decision-Making: Actively involving stakeholders in decision-making processes regarding GRC not only fosters a sense of ownership but also ensures that diverse perspectives are considered. Establishing advisory boards or committees with stakeholder representatives can significantly contribute to this collaborative approach.

vi. Provide Stakeholder Training: To enhance stakeholder understanding of GRC principles, it is beneficial to offer training sessions. These programs can include workshops or webinars designed to educate stakeholders about the importance of GRC, their role in the process, and relevant regulations.

vii. Utilize Technology for Engagement: Leveraging technology enhances stakeholder engagement by providing efficient and collaborative platforms. Online forums, collaborative tools, and project management platforms facilitate virtual engagement, real-time communication, and document sharing.

viii. Seek Stakeholder Feedback: Actively seeking feedback from stakeholders is integral to assessing their satisfaction and identifying areas for improvement. Surveys, feedback forms, and focus groups serve as valuable tools for collecting insights on stakeholder experiences with GRC processes.

ix. Demonstrate Value through Results: Tangibly demonstrating the value of stakeholder engagement involves showcasing measurable results. Success stories, case studies, and key performance indicators can effectively highlight how stakeholder input positively influences GRC outcomes.

x. Foster a Culture of Collaboration: Creating a culture that values collaboration and mutual understanding is foundational for successful stakeholder engagement. Open dialogue, recognition of contributions, and an environment that encourages the sharing of perspectives contribute to a collaborative culture.

xi. Align GRC with Organizational Goals: Aligning GRC initiatives with overall organizational goals and values is crucial for demonstrating the relevance of GRC practices. Communicating how GRC contributes to the organization's mission, vision, and strategic objectives emphasizes a shared purpose with stakeholders.

xii. Create a Two-Way Communication Flow: Establishing a two-way communication flow encourages dialogue between stakeholders and GRC professionals. Providing mechanisms for stakeholders to voice concerns, ask questions, and provide input fosters a dynamic exchange of information, strengthening the collaborative approach to GRC.

xiii. Implementing these strategies collectively ensures a comprehensive and inclusive stakeholder engagement approach in GRC, fostering collaboration, transparency, and shared responsibility across the organization.

11.4.3 Challenges in Stakeholder Engagement and How to Overcome Them

DIVERSE STAKEHOLDER EXPECTATIONS:

Challenge: Meeting the diverse expectations of various stakeholders can be challenging, as different groups may have conflicting interests.

Overcoming: Conduct thorough stakeholder analyses to understand individual expectations. Prioritize transparency in communication and establish clear expectations from the outset.

COMMUNICATION BARRIERS:

Challenge: Language differences, misinterpretation of information, or lack of effective communication channels can hinder engagement efforts.

Overcoming: Use diverse communication channels, ensure language accessibility, and provide regular updates to bridge communication gaps. Foster an open and inclusive communication culture.

RESISTANCE TO CHANGE:

Challenge: Stakeholders may resist new GRC initiatives or changes in existing processes due to fear, uncertainty, or skepticism.

Overcoming: Implement change management strategies, communicate the benefits of changes, and involve stakeholders in decision-making to address concerns and build buy-in.

LIMITED RESOURCES:

Challenge: Organizations may face resource constraints, hindering the ability to dedicate sufficient time and personnel to stakeholder engagement.

Overcoming: Prioritize stakeholder engagement efforts, leverage technology for efficient communication, and seek collaboration with external partners or consultants when necessary.

LACK OF STAKEHOLDER AWARENESS:

Challenge: Some stakeholders may not fully understand the significance of their role in GRC processes.

Overcoming: Conduct awareness campaigns, provide educational resources, and offer training sessions to enhance stakeholder understanding of GRC principles and their impact.

OVERLAPPING INTERESTS AND COMPETING PRIORITIES:

Challenge: Conflicting interests among stakeholders and competing organizational priorities can lead to challenges in aligning GRC efforts.

Overcoming: Facilitate open discussions to identify common ground, establish clear priorities, and seek compromises that balance the interests of different stakeholders.

LACK OF STAKEHOLDER INVOLVEMENT:

Challenge: Some stakeholders may disengage if they feel their input is not valued or if there is a lack of meaningful participation opportunities.

Overcoming: Actively involve stakeholders in decision-making, seek their input in planning processes, and acknowledge and appreciate their contributions to foster a sense of ownership.

DATA PRIVACY CONCERNS:

Challenge: Stakeholders, especially in the context of evolving data privacy regulations, may be concerned about the handling of sensitive information.

Overcoming: Implement robust data protection measures, clearly communicate privacy policies, and ensure compliance with relevant regulations to build trust among stakeholders.

INADEQUATE TECHNOLOGY INFRASTRUCTURE:

Challenge: Limited access to technology or outdated infrastructure can impede effective stakeholder engagement, particularly in virtual environments.

Overcoming: Invest in technology upgrades, provide training on digital platforms, and explore alternative communication methods to accommodate diverse technological capabilities.

RESISTANCE FROM INTERNAL STAKEHOLDERS:

Challenge: Internal stakeholders, such as employees, may resist active engagement due to perceived additional workload or lack of awareness.

Overcoming: Communicate the benefits of engagement, demonstrate the impact of GRC on organizational success, and create a supportive culture that encourages participation.

INADEQUATE FEEDBACK MECHANISMS:

Challenge: Absence of structured feedback mechanisms can hinder the continuous improvement of stakeholder engagement processes.

Overcoming: Implement regular feedback surveys, establish open channels for suggestions, and actively seek input during engagement sessions to create a culture of continuous improvement.

GLOBAL AND CULTURAL DIFFERENCES:

Challenge: Organizations with a global presence may encounter challenges in understanding and accommodating cultural differences that influence stakeholder engagement.

Overcoming: Invest in cultural competency training, leverage local representatives, and tailor engagement strategies to align with cultural norms and expectations.

By addressing these challenges proactively, organizations can enhance their stakeholder engagement efforts, fostering a collaborative and supportive environment conducive to effective GRC practices.

11.5 TECHNOLOGY TOOLS AND PLATFORMS FOR STAKEHOLDER ENGAGEMENT IN GRC

COLLABORATIVE PROJECT MANAGEMENT PLATFORMS:

TOOLS: TRELLO, ASANA, JIRA.

Benefits: These platforms enable stakeholders to collaborate on projects, share updates, and track progress in real-time. Task assignment, document sharing, and centralized communication enhance overall project visibility.

COMMUNICATION AND MESSAGING APPS:

TOOLS: SLACK, MICROSOFT TEAMS, TELEGRAM.

Benefits: Instant messaging apps facilitate quick and direct communication among stakeholders. Channels and groups can be created for specific projects or topics, streamlining communication and reducing email clutter.

VIDEO CONFERENCING SOLUTIONS:

TOOLS: ZOOM, MICROSOFT TEAMS, GOOGLE MEET.

Benefits: Virtual meetings and webinars allow stakeholders to participate remotely, fostering real-time communication. Video conferencing enhances engagement by providing a face-to-face connection, particularly in distributed or remote work environments.

CLOUD-BASED DOCUMENT COLLABORATION:

TOOLS: GOOGLE WORKSPACE, MICROSOFT 365, DROPBOX.

Benefits: Cloud platforms enable collaborative document creation, editing, and sharing. Stakeholders can access and contribute to documents in real-time, ensuring everyone has the latest information and reducing version control issues.

SURVEY AND FEEDBACK TOOLS:

TOOLS: SURVEYMONKEY, TYPEFORM, GOOGLE FORMS.

Benefits: Conducting surveys and collecting feedback becomes efficient with online tools. Stakeholders can express their opinions anonymously, encouraging honest input on GRC processes, initiatives, and overall satisfaction.

VIRTUAL COLLABORATION BOARDS:

TOOLS: MIRO, MURAL, LUCIDCHART.

Benefits: Virtual whiteboards facilitate collaborative brainstorming, ideation, and planning. Stakeholders can visually contribute to discussions, add notes, and work together on diagrams, fostering creativity and engagement.

WEB-BASED GOVERNANCE PORTALS:

TOOLS: DILIGENT BOARDS, BOARDEFFECT, PASSAGEWAYS.

Benefits: Governance portals provide a centralized platform for board members and executives to access important documents, meeting agendas, and strategic plans. They enhance communication, transparency, and collaboration in governance activities.

SOCIAL INTRANET PLATFORMS:

TOOLS: SHAREPOINT, JIVE, CONFLUENCE.

Benefits: Social intranets create a collaborative space for stakeholders within an organization. Features like discussion forums, wikis, and news feeds promote information sharing, knowledge management, and engagement.

ENTERPRISE SOCIAL MEDIA PLATFORMS:

TOOLS: YAMMER, WORKPLACE BY FACEBOOK, CHATTER.

Benefits: Internal social media platforms foster a sense of community among stakeholders. Features like news feeds, group discussions, and real-time updates contribute to open communication and collaboration.

DATA ANALYTICS AND VISUALIZATION TOOLS:

TOOLS: TABLEAU, POWER BI, GOOGLE DATA STUDIO.

Benefits: Analytics tools help stakeholders visualize and interpret data related to GRC metrics. Dashboards and reports provide insights that support informed decision-making and enhance overall understanding of GRC performance.

11.6 How Digital Collaboration Enhances Communication, Information Sharing, and Decision-Making

Real-Time Communication: Digital collaboration tools enable real-time communication, allowing stakeholders to connect instantly regardless of geographical locations. This immediacy fosters quick decision-making and reduces delays in information sharing.

Centralized Information Hub: Digital platforms serve as centralized hubs for information storage, ensuring that stakeholders have access to the latest documents, reports, and updates. This reduces the risk of outdated information and enhances overall information sharing.

Enhanced Accessibility: Cloud-based collaboration tools provide stakeholders with the flexibility to access information from anywhere, at any time. This accessibility promotes continuous engagement, especially in situations where stakeholders may be working remotely or in different time zones.

Improved Collaboration on Documents: Collaboration platforms facilitate simultaneous editing and commenting on documents. This enhances teamwork, as stakeholders can work together on reports, policies, or other GRC-related documents in real-time.

Streamlined Decision-Making Processes: Virtual collaboration tools streamline decision-making by providing a platform for stakeholders to discuss options, share insights, and reach consensus. This transparency in decision-making contributes to more informed and effective outcomes.

Increased Engagement and Participation: Digital collaboration platforms encourage active engagement through features like chat, discussion forums, and collaborative spaces. Stakeholders feel more involved and connected, leading to increased participation in GRC initiatives.

Facilitation of Virtual Meetings and Events: Video conferencing tools enable virtual meetings and events, ensuring that stakeholders can participate in discussions, workshops, and training sessions remotely. This flexibility enhances communication and engagement in a virtual or hybrid work environment.

Data-Driven Decision-Making: Analytics and visualization tools help stakeholders make data-driven decisions. Dashboards and reports provide a clear overview of GRC metrics, enabling stakeholders to analyze trends, identify risks, and make informed decisions based on data insights.

Efficient Project Management: Collaborative project management tools streamline GRC project workflows. Stakeholders can track progress, assign tasks, and communicate within the platform, promoting efficiency in project execution and delivery.

Enhanced Accountability and Transparency: Digital collaboration tools contribute to accountability and transparency by recording discussions, decisions, and document changes. This audit trail ensures that stakeholders are accountable for their contributions and actions, fostering a transparent GRC environment.

11.7 Ethical Dimensions of Engaging Stakeholders in GRC: Ensuring Fairness, Transparency, and Respect for Stakeholders' Rights and Concerns

Engaging stakeholders in Governance, Risk, and Compliance (GRC) processes necessitates a commitment to ethical practices that prioritize fairness, transparency, and respect for stakeholders' rights and concerns. This ethical dimension is crucial for building trust, maintaining organizational integrity, and fostering a positive relationship with stakeholders.

Here's an exploration of key ethical considerations in stakeholder engagement within the GRC context:

FAIRNESS IN DECISION-MAKING:

Ethical Imperative: Ensuring fairness involves treating all stakeholders impartially and providing them with an equal opportunity to voice their opinions and concerns.

Implementation: Establish clear decision-making processes that consider diverse stakeholder perspectives. Avoid favoritism and strive for inclusivity in consultations, taking into account the interests of all affected parties.

TRANSPARENCY IN COMMUNICATION:

Ethical Imperative: Transparency is fundamental to ethical engagement, requiring open and honest communication about GRC policies, decisions, and potential impacts.

Implementation: Clearly communicate the purpose, goals, and outcomes of GRC initiatives. Share relevant information, including risks, compliance measures, and governance structures, in a manner that is accessible and understandable to all stakeholders.

RESPECT FOR STAKEHOLDERS' RIGHTS:

Ethical Imperative: Respecting stakeholders' rights involves recognizing their autonomy, privacy, and freedom of expression throughout the engagement process.

Implementation: Clearly articulate and uphold stakeholders' rights within the engagement framework. Obtain informed consent for data collection, respect confidentiality, and allow stakeholders the freedom to express their views without fear of reprisal.

INCLUSIVITY AND DIVERSITY:

Ethical Imperative: Ethical engagement requires recognizing and valuing the diversity of stakeholders, ensuring their voices are heard regardless of background or identity.

Implementation: Foster inclusivity by actively seeking diverse perspectives. Provide opportunities for input from underrepresented groups, acknowledging the unique concerns and interests that may arise within different stakeholder communities.

RESPONSIVE DECISION-MAKING:

Ethical Imperative: Ethical engagement includes a commitment to responding to stakeholders' concerns and feedback, demonstrating a willingness to adapt decisions based on their input.

Implementation: Establish mechanisms for receiving and addressing stakeholder feedback. Clearly communicate how their input influenced decisions and demonstrate a commitment to continuous improvement based on their concerns.

BALANCING STAKEHOLDER INTERESTS:

Ethical Imperative: Balancing competing stakeholder interests is an ethical challenge, requiring careful consideration of the potential impacts and trade-offs associated with GRC decisions.

Implementation: Implement a fair and transparent decision-making process that considers the interests of all stakeholders. Clearly communicate the rationale behind decisions, acknowledging and addressing conflicts where possible.

EQUITABLE RESOURCE ALLOCATION:

Ethical Imperative: Ethical engagement involves fair and equitable resource allocation, ensuring that benefits and burdens associated with GRC initiatives are distributed justly.

Implementation: Prioritize resource allocation based on a fair assessment of needs and impacts. Avoid disproportionately burdening specific stakeholders and consider the social and economic implications of resource distribution.

ACCOUNTABILITY FOR GRC OUTCOMES:

Ethical Imperative: Ethical engagement requires organizations to be accountable for the outcomes of GRC processes, taking responsibility for both successes and failures.

Implementation: Establish clear accountability mechanisms, communicate transparently about GRC outcomes, and take corrective action when necessary. Demonstrate a commitment to learning from experiences and improving future engagement practices.

AVOIDING CONFLICTS OF INTEREST:

Ethical Imperative: Organizations engaging stakeholders in GRC must actively identify and manage conflicts of interest to ensure unbiased decision-making.

Implementation: Implement robust conflict of interest policies and procedures. Disclose potential conflicts transparently, and take appropriate measures to mitigate or eliminate conflicts that may compromise the integrity of the engagement process.

ENSURING ACCESSIBILITY:

Ethical Imperative: Ethical engagement requires ensuring that all stakeholders, regardless of ability or background, can participate meaningfully in the process.

Implementation: Provide accessible communication channels and materials. Consider the diverse needs of stakeholders, including those with disabilities, and make accommodations to facilitate their participation.

11.8 Cultivating a Culture that Values Stakeholder Input and Collaboration: Aligning Organizational Values with Stakeholder Engagement Principles

Building a culture that values stakeholder input and collaboration is essential for effective Governance, Risk, and Compliance (GRC) practices. Aligning organizational values with stakeholder engagement principles creates a foundation of trust, transparency, and mutual respect. Here's an exploration of strategies to cultivate such a culture:

Define and Communicate Organizational Values: Clearly articulate the core values that guide the organization. Ensure that these values emphasize openness, collaboration, and a commitment to involving stakeholders in decision-making processes.

Leadership Demonstration: Leadership plays a pivotal role in shaping organizational culture. Leaders should actively demonstrate the importance of stakeholder engagement by seeking input, embracing diverse perspectives, and visibly incorporating stakeholder feedback into decision-making.

Incorporate Stakeholder Engagement into Mission and Vision Statements: Align the organization's mission and vision statements with the principles of stakeholder engagement. Communicate a commitment to collaboration, inclusivity, and shared responsibility in achieving the organization's objectives.

Create Formalized Stakeholder Engagement Policies: Develop clear and formalized policies that outline the organization's approach to stakeholder engagement. These policies should define the methods for involving stakeholders, the frequency of engagement, and the mechanisms for addressing stakeholder concerns.

Establish Dedicated Stakeholder Engagement Teams: Form teams or committees responsible for managing stakeholder engagement initiatives. Ensure these teams have the necessary resources and authority to implement engagement strategies effectively.

Provide Training on Stakeholder Engagement: Offer training programs to employees at all levels on the principles and importance of stakeholder engagement. Equip them with the skills needed to facilitate meaningful interactions and collaboration with stakeholders.

Create Open Communication Channels: Establish accessible and open communication channels to encourage stakeholders to voice their opinions and concerns. Utilize various platforms, such as online forums, surveys, and regular town hall meetings, to facilitate two-way communication.

Acknowledge and Celebrate Successes: Recognize and celebrate instances where stakeholder input has positively influenced decision-making or outcomes. This reinforces the value of collaboration and encourages ongoing engagement.

Incorporate Stakeholder Feedback into Performance Metrics: Integrate stakeholder engagement metrics into the organization's performance measurement systems. Acknowledge and reward departments or individuals who excel in engaging stakeholders and incorporating their feedback.

Ensure Diversity and Inclusivity: Foster a culture of diversity and inclusivity, recognizing that stakeholders come from various backgrounds, cultures, and perspectives. Actively seek input from underrepresented groups and ensure that all voices are heard.

Encourage Cross-Functional Collaboration: Break down silos within the organization by encouraging collaboration across different departments and functions. Cross-functional teams can work together to address complex GRC challenges and ensure a holistic approach to stakeholder engagement.

Align Stakeholder Engagement with Business Goals: Demonstrate the strategic importance of stakeholder engagement by aligning it with the achievement of broader business goals. Clearly communicate how collaboration with stakeholders contributes to the organization's success.

Regularly Assess and Improve Engagement Strategies: Continuously assess the effectiveness of stakeholder engagement strategies. Seek feedback from both internal and external stakeholders to identify areas for improvement and implement changes accordingly.

Embed Engagement in Decision-Making Processes: Ensure that stakeholder engagement is integrated into the organization's decision-making processes. Establish protocols for involving stakeholders at key decision points, reinforcing a culture where their input is considered integral to the decision-making process.

Be Transparent about Limitations and Constraints: Communicate openly about any limitations or constraints the organization may face in implementing stakeholder suggestions. This transparency builds trust and demonstrates a commitment to honesty and authenticity.

Emphasize Long-Term Relationship Building: View stakeholder engagement as an ongoing, long-term relationship-building process rather than a one-time effort. Continuously invest in building relationships with stakeholders based on trust, transparency, and shared goals.

Encourage a Bottom-Up Approach: Empower employees at all levels to engage with stakeholders and contribute to the organization's stakeholder engagement initiatives. Encourage a bottom-up approach where ideas and insights from the frontlines are valued.

Regularly Review and Reinforce Organizational Values: Periodically review and reinforce the alignment of organizational values with stakeholder engagement principles. Ensure that these values are consistently communicated and upheld across all levels of the organization.

By integrating these strategies into the organizational fabric, businesses can cultivate a culture that not only values stakeholder input but actively seeks collaboration, fostering a positive environment for effective GRC practices. This alignment of values and engagement principles contributes to the organization's resilience, adaptability, and sustainable success.

CHAPTER TWELVE

TRAINING AND DEVELOPMENT IN GRC: EMPOWERING THE MODERN PROFESSIONAL

The imperative for continuous learning stands as a cornerstone for professional success and organizational resilience. This introduction seeks to illuminate the critical role of continuous learning in GRC and underscore the paramount importance of training and development initiatives in preparing professionals for the dynamic challenges within this complex domain.

12.1 Navigating the GRC Landscape: A Dynamic and Evolving Terrain

The realm of GRC is marked by constant change and complexity. Regulatory landscapes undergo revisions, global markets fluctuate, and the nature of risks evolves in response to emerging threats. In this dynamic environment, professionals operating in GRC roles must not only stay abreast of these shifts but also possess the skills and knowledge to navigate them effectively. Continuous learning becomes the linchpin for professionals to not only keep pace with the changes but to proactively shape and influence GRC strategies in their organizations.

12.1.1 The Crucial Role of Training and Development

At the heart of empowering professionals for GRC challenges lies a robust framework of training and development. As the demands placed on GRC professionals become more intricate, the need for tailored and strategic learning initiatives becomes imperative. Training and development programs serve as catalysts for acquiring the specialized skills, industry insights, and nuanced understanding necessary to thrive in the multifaceted landscape of GRC.

12.1.2 WHY CONTINUOUS LEARNING MATTERS IN GRC

ADAPTABILITY TO REGULATORY SHIFTS:

GRC professionals must anticipate and adapt to regulatory changes that have a profound impact on organizational operations. Continuous learning ensures that professionals are not only aware of these changes but are also equipped to interpret, implement, and comply with new requirements.

MITIGATION OF EMERGING RISKS:

The nature of risks is ever-evolving, from cybersecurity threats to geopolitical instabilities. Continuous learning empowers professionals to identify, assess, and mitigate these risks, fostering a proactive risk management culture within organizations.

12.1.3 ALIGNMENT WITH ETHICAL GOVERNANCE PRACTICES

Ethical considerations are integral to effective GRC. Continuous learning emphasizes the importance of ethical governance, guiding professionals to make principled decisions and contribute to the establishment of a culture of integrity within their organizations.

TECHNOLOGICAL INTEGRATION

The integration of technology in GRC is unavoidable. Training and development initiatives are essential to ensure that professionals are not only tech-savvy but also adept at leveraging advanced tools and analytics for more effective governance and risk management.

ENHANCED DECISION-MAKING SKILLS

GRC professionals are frequently called upon to make critical decisions that impact the entire organization. Continuous learning sharpens decision-making skills by exposing professionals to diverse case studies, simulations, and real-world scenarios.

EMPOWERING PROFESSIONALS FOR THE GRC CHALLENGES OF TOMORROW

As organizations grapple with an increasingly intricate GRC landscape, the commitment to continuous learning emerges as a strategic imperative. The subsequent chapters of this book will delve into the various facets of training and development, exploring effective strategies, emerging trends, and real-world case studies that collectively contribute to the empowerment of GRC professionals. Through these insights, we endeavor to equip readers with the knowledge and tools necessary to thrive in the dynamic world of Governance, Risk, and Compliance.

EVOLUTION AND DIVERSIFICATION OF GRC ROLES

The roles within Governance, Risk, and Compliance (GRC) have undergone a profound transformation over time. Originally viewed as distinct functions with specific mandates, these roles have evolved into more integrated and strategic positions within organizations. The siloed approach to GRC has given way to a more interconnected model, recognizing the inherent interdependencies among governance, risk management, and compliance functions. This evolution has led to the emergence of hybrid roles that demand a broader skill set and a holistic understanding of the organization's operations. Key factors influencing this evolution include:

INCREASED REGULATORY COMPLEXITY

The global business environment has witnessed a surge in regulatory complexity. GRC professionals are now required to navigate a myriad of regulations and standards, necessitating a comprehensive understanding of diverse compliance requirements.

RISING CYBERSECURITY CONCERNS

The escalating threat landscape in cybersecurity has elevated the importance of risk management within GRC. Professionals need to be well-versed in identifying, assessing, and mitigating cybersecurity risks, which have become critical components of the overall risk profile.

EMPHASIS ON ETHICAL GOVERNANCE

The focus on ethical governance has grown significantly, fueled by high-profile corporate scandals. GRC roles now encompass a stronger emphasis on fostering a culture of integrity and ethical decision-making, necessitating a nuanced understanding of ethical principles.

TECHNOLOGICAL ADVANCEMENTS:

The integration of technology has reshaped GRC roles. Professionals must adapt to new technologies, such as data analytics, artificial intelligence, and automation, to enhance the efficiency and effectiveness of governance, risk, and compliance processes.

STRATEGIC ALIGNMENT WITH BUSINESS GOALS:

GRC is no longer confined to a purely risk-averse function. Modern GRC professionals are expected to align their efforts with broader business objectives, contributing to organizational strategies and performance.

KEY SKILLS AND COMPETENCIES REQUIRED IN THE MODERN GRC LANDSCAPE

The evolution and diversification of GRC roles necessitate a comprehensive skill set that goes beyond traditional boundaries. Modern GRC professionals should possess a combination of technical expertise, strategic thinking, and interpersonal skills. Key competencies include:

REGULATORY INTELLIGENCE:

The ability to stay updated on regulatory changes and interpret their implications for the organization.

RISK ASSESSMENT AND MANAGEMENT:

Proficiency in identifying, assessing, and managing risks across various domains, including operational, financial, and cybersecurity.

ETHICAL DECISION-MAKING:

A strong ethical compass to guide decision-making processes, ensuring alignment with organizational values and principles.

DATA ANALYTICS AND TECHNOLOGY PROFICIENCY:

Familiarity with data analytics tools, cybersecurity technologies, and the capacity to leverage emerging technologies for GRC optimization.

COMMUNICATION AND COLLABORATION:

Strong communication skills to articulate complex GRC concepts to diverse stakeholders and foster collaboration across departments.

STRATEGIC THINKING:

The ability to align GRC initiatives with overarching business strategies and contribute to organizational resilience and performance.

ADAPTABILITY AND CONTINUOUS LEARNING:

A mindset of adaptability and a commitment to continuous learning to keep pace with the evolving GRC landscape.

LEADERSHIP AND INFLUENCING SKILLS:

Leadership qualities to drive a culture of compliance, risk awareness, and ethical conduct throughout the organization.

LEGAL AND REGULATORY EXPERTISE:

In-depth knowledge of relevant laws, regulations, and industry standards that impact the organization's GRC framework.

PROBLEM-SOLVING AND CRITICAL THINKING:

The ability to analyze complex situations, identify root causes, and develop effective solutions to mitigate risks and enhance governance practices.

CRISIS MANAGEMENT:

Proficiency in developing and implementing crisis management strategies, ensuring organizational resilience in the face of unexpected challenges.

AUDIT AND ASSURANCE SKILLS:

Familiarity with audit processes and assurance methodologies to evaluate the effectiveness of GRC initiatives.

Modern GRC professionals, equipped with this diverse skill set, play a pivotal role in steering organizations through the complexities of the contemporary business environment. As GRC roles continue to evolve, the demand for professionals who can integrate risk-aware decision-making with strategic business objectives is set to grow, reinforcing the importance of a multidimensional skill set in this dynamic field.

12.3 Understanding the Specific Training Needs of Professionals in GRC Roles

Understanding the training needs of professionals in Governance, Risk, and Compliance (GRC) roles is a crucial step in developing effective and targeted training programs. GRC professionals operate in a dynamic and multifaceted environment, where the landscape of regulations, risks, and governance practices continually evolves. To tailor training initiatives that address their specific needs, it's essential to follow a systematic process:

ROLE ANALYSIS:

Conduct a detailed analysis of different GRC roles within the organization. Identify specific responsibilities, required skills, and the level of expertise expected for each role, whether it be in compliance, risk management, or governance.

SKILL ASSESSMENT:

Evaluate the existing skill set of GRC professionals. This assessment should cover technical skills, such as knowledge of relevant laws and regulations, as well as soft skills like communication, leadership, and critical thinking.

REGULATORY LANDSCAPE:

Stay abreast of the ever-changing regulatory environment. Understand the intricacies of the laws and standards relevant to the industry and the organization. This knowledge is foundational for compliance training needs.

RISK PROFILE:

Analyze the risk profile of the organization. Identify the types of risks it faces, whether operational, financial, or strategic. Tailor training to address the specific risk management needs associated with the organization's risk landscape.

TECHNOLOGY PROFICIENCY:

Assess the technological tools and platforms used in GRC processes. Ensure that professionals are proficient in the use of technology, data analytics, and any specialized software relevant to their roles.

ETHICAL CONSIDERATIONS:

Acknowledge the importance of ethical considerations in GRC roles. Identify training needs related to ethical decision-making, integrity, and fostering a culture of compliance and ethical conduct within the organization.

CONTINUOUS LEARNING:

Recognize the need for continuous learning in the GRC field. GRC professionals should be equipped with the ability to adapt to changes, stay informed about industry trends, and continuously enhance their knowledge and skills.

12.4 CONDUCTING A THOROUGH ANALYSIS TO TAILOR TRAINING PROGRAMS TO ORGANIZATIONAL REQUIREMENTS

Once the specific training needs of GRC professionals are identified, the next step involves conducting a thorough analysis to tailor training programs to organizational requirements. This process ensures that training initiatives align with the strategic objectives and unique characteristics of the organization:

ALIGNMENT WITH ORGANIZATIONAL GOALS:

Understand the overarching goals and objectives of the organization. Tailor training programs to directly contribute to these goals, ensuring that GRC professionals are equipped to support the organization's mission and strategy.

CUSTOMIZATION FOR ORGANIZATIONAL CULTURE:

Consider the organizational culture and values. Customizing training programs to align with the organization's culture helps in creating a cohesive approach to GRC that resonates with employees.

INTEGRATION WITH EXISTING PROCESSES:

Identify how GRC training can seamlessly integrate with existing organizational processes. This integration ensures that the training is practical, relevant, and applicable to day-to-day operations.

FEEDBACK FROM STAKEHOLDERS:

Seek feedback from key stakeholders, including executives, managers, and GRC professionals themselves. Understanding their perspectives and expectations helps in tailoring training programs to meet the specific needs and preferences of different stakeholders.

RISK-BASED TRAINING:

Prioritize training based on the organization's risk profile. Focus on areas that pose the highest risks and vulnerabilities. This risk-based approach ensures that training efforts are directed towards mitigating the most significant threats.

MEASUREMENT AND EVALUATION CRITERIA:

Establish clear criteria for measuring the effectiveness of training programs. Define key performance indicators (KPIs) and evaluation methods to assess the impact of training on GRC competencies and organizational outcomes.

FLEXIBILITY AND ADAPTABILITY:

Design training programs with flexibility and adaptability in mind. The GRC landscape is dynamic, and training initiatives should be responsive to changes in regulations, risks, and industry best practices.

INCORPORATION OF CASE STUDIES AND PRACTICAL SCENARIOS:

Integrate real-world case studies and practical scenarios into training programs. This hands-on approach allows GRC professionals to apply their knowledge in simulated situations, enhancing the practicality of the training.

By conducting a thorough analysis and aligning training programs with both the specific needs of GRC professionals and the organizational context, organizations can ensure that their training initiatives are targeted, effective, and contribute meaningfully to the organization's overall success in navigating the complexities of GRC.

12.5 Developing a Structured Curriculum that Covers Essential GRC Topics

Developing a structured curriculum is foundational to delivering effective Governance, Risk, and Compliance (GRC) training. A well-designed curriculum ensures that GRC professionals receive a comprehensive understanding of essential topics. Here's how to approach the development of such a curriculum:

Identifying Core GRC Domains: Begin by identifying the core domains within GRC, including governance principles, risk management methodologies, and compliance frameworks. This comprehensive approach ensures that professionals gain a holistic understanding of the interconnected nature of GRC.

Defining Learning Objectives: Clearly define learning objectives for each module within the curriculum. These objectives should be specific, measurable, achievable, relevant, and time-bound (SMART). They provide a roadmap for what participants should achieve by the end of each module.

Sequencing Topics: Sequence topics logically to build a structured progression of learning. Start with foundational concepts before progressing to more complex subjects. This sequential arrangement aids in the gradual development of knowledge and skills.

Incorporating Legal and Regulatory Components: Integrate modules that cover legal and regulatory aspects relevant to the industry and organization. Understanding compliance requirements is crucial for GRC professionals, and a dedicated segment of the curriculum should address these components.

Adopting a Risk-Based Approach: Emphasize a risk-based approach by dedicating modules to risk identification, assessment, and mitigation. Provide practical insights into risk management strategies and best practices.

Addressing Ethical Governance: Devote segments to ethical considerations and governance principles. Explore case studies and scenarios that highlight the importance of ethical decision-making and its role in effective governance.

Promoting Continuous Learning: Include elements in the curriculum that foster a culture of continuous learning. Encourage participants to stay updated on emerging trends, technologies, and regulatory changes beyond the formal training program.

12.6 Incorporating Case Studies, Simulations, and Practical Exercises for Hands-on Learning

Case studies, simulations, and practical exercises enhance hands-on learning experiences, allowing GRC professionals to apply theoretical knowledge to real-world scenarios. Here's how to incorporate these elements effectively:

REAL-WORLD CASE STUDIES:

Integrate real-world case studies that reflect diverse GRC challenges. These cases provide practical insights into the application of GRC principles in different organizational contexts.

Simulations of GRC Scenarios: Develop interactive simulations that replicate GRC scenarios. This approach allows participants to navigate simulated situations, make decisions, and observe the consequences of their actions in a controlled environment.

Practical Exercises and Group Activities: Include practical exercises and group activities that require collaboration and problem-solving. These exercises can range from risk assessments to compliance audits, providing participants with hands-on experience.

Scenario-Based Learning: Structure learning modules around realistic scenarios. Participants can analyze, strategize, and make decisions based on these scenarios, mirroring the challenges they might encounter in their roles.

Interactive Workshops: Conduct interactive workshops where participants engage in discussions, share experiences, and collectively problem-solve. This fosters a collaborative learning environment and allows for the exchange of best practices.

Feedback and Reflection Sessions: Incorporate regular feedback and reflection sessions where participants can discuss their experiences, challenges faced, and lessons learned. This iterative process enhances the learning journey.

INTEGRATING TECHNOLOGY FOR INTERACTIVE AND ENGAGING TRAINING EXPERIENCES

Leveraging technology enhances the interactivity and engagement of GRC training programs. Here's how to integrate technology effectively:

E-Learning Platforms: Utilize e-learning platforms that offer flexibility and accessibility. These platforms can host interactive modules, assessments, and resources that participants can access at their convenience.

Virtual Reality (VR) and Augmented Reality (AR): Explore the use of VR and AR for immersive learning experiences. Simulations and virtual environments can provide a realistic setting for GRC professionals to practice their skills.

Online Collaborative Tools: Implement online collaborative tools for group activities and discussions. These tools facilitate real-time collaboration, enabling participants to work together irrespective of geographical locations.

Webinars and Virtual Conferences: Conduct webinars and virtual conferences featuring industry experts and thought leaders. These platforms provide opportunities for participants to engage with experts, ask questions, and stay informed about the latest trends.

Interactive Multimedia Content: Develop interactive multimedia content, including videos, animations, and infographics. Visual and interactive elements enhance engagement and retention of complex GRC concepts.

Gamification Elements: Introduce gamification elements to make learning more enjoyable. Incorporate quizzes, challenges, and badges to create a competitive yet supportive learning environment.

Learning Management Systems (LMS): Implement a robust Learning Management System (LMS) to organize, deliver, and track training materials. An LMS ensures a structured and streamlined learning experience.

By combining a structured curriculum with hands-on learning experiences and leveraging technology, organizations can provide GRC professionals with a well-rounded and engaging training program. This approach not only enhances knowledge retention but also equips professionals with practical skills that can be directly applied in their GRC roles.

12.7.1 Tailoring Training Programs to Address Regulatory Compliance Intricacies

Tailoring training programs to address the intricacies of regulatory compliance is essential for ensuring that professionals are equipped to navigate the complex and ever-evolving landscape of laws and standards. Regulatory compliance, a cornerstone of Governance, Risk, and Compliance (GRC), requires a targeted and comprehensive approach in training.

Here's how organizations can tailor their programs to meet these specific needs:

a. Identifying Industry-Specific Regulations: Begin by identifying the industry-specific regulations that govern the organization. Different sectors have unique compliance requirements, and understanding these specific regulations is crucial for targeted training.

b. Customizing Content for Regulatory Diversity: Customize training content to reflect the diversity of regulatory requirements. Tailor modules to address regional, national, and international regulations that impact the organization's operations.

c. Incorporating Case Studies and Scenarios: Integrate case studies and scenarios that simulate real-world compliance challenges. These practical exercises allow professionals to apply theoretical knowledge to situations they may encounter in their roles.

d. Addressing Compliance Risk Profiles: Assess the organization's compliance risk profile to identify areas of heightened risk. Prioritize training modules based on the criticality and complexity of compliance requirements in these risk-prone areas.

e. Interactive Workshops with Compliance Experts: Conduct interactive workshops with compliance experts. Engage professionals in discussions, Q&A sessions, and collaborative problem-solving to deepen their understanding of intricate compliance nuances.

f. Continuous Updates on Regulatory Changes: Establish mechanisms for providing continuous updates on regulatory changes. Compliance standards evolve, and professionals need to stay informed about amendments, new regulations, and enforcement trends.

g. Simulated Audits and Assessments: Simulate compliance audits and assessments as part of the training. This hands-on approach allows professionals to practice compliance procedures, identify gaps, and understand the audit process.

h. Tailored Training for High-Risk Areas: Identify high-risk areas within the organization and tailor specialized training for professionals operating in these critical zones. This targeted approach ensures that those dealing with the most complex compliance issues receive specific guidance.

i.   Ensuring Professionals are Well-Versed in Latest Compliance Standards and Regulations: Ensuring that professionals are well-versed in the latest compliance standards and regulations requires a proactive and continuous effort.

HERE'S HOW ORGANIZATIONS CAN ACHIEVE THIS GOAL:

Regular Training Updates: Implement regular training updates to cover new compliance standards and regulations. This ongoing education ensures that professionals stay current with the latest requirements impacting their roles.

Access to Regulatory Resources: Provide professionals with access to a repository of regulatory resources. This can include databases, online portals, and subscriptions to regulatory publications that keep them informed about changes in compliance standards.

Mandatory Continuing Education: Establish a culture of mandatory continuing education for professionals in GRC roles. This may involve periodic assessments, refresher courses, and certifications to validate their knowledge of the latest compliance standards.

Industry Networking and Forums: Encourage participation in industry networking events, forums, and conferences. These platforms provide opportunities for professionals to interact with regulatory experts, exchange insights, and gain exposure to emerging compliance trends.

Collaboration with Regulatory Bodies: Foster collaboration with regulatory bodies relevant to the industry. This can involve partnerships, memberships, or participation in working groups, ensuring that professionals have direct access to regulatory insights.

Regular Compliance Briefings: Conduct regular compliance briefings within the organization. These briefings can be led by internal compliance experts or external consultants, providing a platform for professionals to receive targeted updates on the latest standards.

Utilizing Technology for Compliance Tracking: Leverage technology for compliance tracking and monitoring. Implement systems that automatically update professionals on changes in compliance standards and prompt them to undergo relevant training modules.

Benchmarking Against Industry Best Practices: Benchmark the organization against industry best practices in compliance. This involves continuous assessment, benchmarking against peers, and adopting leading-edge compliance strategies.

By tailoring training programs to address regulatory compliance intricacies and ensuring that professionals stay well-versed in the latest standards, organizations can build a compliance-ready workforce. This approach not only mitigates compliance risks but also contributes to the overall effectiveness of the GRC framework within the organization.

12.8 Risk Management Training: Building Resilience

Risk management training is a critical component of developing a resilient organization. By focusing on risk identification, assessment, and mitigation strategies, and providing scenario-based training to enhance decision-making in risk-prone situations, organizations can empower their teams to navigate uncertainties effectively.

1. **Risk Identification:**

   Importance of Awareness: Start by emphasizing the importance of awareness in risk identification. Train individuals to recognize both internal and external factors that could impact the organization's objectives. This includes financial, operational, strategic, and compliance risks.

Early Warning Signs: Provide guidance on recognizing early warning signs of potential risks. This could involve changes in industry trends, emerging technologies, geopolitical shifts, or internal operational shifts.

Cultivate a Risk-Aware Culture: Foster a risk-aware culture where all employees understand their role in identifying and reporting potential risks. This culture encourages open communication and ensures that risks are not only identified at the top level but throughout the organization.

2. Risk Assessment:

Quantitative and Qualitative Assessment: Train individuals in both quantitative and qualitative methods of risk assessment. This includes financial modeling for quantitative analysis and scenario analysis for qualitative understanding.

Impact and Probability Analysis: Teach the analysis of risks based on their potential impact and probability of occurrence. This allows for the prioritization of risks and efficient allocation of resources for mitigation.

Risk Heat Maps: Introduce the use of risk heat maps to visually represent the magnitude and distribution of risks. This tool aids in creating a comprehensive overview that is easily understandable for stakeholders at all levels.

3. Mitigation Strategies:

Developing Mitigation Plans: Train teams to develop robust mitigation plans that address identified risks. This involves understanding the root causes of risks and designing strategies that reduce the likelihood of occurrence or minimize the impact.

Risk Transfer and Acceptance: Educate individuals on the concepts of risk transfer and risk acceptance. Understanding when to transfer risk through insurance or contracts and when to accept certain risks is crucial in effective risk management.

Continuous Monitoring: Emphasize the importance of continuous monitoring and adjustment of mitigation strategies. Risks evolve, and an effective risk management plan should be dynamic, adapting to changing circumstances.

4. **Scenario-Based Training:**

Realistic Simulations: Provide scenario-based training through realistic simulations. Simulations allow individuals to practice their decision-making skills in a controlled environment, mirroring the complexities of real-world situations.

Cross-Functional Collaboration: Develop scenarios that require cross-functional collaboration. This promotes a holistic understanding of risks and encourages different departments to work together in mitigating potential threats.

Learning from Past Incidents: Incorporate case studies from past incidents into training scenarios. Analyzing real-life situations enhances the practical application of risk management principles.

5. **Decision-Making in Risk-Prone Situations:**

Balancing Risks and Rewards: Train individuals to balance risks and rewards in decision-making. This involves considering the potential benefits against the associated risks and making informed choices that align with organizational objectives.

Communication Skills: Enhance communication skills in the context of risk management. Being able to articulate risks, mitigation strategies, and potential impacts is essential for effective decision-making and collaboration.

Ethical Considerations: Discuss ethical considerations in decision-making, especially in situations where risk management may involve difficult choices. This ensures that decisions align with the organization's values and principles.

By integrating these elements into risk management training, organizations can build a resilient workforce capable of identifying, assessing, and mitigating risks effectively. This proactive approach not only safeguards the organization against potential threats but also fosters a culture of continuous improvement and adaptability in the face of uncertainties.

12.9 GOVERNANCE TRAINING: CULTIVATING ETHICAL LEADERSHIP

Governance training is a pivotal component in shaping ethical leadership within Governance, Risk, and Compliance (GRC) roles. By developing programs that emphasize the principles of good governance and instilling ethical decision-making and responsible leadership in GRC professionals, organizations can foster a culture of integrity and excellence. Here's how to approach this training:

1. **Developing Programs Emphasizing Principles of Good Governance:**

   Understanding Governance Fundamentals: Begin with a thorough understanding of governance fundamentals. This includes the roles and responsibilities of governing bodies, the importance of transparency, accountability, and the overall framework that guides decision-making.

   Legal and Regulatory Compliance: Incorporate modules on legal and regulatory compliance within the governance context. This ensures that professionals are well-versed in the laws and standards that govern organizational conduct, preventing legal pitfalls.

   Board Effectiveness and Dynamics: Provide insights into board effectiveness and dynamics. This involves understanding the structure of the board, effective communication within the board, and strategies for enhancing board performance.

Stakeholder Engagement: Emphasize the significance of stakeholder engagement in governance. This includes training on effective communication with stakeholders, addressing their concerns, and incorporating their perspectives into decision-making processes.

Risk Governance: Integrate risk governance principles into the training. This involves understanding how governance practices intersect with risk management strategies and ensuring that governance structures are resilient in the face of uncertainties.

2. **Instilling Ethical Decision-Making and Responsible Leadership:**

Ethical Decision-Making Frameworks: Introduce ethical decision-making frameworks. Train GRC professionals on models such as consequentialist, deontological, and virtue ethics, providing tools for analyzing ethical dilemmas and making principled decisions.

Case Studies in Ethical Leadership: Incorporate case studies that highlight instances of ethical leadership. Analyzing real-world examples allows professionals to learn from both positive and negative ethical leadership experiences.

Integrity in Decision-Making: Emphasize the role of integrity in decision-making. Train professionals to prioritize honesty, transparency, and fairness in their actions, aligning their decisions with organizational values and ethical standards.

Responsible Leadership: Cultivate responsible leadership qualities. This involves understanding the impact of decisions on various stakeholders, taking a long-term perspective, and considering the social and environmental responsibilities of the organization.

Navigating Ethical Dilemmas: Provide tools for navigating ethical dilemmas. Ethical scenarios and role-playing exercises help GRC professionals develop the skills needed to address complex situations where ethical considerations are paramount.

3. **Integrating Practical Exercises and Continuous Learning:**

    Interactive Workshops: Conduct interactive workshops that involve group discussions, problem-solving exercises, and collaborative decision-making. This promotes engagement and allows professionals to learn from each other's perspectives.

    Continuous Learning Platforms: Establish continuous learning platforms. These can include webinars, forums, and other online resources that enable GRC professionals to stay updated on evolving governance principles, ethical standards, and industry best practices.

    Feedback and Reflection Sessions: Incorporate feedback and reflection sessions. These sessions allow professionals to discuss their experiences, challenges faced, and lessons learned, fostering a culture of continuous improvement.

    Scenario-Based Learning: Develop scenario-based learning modules that require GRC professionals to apply governance and ethical principles in simulated situations. This hands-on approach enhances the practical application of theoretical knowledge.

4. **Leadership Development and Mentoring:**

    Leadership Development Programs: Implement leadership development programs that specifically focus on GRC professionals. These programs can include mentorship opportunities, leadership training, and exposure to executive decision-making processes.

    Mentorship and Coaching: Pair GRC professionals with mentors who exemplify ethical leadership. Mentorship provides a platform for guidance, support, and the transfer of leadership values from experienced leaders to emerging professionals.

Leadership Assessments: Conduct leadership assessments to identify strengths and areas for development. This personalized approach allows GRC professionals to receive targeted training that aligns with their leadership goals.

Succession Planning: Integrate succession planning into leadership development. Ensure that there is a pipeline of ethical leaders within the GRC function, ready to take on increased responsibilities and contribute to organizational success.

By strategically combining governance training with a focus on ethical leadership, organizations can cultivate a GRC workforce that not only understands the principles of good governance but also embodies ethical decision-making and responsible leadership. This approach contributes to the establishment of a resilient and ethically-driven organizational culture, ensuring sustained success in the complex and dynamic business environment.

12.9.1 Technology and Tools Training for GRC Professionals

In the modern landscape of Governance, Risk, and Compliance (GRC), technology plays a pivotal role in enhancing efficiency, mitigating risks, and ensuring compliance. Training GRC professionals in digital literacy, GRC software, analytics tools, and emerging technologies is essential to equip them with the skills needed to navigate the complexities of the digital age.

Here's how organizations can approach technology and tools training for GRC professionals:

1. **Exploring the Role of Technology in GRC:**

   Digital Transformation Overview: Begin with an overview of the digital transformation landscape. Help GRC professionals understand the broader context of how technology is reshaping the business environment and influencing GRC practices.

   Impact on Governance, Risk, and Compliance: Explore the specific impact of technology on governance, risk management, and compliance. Discuss how digital tools can streamline processes, enhance data accuracy, and improve decision-making within the GRC framework.

   Importance of Data and Analytics: Emphasize the importance of data and analytics in GRC. Discuss how data-driven insights can empower professionals to make informed decisions, identify emerging risks, and optimize compliance strategies.

   Integration of Technology with GRC Practices: Illustrate how technology integrates with various GRC practices, including policy management, risk assessments, compliance monitoring, and incident response. Highlight practical examples of successful technology integration in GRC.

2. **Need for Digital Literacy in GRC:**

   Digital Literacy Fundamentals:

   Provide foundational training on digital literacy. Ensure that GRC professionals have a solid understanding of basic digital concepts, terminologies, and the overall digital landscape.

   Cybersecurity Awareness:

   Integrate cybersecurity awareness into digital literacy training. GRC professionals should be aware of cybersecurity threats and best practices to safeguard sensitive information.

Adapting to Technological Change:

Train professionals to adapt to technological changes. This includes staying current with software updates, understanding new tools, and embracing a mindset of continuous learning in the ever-evolving digital environment.

3. **Training on GRC Software and Analytics Tools:**

Introduction to GRC Software:

Familiarize GRC professionals with GRC software solutions available in the market. Provide an overview of their functionalities and how they can be customized to meet organizational needs.

Hands-On Training:

Conduct hands-on training sessions on GRC software. Allow professionals to navigate through the software interface, input data, generate reports, and simulate real-world scenarios to reinforce their learning.

Analytics Tools for Risk Management:

Introduce analytics tools for risk management. Train professionals to use data analytics to identify patterns, assess risk probabilities, and enhance predictive modeling for more effective risk management.

Compliance Monitoring Tools:

Train on tools for compliance monitoring. Showcase how these tools can automate compliance tracking, provide real-time updates on regulatory changes, and facilitate reporting for auditing purposes.

4. **Emerging Technologies Shaping the Field:**

Introduction to Emerging Technologies:

Explore emerging technologies shaping the GRC field. This may include artificial intelligence, machine learning, blockchain, and robotic process automation. Discuss their potential applications and impact on GRC practices.

Case Studies and Use Cases:

Provide case studies and use cases highlighting the successful implementation of emerging technologies in GRC. Illustrate how organizations have leveraged these technologies to enhance efficiency, accuracy, and agility in GRC processes.

Interactive Sessions with Tech Experts:

Facilitate interactive sessions with technology experts. Allow GRC professionals to engage with experts who can provide insights into the practical applications of emerging technologies in GRC.

Preparing for Future Technological Trends:

Encourage professionals to stay informed about future technological trends. Discuss how anticipating and preparing for these trends is crucial for maintaining a proactive and resilient GRC framework.

5. **Integration of Technology Training into Continuous Learning:**

Continuous Learning Platforms:

Integrate technology training into continuous learning platforms. Provide online courses, webinars, and forums where GRC professionals can access resources and stay updated on the latest technological advancements.

Certifications in Technology and Tools:

Offer certifications in technology and tools. Recognize and reward professionals who demonstrate proficiency in utilizing GRC software, analytics tools, and emerging technologies.

Feedback Mechanisms:

Establish feedback mechanisms to gather insights on the effectiveness of technology training. Regularly assess the impact of the training programs and use feedback to refine and enhance future training initiatives.

By investing in comprehensive technology and tools training, organizations can ensure that their GRC professionals are well-equipped to harness the potential of digital advancements. This not only enhances the efficiency of GRC processes but also contributes to the organization's overall resilience in an increasingly digitized business environment.

12.9.2 Encouraging a Culture of Continuous Learning within the Organization

Fostering a culture of continuous learning within the organization is crucial, especially in the dynamic field of Governance, Risk, and Compliance (GRC). This culture not only empowers GRC professionals to stay abreast of industry developments but also enhances adaptability and innovation. Here's how organizations can encourage continuous learning:

1. **Leadership Endorsement:**

   Setting the Tone from the Top: Leadership should actively endorse and participate in continuous learning. When leadership prioritizes learning, it sends a clear message that ongoing development is integral to the organization's success.

Leading by Example: Leaders should lead by example. Demonstrating a commitment to learning through participation in training programs, certifications, and skill development initiatives encourages others to follow suit.

2. **Establishing Learning Culture:**

Communication and Awareness: Clearly communicate the importance of continuous learning. Create awareness campaigns, internal communications, and workshops to highlight how learning contributes to individual growth and organizational success.

Recognizing and Celebrating Learning Achievements: Establish a system to recognize and celebrate learning achievements. This can include internal awards, acknowledgment in company newsletters, or public recognition during team meetings.

Making Learning Resources Accessible: Provide easy access to learning resources. Establish a centralized learning management system (LMS) where employees can find courses, webinars, and other educational materials relevant to GRC.

3. **Ongoing Professional Development in GRC:**

Tailored Training Programs: Develop tailored training programs specific to GRC. These can cover areas such as regulatory changes, emerging technologies, risk management methodologies, and ethical governance practices.

Certifications and Accreditation: Encourage GRC professionals to pursue relevant certifications and accreditations. This not only enhances their knowledge but also adds credibility to their expert.

Industry Conferences and Seminars: Support attendance at industry conferences and seminars. These events provide opportunities to learn from experts, stay informed about industry trends, and network with peers.

Professional Memberships: Encourage membership in professional organizations related to GRC. Membership often comes with access to resources, networking events, and forums for continuous learning.

4. **Flexibility and Autonomy:**

Flexible Learning Paths: Offer flexibility in learning paths. Recognize that individuals have different learning preferences and provide options such as online courses, workshops, mentorship programs, and self-directed learning.

Encouraging Personal Development Plans: Encourage employees to create personal development plans. This involves setting individual learning goals, identifying areas for improvement, and planning a roadmap for achieving those objectives.

Time and Resources Allocation: Allocate dedicated time and resources for learning. This may include designated learning hours, budget for external courses, or support for higher education and advanced degrees.

5. **Collaborative Learning:**

Internal Knowledge Sharing: Facilitate internal knowledge sharing. Encourage GRC professionals to share insights, case studies, and best practices through regular team meetings, forums, or collaborative platforms.

Cross-Functional Learning Initiatives: Promote cross-functional learning initiatives. Encourage collaboration between different departments, allowing employees to learn from colleagues with diverse expertise.

Mentorship and Peer Learning: Establish mentorship programs and peer learning circles. Pairing less experienced employees with seasoned professionals creates a supportive learning environment.

6. **Continuous Evaluation and Feedback:**

Feedback Mechanisms: Implement feedback mechanisms for learning programs. Regularly gather input from participants to understand the effectiveness of training initiatives and make improvements based on their feedback.

Performance Reviews with Learning Goals: Integrate learning goals into performance reviews. Align individual learning achievements with career development plans, reinforcing the connection between continuous learning and career progression.

Adapting to Changing Needs: Be adaptable in learning initiatives. As GRC requirements evolve, ensure that the organization's learning programs are agile and responsive to changing needs.

Encouraging a culture of continuous learning is an investment in the organization's long-term success. In the dynamic field of GRC, where staying informed is critical, fostering a commitment to ongoing professional development ensures that the workforce remains agile, innovative, and well-prepared to meet evolving challenges.

12.9.3 EMBRACING E-LEARNING PLATFORMS FOR FLEXIBLE AND ACCESSIBLE TRAINING

In the realm of Governance, Risk, and Compliance (GRC), embracing e-learning platforms offers organizations the opportunity to provide flexible and accessible training solutions. E-learning has become a cornerstone in modern education and professional development, offering a range of benefits for GRC professionals and organizations alike.

12.9.4 Benefits of Online Courses, Webinars, and Virtual Training Environments

1. **Flexibility and Accessibility:**

Anytime, Anywhere Learning:

E-learning platforms enable GRC professionals to access training materials at their convenience, breaking the constraints of traditional schedules. This flexibility allows individuals to engage in learning activities from anywhere in the world.

Self-Paced Learning:

Online courses and webinars often allow for self-paced learning. This accommodates individuals with varying learning speeds, ensuring a personalized approach to knowledge acquisition.

Reduced Geographic Barriers:

Virtual training environments eliminate geographic barriers. GRC professionals, regardless of their location, can participate in training programs without the need for extensive travel, making education more inclusive.

2. **Cost-Effective Solutions:**

Reduced Travel Expenses:

Online courses and virtual training environments eliminate the need for travel. This not only reduces expenses associated with transportation and accommodation but also minimizes time away from work.

Scalable Training Programs:

E-learning platforms offer scalable solutions. Organizations can efficiently train a large number of GRC professionals simultaneously without incurring significant costs associated with physical classrooms and materials.

3. **Diverse Learning Materials:**

Multimedia Integration:

E-learning platforms often incorporate multimedia elements. This includes videos, interactive simulations, and engaging graphics that cater to diverse learning styles, enhancing the overall learning experience.

Rich Content Library:

Virtual training environments provide access to a rich content library. GRC professionals can access a wide array of resources, from regulatory documents and case studies to interactive modules, enhancing the depth and breadth of their knowledge.

4. **Real-time Updates and Interactivity:**

Timely Updates:

Online courses and webinars can be updated in real-time to reflect changes in regulations, industry standards, or best practices. This ensures that GRC professionals are consistently provided with the most current information.

Interactive Learning Modules:

Virtual training environments often include interactive elements. This interactivity, such as quizzes, discussions, and real-world simulations, engages learners actively, reinforcing their understanding of GRC concepts.

5. **Tracking and Assessments:**

Progress Tracking:

E-learning platforms provide robust tracking mechanisms. Organizations can monitor the progress of GRC professionals, ensuring that individuals complete required training modules and identifying areas for improvement.

Assessment Tools:

Virtual training environments often include assessment tools. These tools enable organizations to evaluate the comprehension and application of GRC knowledge, facilitating a more targeted approach to further training.

6. **Customization for Organizational Needs:**

Tailored Training Programs:

E-learning platforms allow organizations to customize training programs based on their specific GRC needs. This ensures that training aligns with the organization's unique challenges, goals, and compliance requirements.

Adaptability to Skill Levels:

Virtual training environments can be adapted to different skill levels. Whether it's foundational courses for newcomers or advanced modules for experienced professionals, customization supports a diverse workforce.

7. **Sustainable and Environmentally Friendly:**

Reduced Carbon Footprint:

By eliminating the need for travel and printed materials, e-learning contributes to environmental sustainability. Organizations embracing virtual training environments align with eco-friendly practices, reducing their carbon footprint.

Paperless Learning:

E-learning platforms promote a paperless learning environment. This not only saves resources but also aligns with modern sustainability goals.

Embracing e-learning platforms for GRC training provides a strategic advantage for organizations seeking flexible, cost-effective, and impactful solutions. The benefits of online courses, webinars, and virtual training environments extend beyond traditional methods, offering a dynamic and adaptive approach to continuous professional development.

12.9.5 Implementing Metrics and Key Performance Indicators (KPIs) to Measure Training Success

In the context of Governance, Risk, and Compliance (GRC) training programs, measuring success is paramount. Implementing metrics and Key Performance Indicators (KPIs) provides organizations with valuable insights into the effectiveness of their training initiatives.

Here's how to establish a robust framework for measuring training success:

1. **Define Clear Objectives:**

   Identify Training Objectives: Clearly define the objectives of the GRC training program. These objectives should align with organizational goals and the specific skills and knowledge areas targeted by the training.

   Quantifiable Goals: Ensure that training objectives are quantifiable. This allows for the creation of measurable metrics that directly reflect the achievement of these goals.

2. **Select Relevant Metrics and KPIs:**

   Completion Rates: Measure the percentage of GRC professionals who successfully complete the training program. This provides an initial assessment of program engagement.

   Knowledge Retention: Assess knowledge retention through pre- and post-training assessments. Evaluate how much information GRC professionals have gained and retained after completing the training.

   Application of Learning: Track the application of learning in real-world scenarios. This can be measured through case studies, simulations, or on-the-job performance evaluations.

Time-to-Competency: Measure the time it takes for GRC professionals to reach a level of competency after completing the training. A shorter time-to-competency indicates more efficient learning.

3. **Utilize Learning Analytics:**

    User Engagement Analytics: Monitor user engagement within e-learning platforms. Track how frequently GRC professionals access training materials, participate in discussions, and interact with course content.

    Assessment Performance: Analyze individual performance in assessments. Identify trends in performance to understand which areas may require additional focus or clarification.

    Progress Tracking: Use learning analytics to track the progress of each participant throughout the training program. This provides a comprehensive view of individual and collective advancements.

4. **Gather Feedback:**

    Participant Surveys: Conduct surveys to gather feedback from GRC professionals. These surveys should assess the relevance of the training content, the effectiveness of delivery methods, and overall satisfaction.

    Feedback Sessions: Organize feedback sessions where participants can share their experiences and insights. Open dialogue allows for a more in-depth understanding of the strengths and areas for improvement in the training program.

    Peer Reviews: Implement peer review mechanisms where participants can provide constructive feedback to their colleagues. Peer insights offer a unique perspective on the impact of training on real-world performance.

5. **Adapt Training Strategies:**

Continuous Improvement Cycle:

Establish a continuous improvement cycle for training programs. Regularly review feedback, assess metrics, and identify areas for enhancement.

Dynamic Content Updates:

Use feedback to make dynamic updates to training content. If certain modules are consistently challenging for participants, consider revising or adding supplementary materials.

Personalized Learning Paths:

Leverage feedback to personalize learning paths. Identify areas where participants may need additional resources or alternative approaches to meet their unique learning needs.

6. **Align with Organizational Goals:**

Link to Organizational KPIs:

Align training metrics and KPIs with broader organizational KPIs. Demonstrating how training contributes to organizational success reinforces the value of continuous learning.

Strategic Impact Assessment:

Assess the strategic impact of training programs on GRC objectives. Measure how well the training aligns with and contributes to the organization's strategic goals.

7. **Regularly Review and Report:**

Scheduled Reviews:

Schedule regular reviews of training metrics and KPIs. This ensures that the organization stays proactive in adapting to evolving needs and industry trends.

Report Generation:

Generate comprehensive reports that highlight key findings from the metrics and KPI assessments. Share these reports with relevant stakeholders, including leadership, to maintain transparency and support decision-making.

Implementing metrics and KPIs for GRC training programs is an integral part of a continuous improvement strategy. By regularly assessing the success of training initiatives, organizations can refine their approaches, address emerging challenges, and cultivate a culture of continuous learning and improvement within the GRC domain.

12.9.6 ANTICIPATING EMERGING TRENDS IN GRC EDUCATION AND SKILLS DEVELOPMENT

As Governance, Risk, and Compliance (GRC) continue to evolve, so do the educational and skills development practices within the field. Anticipating emerging trends is crucial for staying ahead in preparing GRC professionals for the challenges of the future. Here are some trends to consider, taking into account the impact of technology, remote work, and evolving GRC practices on training methodologies:

1. **Integration of Technology in Training:**

   Virtual Reality (VR) and Augmented Reality (AR):

   Anticipate the integration of VR and AR technologies in GRC training. Simulations and immersive experiences can enhance practical understanding, especially in risk assessment and crisis management scenarios.

   AI-Powered Personalized Learning:

   AI algorithms will likely play a role in personalizing learning paths for GRC professionals. This ensures that individuals receive targeted training based on their specific needs, strengths, and areas for improvement.

Blockchain for Training Certifications:

Utilize blockchain technology for secure and transparent certification processes. This enhances the credibility of certifications in the GRC space and provides a tamper-proof record of an individual's training achievements.

2. **Remote and Flexible Learning:**

Hybrid Learning Models:

Expect the continued growth of hybrid learning models, combining both online and in-person elements. This accommodates diverse learning preferences and enables professionals to engage in training regardless of their location.

Mobile Learning Platforms:

Embrace mobile-friendly learning platforms. GRC professionals, often working remotely, can access training materials on their mobile devices, facilitating learning on-the-go and during flexible work hours.

Virtual Instructor-Led Training (VILT):

Expand the use of VILT to replicate the classroom experience in a virtual environment. This allows for real-time interaction, discussions, and engagement with trainers and peers, even in remote settings.

3. **Continuous Adaptive Learning:**

Microlearning Modules:

Shift towards microlearning modules. Short, focused bursts of content allow for continuous learning without disrupting daily work routines, catering to the attention spans and time constraints of busy professionals.

Adaptive Learning Platforms:

Implement adaptive learning platforms that adjust content based on individual progress and performance. This ensures that GRC professionals receive customized training experiences tailored to their evolving skill levels.

Gamification Elements:

Integrate gamification elements into training programs. Points, badges, and leaderboards can motivate learners and make the training experience more engaging, fostering a sense of competition and achievement.

12.9.7 ADDITIONAL RESOURCES

Continuous learning is essential for Governance, Risk, and Compliance (GRC) professionals to stay updated on industry trends, regulations, and best practices. Here are recommendations for further readings, courses, and resources to support their continuous learning journey:

i. **Books:**

Title: "Governance, Risk Management, and Compliance: It Can't Happen to Us - Avoiding Corporate Disaster While Driving Success"

Author: Leighton Johnson

Overview: This book provides insights into practical strategies for implementing effective GRC practices and avoiding common pitfalls.

Title: "The Basics of IT Audit: Purposes, Processes, and Practical Information"

Author: Stephen D. Gantz

Overview: A comprehensive guide that explores the fundamentals of IT audit, an integral component of GRC in the modern business landscape.

Title: "Enterprise Risk Management: Today's Leading Research and Best Practices for Tomorrow's Executives"

Author: John Fraser, Betty Simkins

Overview: This book delves into the latest research and best practices in enterprise risk management, providing valuable insights for GRC professionals.

ii. **Online Courses:**

Course: "Certified in Risk and Information Systems Control (CRISC)"

Provider: ISACA

Overview: This certification focuses on risk management and information systems control, providing GRC professionals with valuable skills in identifying and managing IT-related risks.

Course: "Certified Information Systems Security Professional (CISSP)"

Provider: (ISC)^2

Overview: CISSP is a globally recognized certification that covers various aspects of information security, contributing to a holistic understanding of risk management.

Course: "Advanced Risk Management"

Provider: Risk Management Society (RIMS)

Overview: This course offers advanced insights into risk management strategies, providing GRC professionals with practical knowledge for effective risk mitigation.

iii. Websites and Resources:

Website: Risk.net

Overview: Risk.net is a comprehensive platform that covers risk management news, articles, and insights. It's a valuable resource for staying updated on industry trends and emerging risks.

Website: Compliance Week

Overview: Compliance Week provides news, analysis, and resources on compliance-related topics. It offers insights into regulatory changes and best practices in compliance management.

Resource: Gartner's Risk Management Research

Overview: Gartner offers in-depth research reports and analysis on risk management trends. Accessing Gartner's research can provide GRC professionals with valuable strategic insights.

iv. Professional Organizations:

Organization: ISACA (Information Systems Audit and Control Association)

Overview: ISACA provides resources, certifications, and networking opportunities for GRC professionals. Membership offers access to a wealth of knowledge and a global community.

Organization: The Risk Management Society (RIMS)

Overview: RIMS is a leading professional organization dedicated to advancing risk management. It offers educational resources, events, and networking opportunities for GRC professionals.

Organization: The Institute of Internal Auditors (IIA)

Overview: IIA is a global organization focused on internal audit excellence. GRC professionals can benefit from IIA's resources, certifications, and industry insights.

v.   Journals and Publications:

Journal: "Journal of Risk Management in Financial Institutions"

Overview: This journal publishes research articles and case studies on risk management in financial institutions, providing insights relevant to GRC professionals.

Publication: "Compliance & Ethics Professional"

Overview: This publication by the Society of Corporate Compliance and Ethics (SCCE) covers topics related to compliance and ethics, offering practical insights and best practices.

Continuous learning in GRC involves a combination of theoretical knowledge, practical insights, and staying informed about industry developments. These recommended readings, courses, and resources provide a well-rounded approach to support GRC professionals in their continuous learning journey.

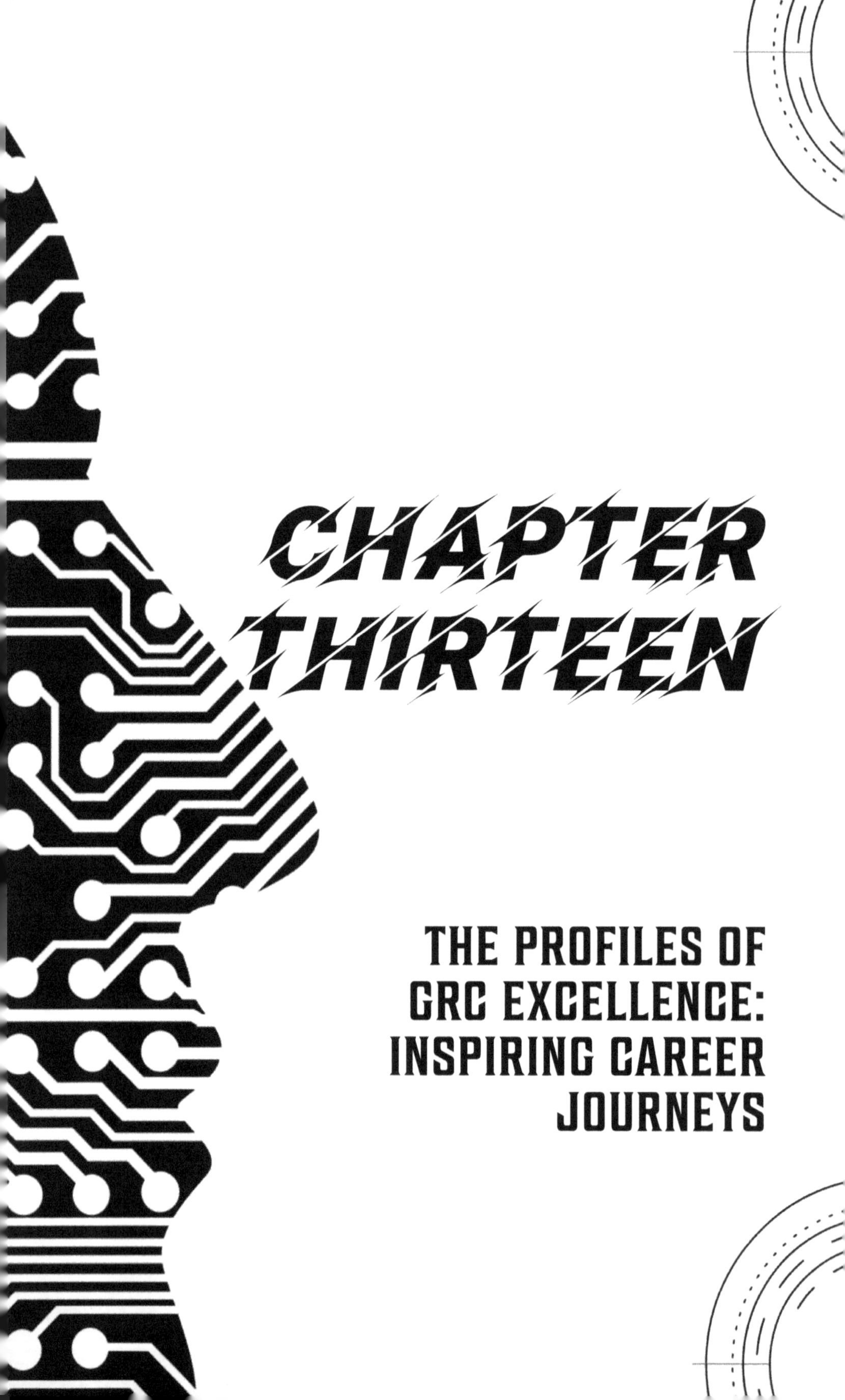

CHAPTER THIRTEEN

THE PROFILES OF GRC EXCELLENCE: INSPIRING CAREER JOURNEYS

Success is often shaped by the lessons learned, challenges overcome, and innovations introduced by trailblazing professionals. This chapter delves into the inspiring career trajectories of a select group of GRC professionals, offering you a unique opportunity to glean insights from the journeys of those who have made significant contributions to the field.

13.1 THE SIGNIFICANCE OF LEARNING FROM GRC LEADERS

The importance of learning from successful GRC professionals cannot be overstated. In an ever-evolving regulatory environment and amidst the complexities of risk management, drawing from the experiences of those who have navigated similar terrain provides a valuable roadmap for both seasoned practitioners and those embarking on their GRC careers.

Navigating Uncertainties: GRC professionals are confronted with an array of uncertainties, from regulatory shifts to emerging risks. Learning from those who have successfully navigated such uncertainties equips individuals with a strategic mindset and adaptive skills.

Innovation and Best Practices: Pioneers in the GRC realm often introduce innovative approaches and best practices that set new standards for the industry. Understanding their methodologies can inspire fresh perspectives and a commitment to excellence.

Leadership and Collaboration: Successful GRC professionals exhibit leadership qualities and a penchant for collaboration. Exploring their career trajectories sheds light on the crucial role of effective leadership and collaboration in driving impactful GRC initiatives.

This chapter will spotlight the following GRC professionals, each distinguished by their unique contributions and career paths:

1.   **Michael Rasmussen: A GRC Thought Leader**

Michael Rasmussen's journey into the Governance, Risk, and Compliance (GRC) field reflects a trajectory shaped by a blend of academic foundation and hands-on experience. His early career showcased a deep interest in understanding the dynamics of risk, compliance, and governance.

Michael's educational background laid a solid foundation for his future endeavors. Armed with a degree in business and computer science, he began his career exploring the intersection of technology and business processes. This intersection became a pivotal space where he would later contribute significantly to the GRC landscape.

Key Milestones:

Throughout his career, Michael Rasmussen has achieved several key milestones that have left an indelible mark on the GRC profession:

Formation of GRC 20/20: One of the defining moments in Michael's career was the establishment of GRC 20/20 Research, LLC. Founding this research and advisory firm signaled his commitment to providing organizations with independent insights into GRC solutions and strategies.

Authorship and Thought Leadership: Michael has authored numerous articles, blog posts, and papers, solidifying his reputation as a thought leader. His book, "GRC 20/20 Research - 2020 GRC Buyers Guide," reflects his commitment to sharing knowledge and guiding organizations in navigating the complexities of GRC.

Educational Contributions: As a GRC educator, Michael has played a crucial role in enhancing the understanding of GRC concepts. His contributions to GRC education include webinars, training programs, and speaking engagements at industry conferences.

Michael Rasmussen's leadership journey in the GRC field has been characterized by a progression from individual contributor roles to influential leadership positions. Michael started by gaining hands-on experience in technology and business processes. This foundation allowed him to appreciate the practical challenges organizations face in managing governance, risk, and compliance.

Transitioning into consultancy roles, Michael began providing strategic guidance to organizations seeking to improve their GRC capabilities. This phase allowed him to witness diverse GRC challenges across industries and develop a nuanced understanding of effective solutions.

Formation of GRC 20/20:

The founding of GRC 20/20 marked a leadership move where Michael took the helm of an organization dedicated to providing research, advisory, and consulting services in the GRC domain. This step positioned him as a leader shaping the discourse in the GRC community.

His background in both business and technology underscores the importance of interdisciplinary knowledge in the GRC field. Understanding how these areas intersect is crucial for effective GRC management.

Through his commitment to continuous learning and thought leadership, Michael emphasizes the importance of staying current in a field that is ever-evolving. GRC professionals can benefit from this mindset by actively engaging in industry discussions and staying informed about emerging trends.

Michael's early career roles in technology and business processes highlight the significance of practical experience. GRC professionals can leverage this lesson by seeking hands-on experience to complement theoretical knowledge.

The establishment of GRC 20/20 reflects Michael's entrepreneurial spirit. GRC professionals can draw inspiration from this, recognizing the potential impact of their contributions and exploring entrepreneurial avenues within the GRC landscape.

Michael Rasmussen's journey offers valuable insights and lessons for aspiring GRC professionals:

2. Douglas W. Hubbard

Early Career:

A pioneer in Risk Management and Decision Science, Douglas W. Hubbard's entry into the Governance, Risk, and Compliance (GRC) field is characterized by a unique blend of quantitative expertise and a dedication to understanding risk and decision-making. His early career laid the groundwork for his later contributions to risk management.

Hubbard's academic background in economics and decision sciences provided him with a strong quantitative foundation. This early education set the stage for his future endeavors in applying mathematical principles to risk assessment and decision-making.

In his early career, Hubbard immersed himself in roles that allowed him to apply quantitative methods to real-world challenges. These roles often involved working at the intersection of business processes and data analysis, shaping his perspective on risk and uncertainty.

Douglas W. Hubbard's career is marked by several key milestones that have significantly influenced the GRC landscape:

A pivotal moment in Hubbard's career was the publication of his influential book, "How to Measure Anything." This work challenged traditional notions around measuring intangibles, introducing practical approaches to quantifying uncertainties and risks.

Hubbard's decision to establish Hubbard Decision Research marked a significant milestone. This consultancy firm focuses on helping organizations make more informed decisions by applying quantitative methods to assess and manage risk.

Hubbard's thought leadership extends beyond his consultancy work. He has authored multiple books, articles, and research papers that contribute to the understanding of risk management, decision science, and the measurement of uncertainties.

Douglas W. Hubbard's journey in the GRC domain reflects a progression from individual contributor to influential leadership roles:

Hubbard's early career roles involved hands-on work in applying quantitative methods to measure uncertainties and risks. This phase allowed him to develop a deep understanding of the practical challenges organizations face in quantifying and managing risk.

The establishment of Hubbard Decision Research showcased Hubbard's leadership and entrepreneurial spirit. Leading a consultancy firm allowed him to guide organizations in adopting quantitative approaches to enhance decision-making and risk management.

Hubbard's emphasis on quantitative methods underscores the importance of developing and applying strong analytical skills in the GRC field. GRC professionals can benefit by incorporating quantitative approaches into risk assessment and decision-making processes.

The publication of "How to Measure Anything" reflects Hubbard's willingness to challenge traditional assumptions. GRC professionals can learn the importance of questioning established norms and exploring innovative approaches to risk management.

Hubbard's entrepreneurial journey highlights the impact that individuals can have when they apply their expertise to real-world challenges. GRC professionals can draw inspiration from this, considering entrepreneurial avenues within the GRC landscape.

Hubbard's commitment to thought leadership and ongoing learning is evident in his extensive body of work. GRC professionals can embrace a similar commitment to staying informed, sharing insights, and contributing to the evolving discourse in the field.

3. **Norman Marks: A Visionary in Governance, Risk, and Compliance (GRC)**

Norman Marks' journey into the Governance, Risk, and Compliance (GRC) field is marked by a dynamic blend of early roles that cultivated his passion for effective risk management and governance.

Marks began his journey with a strong educational background, earning a degree in business studies. This foundational knowledge provided him with a solid base for his future endeavors in navigating the complexities of GRC.

Marks' early career involved roles where he could actively contribute to the strategic aspects of risk and governance. These roles often required a multidisciplinary approach, bridging the realms of business operations, risk management, and governance.

Norman Marks' career is punctuated by several key milestones that have had a lasting impact on the GRC landscape:

Serving as the Vice President of Internal Audit at various organizations, Marks played a crucial role in establishing effective internal audit functions. This phase laid the groundwork for his broader contributions to risk management and governance.

He emerged as a prolific author, sharing his insights and expertise through books, blogs, and articles. His writings, such as "World-Class Risk Management," have become influential resources for GRC professionals seeking practical guidance.

He then assumed advisory roles, providing guidance to organizations seeking to enhance their risk management and governance practices. This transition from hands-on roles to advisory positions highlighted his ability to influence strategic decisions.

Marks' leadership journey in the GRC field traces a progression from individual contributor to influential leadership roles. In his early roles, Marks functioned as an individual contributor, actively involved in shaping internal audit functions and risk management practices. This hands-on experience provided him with a deep understanding of the challenges organizations face.

Marks' leadership, including Vice President of Internal Audit, marked a shift towards strategic leadership. He demonstrated an ability to align risk management and governance with broader organizational goals, emphasizing the integration of these functions.

Transitioning to advisory and consultancy roles, Marks leveraged his expertise to guide organizations in developing world-class risk management practices. This phase showcased his influence on the strategic direction of GRC initiatives.

Marks' career emphasizes the importance of adopting a holistic approach to GRC. Integrating risk management and governance with overall business strategy is essential for creating resilient organizations.

Marks' ability to articulate complex GRC concepts in his writings and advisory roles underscores the importance of effective communication. GRC professionals can benefit from honing their communication skills to convey the value of risk management to diverse stakeholders.

Furthermore, Marks' leadership journey highlights the significance of aligning GRC efforts with organizational strategy. GRC professionals should seek opportunities to contribute strategically, demonstrating how risk management enhances overall business performance.

Likewise, Marks' commitment to continuous learning, evident in his writings and advisory roles, underscores the importance of staying informed in the dynamic GRC landscape. GRC professionals can learn from this mindset, embracing adaptability and a willingness to evolve with industry trends.

4. **Richard Chambers: A Trailblazer in Internal Auditing and GRC**

Richard Chambers' journey into the Governance, Risk, and Compliance (GRC) field is characterized by a commitment to excellence in internal auditing and a passion for promoting effective governance and risk management.

Chambers' career began with a strong educational foundation, earning a degree in business administration. This academic background laid the groundwork for his subsequent contributions to internal auditing and GRC.

Chambers' early career involved pivotal roles that shaped his entry into the GRC field. Notably, his roles in internal auditing provided valuable hands-on experience in assessing and improving organizational processes, controls, and risk management.

Richard Chambers' career is marked by several key milestones that have left a lasting impact on the GRC landscape:

Chambers served as the President and CEO of The Institute of Internal Auditors (IIA), a global professional association. Under his leadership, the IIA expanded its influence, advocating for the value of internal auditing and setting standards for the profession.

Chambers became a thought leader in the GRC community, advocating for the crucial role of internal auditors in organizational governance and risk management. His writings, speeches, and engagements underscored the importance of professionalism and ethical conduct in the field.

During Chambers' tenure at the IIA, the organization made significant strides in advancing internal audit standards globally. The introduction of the International Professional Practices Framework (IPPF) and the Common Body of Knowledge (CBOK) reflected his commitment to standardizing and elevating the profession.

Chambers' leadership journey in the GRC field traces a progression from individual contributor to influential leadership roles. Chambers began his career in internal auditing, where he honed his skills in assessing risk, evaluating controls, and contributing to organizational governance. This phase provided him with a deep understanding of the foundational elements of GRC.

As President and CEO of the IIA, Chambers assumed a leadership role that extended beyond internal auditing. His influence reached a global scale as he championed the broader GRC agenda, emphasizing the interconnected nature of governance, risk, and compliance.

His leadership extended to advocacy for the internal audit profession worldwide. By driving global initiatives, he played a pivotal role in positioning internal auditors as strategic partners in organizational success.

His dedication to elevating the internal audit profession highlights the importance of professionals actively contributing to the growth and recognition of their field within the broader GRC landscape.

Chambers' global perspective underscores the interconnected nature of GRC on a worldwide scale. GRC professionals can draw inspiration from his commitment to global standards and collaboration.

Chambers' ongoing advocacy for internal auditing illustrates the importance of professionals continually championing their roles. GRC professionals should actively engage in promoting the value of their contributions to organizational success.

5. **Carole Switzer: A Trailblazer in GRC and Ethical Governance**

Carole Switzer's journey into the Governance, Risk, and Compliance (GRC) field is characterized by a commitment to ethical governance and the co-founding of an organization that has become influential in shaping GRC practices.

Switzer's career began with a solid educational background, providing her with the foundational knowledge needed to navigate the complexities of GRC. Her academic pursuits likely contributed to her future roles in the field.

Her early career involved pivotal roles that shaped her entry into the GRC field. Her experiences may have included positions that exposed her to the challenges of organizational governance, risk management, and compliance.

Switzer's career is marked by several key milestones that have left a lasting impact on the GRC landscape. A pivotal moment in her career was the co-founding of OCEG. This organization, dedicated to providing frameworks and resources for integrating governance, risk management, and compliance, has become a leading voice in the GRC community.

She emerged as a thought leader, advocating for the importance of ethical governance. Her contributions through OCEG have significantly influenced how organizations approach GRC, emphasizing the integration of ethical principles into business practices.

Under Switzer's leadership, OCEG has been involved in educational initiatives, providing resources, training, and guidance to professionals seeking to enhance their GRC capabilities. This commitment to education has contributed to OCEG's role as a knowledge hub in the field.

Switzer's leadership journey began with the co-founding of OCEG, a testament to her entrepreneurial spirit and vision for a comprehensive approach to GRC. This marked a leadership move that positioned her as a driving force in shaping the discourse around GRC.

Her leadership extended beyond organizational roles to advocacy for ethical governance. Her influence through OCEG underscores the interconnected nature of governance, risk, and compliance, emphasizing the need for an ethical foundation.

Switzer's founding of OCEG emphasizes the importance of aligning with core principles. GRC professionals can learn the value of establishing organizations, frameworks, or initiatives that are grounded in foundational principles and values.

Switzer's emphasis on ethical governance underscores the critical role of ethics in the GRC landscape. GRC professionals should prioritize the integration of ethical principles into their practices, recognizing that ethical governance is foundational to organizational success.

Switzer's collaborative leadership, evident in her role at OCEG, showcases the power of collaboration in shaping GRC standards and practices. GRC professionals can draw inspiration from this, recognizing the collective effort required to advance the field.

Switzer's commitment to education through OCEG highlights the importance of continuous learning in GRC. Professionals should actively seek educational opportunities to stay informed about evolving practices and standards.

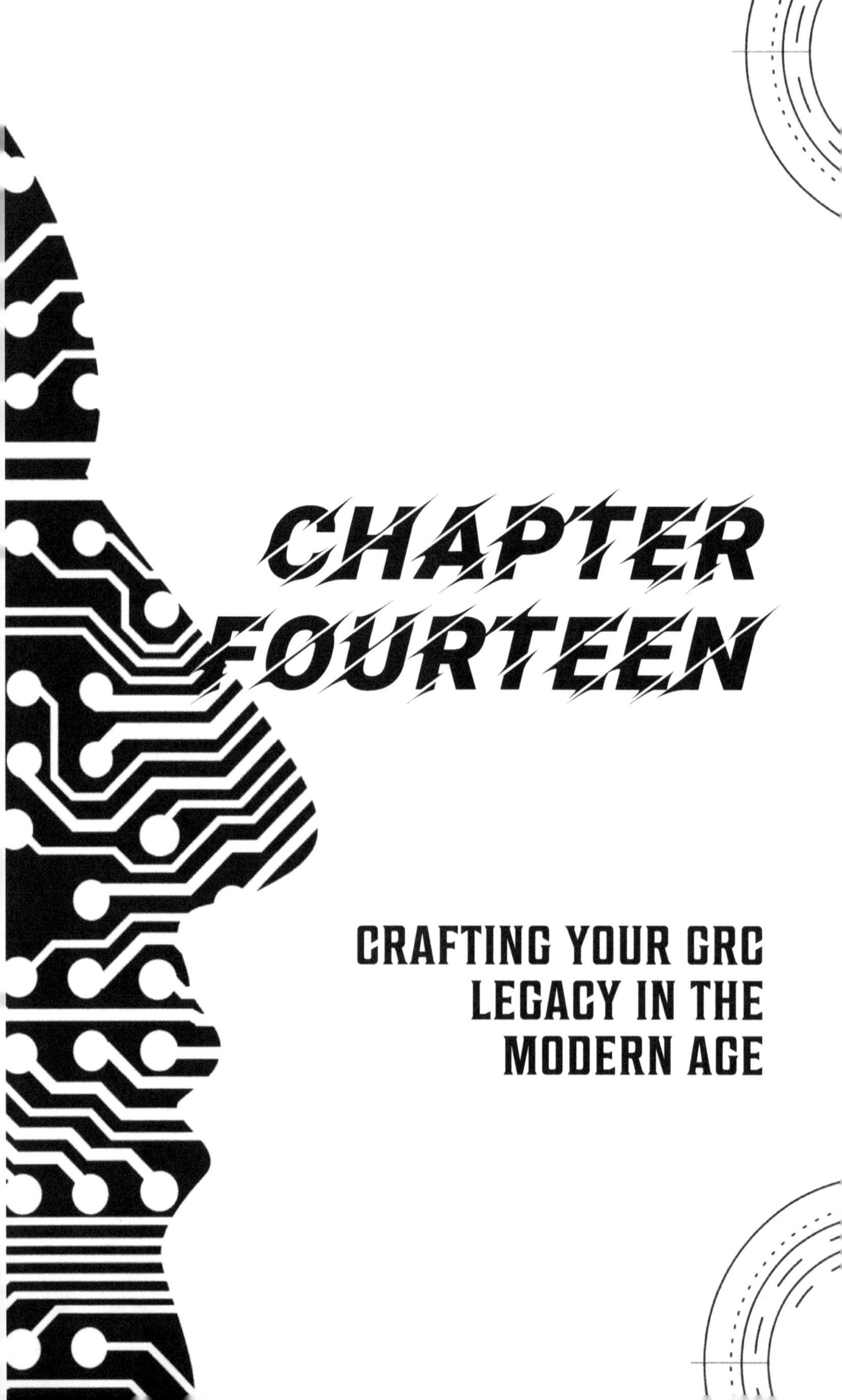

CHAPTER FOURTEEN

CRAFTING YOUR GRC LEGACY IN THE MODERN AGE

Within the dynamic realm of Governance, Risk, and Compliance (GRC), the significance of leaving an enduring impact is paramount. GRC professionals stand as architects of ethical governance, and the transformative influence of individual contributions resonates deeply within the landscape of organizational practices.

Let's delve into the vital importance of creating a lasting mark and explore how the distinctive efforts of each professional can collectively mold the future of GRC practices.

1. **Guiding Organizational Integrity**

   Individual contributions in GRC serve as beacons guiding organizations towards integrity. By championing ethical principles, professionals can instill a culture of responsibility, transparency, and accountability. This commitment to integrity forms the bedrock of sustainable and principled organizational governance.

2. **Shaping Industry Standards**

   GRC practices are continually refined and standardized, and individual contributions play a central role in shaping these standards. By pushing the boundaries of conventional practices, professionals can influence the development of frameworks, methodologies, and best practices that set the benchmark for the entire industry.

3. **Fostering Innovation and Adaptability**

    Innovation is key to the future of GRC, and individual contributions fuel this innovation engine. Professionals who bring fresh perspectives, embrace technological advancements, and champion adaptive strategies contribute to the industry's ability to thrive in an ever-changing landscape.

4. **Advocating for Ethical Leadership**

    Individuals in the GRC field have the power to be advocates for ethical leadership. By modeling ethical behavior, promoting transparency, and holding organizations accountable, professionals contribute to the establishment of ethical norms that elevate the entire profession and foster a culture of trust.

5. **Influencing Organizational Resilience**

    GRC is a cornerstone of organizational resilience, and individual contributions can significantly impact an organization's ability to navigate uncertainties. Professionals who proactively identify risks, implement effective controls, and contribute to strategic planning enhance an organization's resilience in the face of challenges.

6. **Building a Knowledge Legacy**

    Every insight, lesson learned, and best practice shared contributes to the knowledge legacy of the GRC community. Individual efforts in knowledge dissemination through publications, presentations, and mentorship create a collective wisdom that benefits both current and future generations of GRC professionals.

7. **Catalyzing Cultural Shifts**

    Individual contributions can catalyze cultural shifts within organizations. Whether it's fostering a culture of compliance, risk awareness, or a commitment to ethical behavior, professionals have the power to influence the very fabric of organizational culture, creating environments that prioritize GRC principles.

8. **Inspiring Future Leaders**

    Through mentorship, knowledge sharing, and leadership, individuals in GRC inspire the next generation of professionals. By cultivating a community of forward-thinking and ethical leaders, current professionals contribute to a sustainable legacy that propels the field forward.

14.1 NAVIGATING THE ETHICAL COMPASS: PERSONAL VALUES IN GRC DECISION-MAKING

Decision-making is an art crafted not only from the statutes of regulations but profoundly influenced by the personal values and principles that individuals bring to the table. This journey entails the thoughtful exploration of deeply ingrained beliefs, the articulation of these values into guiding principles, and a commitment to aligning professional practices with unwavering ethical standards. Let's navigate the ethical compass that guides GRC professionals, understanding the significance of this alignment in shaping a landscape where decisions transcend mere compliance to embody the very essence of ethical righteousness.   Identifying Personal Values:

At the core of every GRC professional lies a set of personal values that serve as a moral compass. Identifying these values is a self-reflective journey, requiring a thoughtful exploration of beliefs, priorities, and the fundamental principles that shape one's character. Whether it's integrity, transparency, or accountability, acknowledging these values lays the groundwork for principled decision-making.

14.1.1 Articulating Principles Guiding GRC Decisions

Once identified, the next crucial step is articulating these values into clear, actionable principles that guide GRC decision-making. These principles become the touchstones when navigating complex risk scenarios, formulating governance strategies, or ensuring compliance. Articulation transforms values from abstract concepts into tangible guidelines, fostering consistency and clarity in decision-making processes.

14.1.2 The Significance of Ethical Alignment

Aligning personal values with ethical standards is the linchpin that sustains the integrity of GRC practices. It ensures that decision-making transcends mere adherence to rules, extending into a realm where actions are inherently grounded in a commitment to what is morally right. This alignment is the bedrock upon which trust is built – trust from stakeholders, colleagues, and the broader community.

14.1.3 Upholding Integrity in GRC Decisions

Integrity, as a fundamental value, takes center stage in GRC decision-making. It involves the steadfast adherence to ethical principles, even when faced with challenging circumstances. Upholding integrity in every decision not only safeguards personal and professional reputation but also contributes to the overarching reputation of the organization within the GRC ecosystem.

14.1.4 Fostering a Culture of Accountability

Accountability, another pivotal value, ensures that decisions made in the GRC realm are transparent, responsible, and accountable to stakeholders. By aligning personal practices with ethical standards, GRC professionals become standard-bearers for accountability, cultivating a culture where responsibility is paramount, and the consequences of decisions are understood and accepted.

14.1.5 THE RIPPLE EFFECT: IMPACT ON STAKEHOLDERS AND BEYOND

The significance of aligning professional practices with ethical standards extends beyond individual choices. It permeates the fabric of organizational culture, influencing colleagues and stakeholders. The ripple effect of ethically aligned decision-making resonates far beyond immediate scenarios, contributing to the creation of a resilient and principled GRC environment.

14.2 FORGING A GRC LEGACY: NAVIGATING LONG-TERM CAREER GOALS AND SHORT-TERM OBJECTIVES

Establishing long-term career goals involves a strategic vision that not only propels individual advancement but contributes meaningfully to the broader GRC landscape. Yet, this voyage is not one of singular focus; it is a delicate dance, harmonizing short-term objectives with a panoramic vision for professional impact.

14.2.1 ESTABLISHING LONG-TERM CAREER GOALS

At the heart of career aspirations lies the cultivation of long-term goals that extend beyond the confines of immediate roles. For GRC professionals, these goals may encompass becoming industry leaders, spearheading transformative initiatives, or influencing regulatory landscapes. The process involves a meticulous consideration of personal strengths, passions, and the broader needs of the GRC ecosystem.

14.2.2 CONTRIBUTING TO INDUSTRY-WIDE ADVANCEMENTS

Long-term goals in the GRC domain should echo a commitment to industry-wide advancements. This could entail active participation in the creation of frameworks, championing ethical practices, or contributing research that shapes the future of GRC. By aligning personal aspirations with the betterment of the industry, professionals become architects of a landscape that thrives on innovation and excellence.

14.2.3 BALANCING SHORT-TERM OBJECTIVES

While the horizon is adorned with long-term ambitions, the pragmatic GRC professional understands the importance of balancing these lofty goals with short-term objectives. These objectives could involve acquiring specific certifications, mastering evolving regulatory frameworks, or leading projects that address immediate organizational needs. Short-term wins not only bolster professional confidence but also lay the groundwork for broader impacts.

14.2.4 NAVIGATING THE DELICATE DANCE

The delicate dance between short-term objectives and long-term goals is an art that demands strategic finesse. While short-term wins are crucial for immediate success, they should seamlessly align with the overarching vision. Each tactical move, whether it's mastering a new skill or successfully executing a project, becomes a stepping stone toward the grander symphony of professional impact.

14.2.5 BUILDING EXPERTISE FOR LONG-TERM IMPACT

A cornerstone of long-term career goals is the continual pursuit of expertise. Whether through educational pursuits, specialized training, or hands-on experience, building a reservoir of knowledge contributes not only to personal growth but also positions individuals as thought leaders capable of steering the industry toward new horizons.

14.2.6 Fostering Adaptability and Resilience

In the dynamic landscape of GRC, the ability to adapt and pivot is as crucial as the pursuit of long-term goals. Professionals must cultivate resilience, understanding that industry shifts, regulatory changes, and organizational dynamics necessitate a nimble approach. Short-term objectives should, therefore, align with developing adaptability – a skill set that fortifies the foundation for enduring impact.

14.2.7 Cultivating Excellence: The Vital Role of Mentorship in GRC

Within the dynamic landscape of Governance, Risk, and Compliance (GRC), the torchbearers of experience have a profound responsibility to illuminate the paths of those venturing into the field. Mentorship stands as a beacon, guiding emerging talent through the intricacies of GRC, and its importance reverberates across the entire community. Let's delve into why mentorship is a linchpin in fostering excellence and encourage seasoned professionals to generously share their knowledge, wisdom, and insights with the next generation.

14.3 Navigating the Complexities of GRC

The GRC terrain is rife with complexities, from intricate regulatory frameworks to the delicate balance of risk management and compliance. For emerging professionals, this landscape can be both challenging and daunting. Mentorship serves as a guiding compass, providing a navigational tool for understanding, interpreting, and thriving within the intricate GRC ecosystem.

ACCELERATING PROFESSIONAL GROWTH:

In the GRC community, experience is a treasure trove, and mentorship is the key to unlocking its vast potential. Seasoned professionals have weathered diverse challenges, honed their skills, and acquired invaluable insights. By sharing this wealth of experience, mentors accelerate the professional growth of their mentees, providing a shortcut to wisdom that might otherwise take years to accumulate.

TRANSFER OF SPECIALIZED KNOWLEDGE:

GRC is a domain where specialized knowledge is paramount. Mentorship facilitates the transfer of this specialized wisdom from mentors, who have delved deep into the nuances of the field, to mentees eager to absorb and apply this knowledge. This transfer is not just a passing of information but a legacy-building endeavor that fortifies the collective expertise of the GRC community.

CULTIVATING ETHICAL LEADERSHIP:

Beyond technical skills, mentorship in GRC is instrumental in cultivating ethical leadership. Professionals with seasoned backgrounds not only instill ethical principles but also serve as living examples of how to navigate the ethical minefields inherent in governance, risk management, and compliance. The mentor-mentee relationship becomes a crucible for the development of leaders committed to integrity.

CREATING A COLLABORATIVE COMMUNITY:

Mentorship transforms the GRC community into a collaborative ecosystem where knowledge flows seamlessly between generations. This collaboration is not confined to a unidirectional exchange; rather, it creates a reciprocal relationship where mentors glean fresh perspectives from mentees, fostering an environment of innovation and adaptability.

ENCOURAGING A LEGACY OF GENEROSITY:

Experienced professionals are the architects of the GRC legacy, and mentorship is a legacy of generosity. By imparting knowledge and insights to emerging talent, seasoned practitioners contribute to the perpetuity of excellence within the GRC community. This act of generosity transcends individual careers, shaping the very fabric of the profession for generations to come.

14.4 Forging Alliances: The Power of Networks and Collaborations in GRC

Cultivating robust connections within the GRC community is not merely a transactional pursuit; it is the heartbeat of innovation, resilience, and the collective capacity to address complex challenges. Let's explore the significance of forging strong professional networks and collaborations, recognizing their pivotal role in navigating the intricate GRC landscape.

BUILDING BRIDGES THROUGH PROFESSIONAL NETWORKS:

Professional networks in GRC are more than a list of contacts; they are bridges that connect individuals, organizations, and ideas. These networks serve as conduits for the exchange of knowledge, insights, and best practices. They create a vibrant tapestry where professionals can draw on the collective wisdom of the community, fostering an environment of continuous learning and growth.

ACCELERATING KNOWLEDGE TRANSFER:

Within the GRC community, information is a currency, and professional networks are the banks where this currency is exchanged. Networks facilitate the rapid transfer of knowledge, allowing practitioners to stay abreast of industry trends, regulatory shifts, and emerging best practices. This accelerates the learning curve and ensures that the community as a whole remains at the forefront of GRC advancements.

CATALYZING COLLABORATIONS FOR COLLECTIVE STRENGTH:

Collaboration within the GRC community is not just a strategic choice; it is a necessity. The challenges faced in governance, risk management, and compliance are multifaceted and often transcend the capabilities of individual practitioners or organizations. Collaborations harness the collective strength of diverse perspectives, skill sets, and experiences, fostering an environment where complex challenges are met with innovative solutions.

NAVIGATING REGULATORY COMPLEXITY:

In the ever-evolving landscape of regulations, navigating complexity requires a collective effort. Professional networks become invaluable sources of insights and interpretations, helping practitioners stay ahead of regulatory changes. Collaborations further amplify this capacity, enabling the GRC community to collectively respond to and influence regulatory landscapes.

INNOVATION THRIVES IN COLLABORATIVE SPACES:

The GRC professionals of today are the innovators of tomorrow, and innovation thrives in collaborative spaces. Networks provide fertile ground for the cross-pollination of ideas, fostering an environment where innovative approaches to governance, risk, and compliance challenges can take root and flourish. Collaborations amplify this potential, turning individual sparks of creativity into transformative initiatives.

STRATEGIC PARTNERSHIPS FOR COMPREHENSIVE SOLUTIONS:

Addressing complex GRC challenges requires a holistic approach, and strategic partnerships are the linchpin of comprehensive solutions. By forming alliances with complementary expertise, organizations within the GRC community can create a synergy that transcends individual capabilities. These partnerships enhance resilience and provide a multifaceted response to the multifaceted challenges that characterize the GRC landscape.

RECOGNIZING THE INTERCONNECTEDNESS OF SUCCESS:

Success in GRC is not a solitary achievement but an interconnected outcome. Recognizing the value of professional networks and collaborations is an acknowledgment of this interconnectedness. It is an understanding that the successes of one contribute to the successes of all, creating a community where the rising tide lifts all ships.

14.5 Closing Thoughts: Shaping Tomorrow through Your GRC Legacy

As you conclude this chapter on crafting your GRC legacy in the modern age, remember that your journey is not just a series of career milestones; it's a narrative that contributes to the evolving story of Governance, Risk, and Compliance. The choices you make, the values you uphold, and the innovations you introduce collectively shape the future of GRC practices.

By reflecting on your experiences, clarifying your values, and setting strategic goals, you are not only advancing your own career but also influencing the trajectory of the entire GRC community. As you navigate challenges with resilience, embrace diversity and inclusion, and advocate for ethical practices, you become a beacon for others in the field.

Your legacy extends beyond individual accomplishments; it's about nurturing a culture of mentorship, fostering innovation, and leaving a positive impact on future GRC professionals. In the dynamic intersection of tradition and innovation, your ability to balance both will define your lasting influence on the GRC landscape.

As you embark on the journey of crafting your GRC legacy, remember that every decision, every relationship, and every contribution matters. Your commitment to ethical leadership, continuous learning, and responsible governance echoes beyond your immediate sphere, resonating in the broader narrative of industry progress.

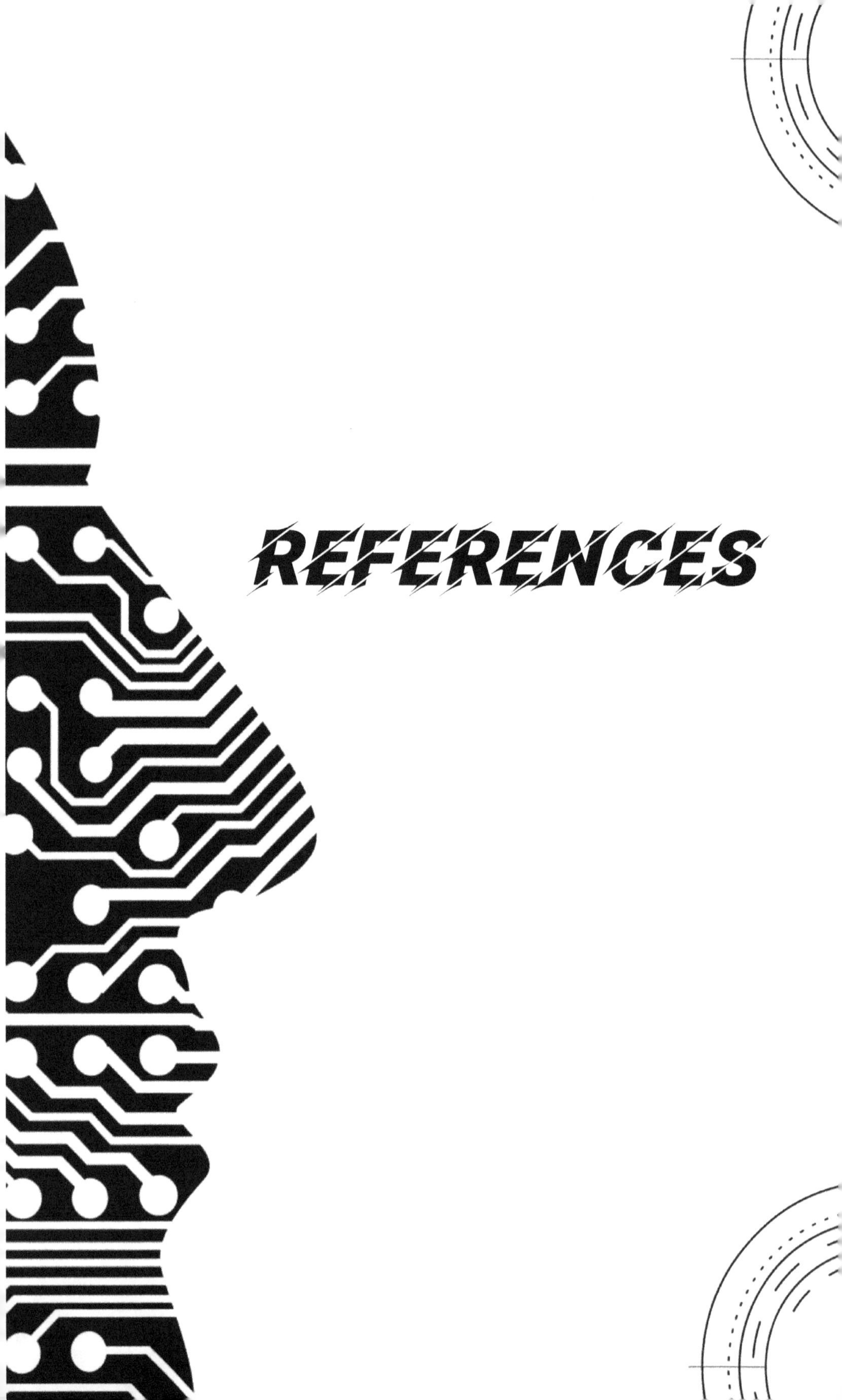

REFERENCES

2017 Equifax data breach. (2020, August 2). Retrieved from Wikipedia website: https://en.wikipedia.org/wiki/2017_Equifax_data_breach

AWS. (n.d.). What is Governance, Risk, and Compliance? - GRC Explained - AWS. Retrieved from Amazon Web Services, Inc. website: https://aws.amazon.com/what-is/grc/

Governance Risk Management & Compliance (GRC) Market By 2031 Size, Share, Trend. (n.d.). Retrieved November 19, 2023, from www.businessresearchinsights.com website: https://www.businessresearchinsights.com/market-reports/governance-risk-management-and-compliance-grc-market-102540

MOYLE, E. (n.d.). Buyer Beware: The Complexities of Evaluating GRC. Retrieved from http://cdn.ttgtmedia.com/searchSecurity/downloads/12_10L_ebook_GRC_ebook_landscape.pdf

Palmer, J. (2023, August 8). How to Build a GRC Framework (Step-by-Step) | OnBoard Board Intelligence. Retrieved from OnBoard Board Management Software | Board Portal | Board Intelligence website: https://www.onboardmeetings.com/blog/grc-framework/

PWC. (n.d.). Governance, Risk Management and Compliance: Sustainability and Integration supported by Technology. Retrieved from https://www.pwc.com.au/consulting/assets/risk-controls/governance_mar09.pdf

Steinberg, R. M. (2011). *Governance, risk management, and compliance : it can't happen to us-avoiding corporate disaster while driving success.* Hoboken, N.J.: Wiley.

Swetha Amaresan. (2019). Data Silos: What They Are and How to Get Rid of Them. Retrieved from Hubspot.com website: https://blog.hubspot.com/service/data-silos

The GRC Framework: A Practical Guide to GRC. (2022, February 25). Retrieved from CIO Insight website: https://www.cioinsight.com/it-management/grc-framework/

Wikipedia. (2019, March 4). Industrial Revolution. Retrieved from Wikipedia website: https://en.wikipedia.org/wiki/Industrial_Revolution

Wikipedia Contributors. (2019, March 31). Enron scandal. Retrieved from Wikipedia website: https://en.wikipedia.org/wiki/Enron_scandal

ABOUT
THE
AUTHOR

The Author, Tolulope Michael, is a proud Computer Science graduate from the esteemed and prestigious Lagos State University. His love for technology, combined with a strong interest in cybersecurity, has driven him to dedicate close to two decades of his life to this field.

Over the years, he has gained valuable experience in various domains of cybersecurity, including Penetration Testing, Application Security Engineering, Cloud Security Engineering, and Governance, Risk and Compliance (GRC). He is proud to say that he has contributed to the growth of the industry, leaving a lasting impact with his expertise and knowledge.

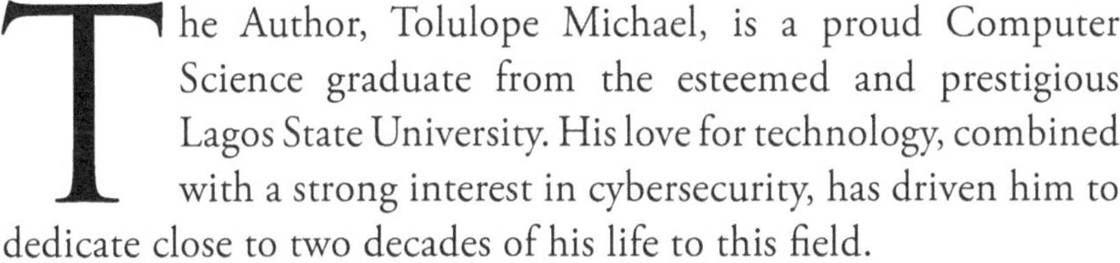

In his quest to help others succeed in cybersecurity, he created ExcelMindCyber, a platform designed to provide comprehensive education in this field. His flagship program, "The Ultimate Cybersecurity Program" has already made a significant impact, helping many individuals realize their potential and earn multiple six figures.

He is grateful for the opportunity to share his passion and knowledge with others, and it brings him immense joy to see his students find success and fulfillment in this field. His journey in cybersecurity has been a rewarding one, and he is proud to be a part of this industry. He hopes to continue making a difference in the lives of those who share his love for cybersecurity, and is committed to helping them achieve their goals. This is his story, and he is proud to tell it.

With a clear and accessible writing style, he provides a roadmap for individuals looking to break into the field of cybersecurity, offering practical advice and actionable tips that will help you succeed in your journey. Whether you're a student, a professional looking for a change, or simply someone with an interest in cybersecurity, the author's insights and guidance will help you build the foundation you need for an exciting and rewarding career.